$25·   10/85

**Profit Cycles,
Oligopoly, and
Regional Development**

Profit Cycles, Oligopoly, and Regional Development

Ann Roell Markusen

The MIT Press
Cambridge, Massachusetts
London, England

Library of Congress Cataloging in Publication Data

Markusen, Ann R.
    Profit cycles, oligopoly, and regional development.

    Bibliography: p.
    Includes index.
    1. Regional economics. 2. Regional economic
disparities. 3. Corporate profits. 4. Oligopolies.
5. United States—Economic conditions—1945-   —Regional disparities. 6. United States—Industries—Location. 7. Corporate profits—United States.
8. Oligopolies—United States. I. Title.
HT391.M36 1985   330.973   84-19395
ISBN 0-262-13201-X

For Marc Weiss

Contents

List of Figures

Tables

Preface

This book is about the relationship between industrial dynamics and regional change. It is part of a larger, international project to propose more powerful ways of understanding contemporary displacement than we have had in regional science in the past. Doreen Massey and Ben Harrison's arguments that we must search for the key to regional fortunes in industrial restructuring and corporate decisionmaking struck me as crucial at the outset. I would like to thank Peter Hall for reintroducing me to Schumpeter, Candace Howes for convincing me of the value of doing industry studies, and Walter Adams for his encouragement to study the steel industry. My ideas on this subject have been developed with the benefit of continual exposure to my colleagues in the Union for Radical Political Economics, especially Matt Edel and Rick Simon, and the Berkeley National Urban Policy Collective—Dick Walker, David Wilmoth, Michael Storper, Annalee Saxenian, Marc Weiss, Amy Glasmeier, Madeline Landau, Erica Schoenberger, Candace Howes, Michael Luger, Marsh Feldman, Becky O'Malley and Kit Muller.

The empirical research relied heavily upon the painstaking compilation, manipulation and tabulation of data by Marjorie Bennett and Richard Osborne. The work of several of my students on specific industries—Annalee Saxenian on semiconductors, David Fogarty on brewing, and Marjorie Bennett on lumber milling, helped inform my own case studies. Vijaya Nagarajan and Linda Wheaton mopped up the incomplete references and proofread the final draft. Special thanks to the Data Center in Oakland for access to their files.

My regionalist colleagues around the country shared lots of important insights after thorough readings of major portions of the manuscript: Michael Teitz, Doreen Massey, Ben Harrison, Niles Hansen, John Mollenkopf, Roger Bolton, Norman Glickman, Erica Schoenberger, Mike Luger, Joan Hoffman, John Friedmann, Gordon

Clark, Sandra Kanter, Candace Howes, Mary Beth Pudup, Evan Jones, and Ed Soja. My content editor, David Plotke, deserves credit for painlessly blunt suggestions on cutting and reorganizing and for perceptive detection of weak links in the argument.

Environments contributed mightily to this project. My Cromwell, Minnesota neighbors provided an ever ready pot of coffee and homemade sweets for the unpredictable summertime writer's cramp. David Taylor lent me an inviolable haven on Fulton Street in the center of Berkeley, and Hilda and David Dobbs made me highballs and tolerated my tromping into their cabin to use the phone for a month in the northern Sierras. In Los Angeles, Geotz Wolff and Dolores Hayden provided quiet, workable space during my visit to UCLA.

As befits a text preoccupied with innovation, the production process was a frustrating but largely successful experiment. My great thanks to Dorothy Heydt for teaching me to use UNIX, and to Mel Webber, Kathy Crum and Lynne Charlot for making sure I had the hardware and staff assistance I needed. The IURD staff over the years—Alyce Miller, Kate Herman, Maureen Jurkowski, Linda Reichman-Garcia, Roger Sender, Eric Billitzer, Nancy Albert, Liz Prince, Tad Stratford, Barbara Hadenfeldt, Tawnya Pickett, Toni Brock and Jeff Segol—punctuated the drafts with a good bit of welcome humor and partying, while they were consistently conscientious about product. Adrienne Morgan drafted the figures deftly. I am particularly indebted to Nene Ojeda for her impressive organizational and technical skills in revising and typesetting the entire book. Bob Bolick, my editor at M.I.T. Press, was consistently encouraging and responsive.

My friends and family provided the adventure and emotional counterpart to the isolation of writing. I'd like to thank in particular Amy Glasmeier for her unique blend of energy and pragmatism, Candace Howes for her consistently surprising insights into the process of creation and its social fetters, and my Markusen cousins for their nonchalance and affection. I could never have started this project without the education my parents, Jeanne and David Markusen, gave me, would never have kept at it without the women's movement, and could never have finished it without my two most loyal boosters, Marc Weiss and David Markusen-Weiss.

**Profit Cycles,
Oligopoly, and
Regional Development**

1   The Dynamics
of Regional Development

The economic events of the past fifteen years—roughly since the late 1960s—have presented a serious challenge to the existing body of regional theory. The consistently poor performance of the heartland industrial regions in advanced capitalist countries contradicts those theoretical approaches, from geographers' models to Marxist dependency theories, which predict the continued leadership and superior performance of advanced industrial regions. The sorry state of these regional economies, registered by high unemployment rates, local public sector crisis, and high rates of out-migration, provocatively questions the ability of capitalist industrial development to reproduce permanent growth and economic well-being, especially at the regional scale. Even if these regional economies should stabilize, their structures and specializations will be markedly different from the past, at the same time that newer regions will sport industrial structures reminiscent of that same fleeting past. Another sanguine view—that although more advanced regions will lose jobs to lower-cost regions, they will continue to be seedbeds of innovation that will ensure their lead—has also been called into question as innovation has occurred in relatively new, outlying regions. A central thesis of this book is that in these modern times, we require a theory that radically reconceptualizes the causal forces driving regional economic change.

The theoretical perspective presented in this book addresses the deindustrialization debate currently waging. It suggests that regional shifts in production and employment are not simply the product of changing factor endowments or shifting consumer demands but of disparate strategies undertaken by corporations experiencing different historical moments of longer-term profitability cycles. Regional shifts in the aggregate are composed of two major impulses: the tendency to rationalize and cheapen production on the part of more mature, profit-squeezed sectors and the tendency to innovate and concentrate production at virgin sites by young, superprofit sectors. The resulting regional adjustment problems are compounded by oligopolistic practices which overconcentrate production in original sites, retard the rate of dispersion of production, underdevelop capacity in outlying areas, monopsonize the resources of its host regions, and restructure ruthlessly when market control erodes.

1.1 A Theory of Regional Differentiation and Change

Traditional theories treat regional development as the product of the interaction of demand and supply. As deductive theories they have three major problems: they inadequately cope with long-run structural change and with innovation in particular; they demote corporate decision makers to relatively passive agents whose spatial behavior is dictated by free market conditions; and they ignore the increasingly ubiquitous presence of oligopoly as an important distortion in the market economy. These theories and their inadequacies are the subject of chapter 2.

The theoretical approach of this book seeks to improve on this situation in the following ways. First, it casts business strategies in the lead role, assuming that managerial decision making is not perfectly dictated by the market but that risk-taking, organization-building, and market-dominating efforts, political influence, and mistakes may all be important contributors to regional fortunes. Second, it handles corporate decision making by disaggregating firms into common industrial groupings, approximating as closely as possible the competition that each experiences in general product lines. Third, it incorporates an evolutionary dimension wherein profitability has very different determinants at different historical moments. Finally, it incorporates the phenomenon of market power by explicitly hypothesizing the spatial behavior of oligopolistic firms at different points in their historical evolution. This synthetic theory, presented in chapter 3, builds on Schumpeterian and Marxist work on innovation and capitalist dynamics, on the product cycle theories of business economists, and on theories of oligopolistic behavior from industrial organization. It is embodied in a model, called the profit cycle, that differentiates variations in levels and sources of profitability throughout a sector's evolution.

Four sequential profitability experiences, arising from disparate competitive conditions, dictate different responsive strategies. In initial innovative eras new industries can garner superprofits from the novelty of their commodity and the absence of immediate competition. While rates of return may be high, looming competitive pressures dictate further innovation plus intense organization building. A second era, of normal profits, corresponds to the competitive economic model and produces relatively conventional pressures to cut costs and move toward optimal scale production. A third era, sometimes preempting the second, is one in which market power, rather than innovative edge, permits greater-than-normal profitability, with distinct business strategies coloring industry performance. Such oligopolistic forms do not emerge in all industries but have characterized significant portions of the U.S. industrial structure. A fourth era of profit squeeze results from renewed competition from outsiders or substitutes and produces pressures to rationalize and often to close down capacity. Bracketed by two stages of unrealized profit, an inventive, precommodity stage and a postsqueeze obsolescence stage, these eras are hypothesized to comprise the normal evolutionary history of an industry.

The passage of an industry through its cycle can best be gauged by the expansionary path of employment. In place of output growth—the basic measure used, sometimes implicitly, in the product cycle model—my model stresses the regularity of rapid job creation followed by periods of retrenchment and then absolute declines, corresponding to eras of profit performance in an industry. Absolute job losses are consistent with the continuation of output growth in eras where corporations place heavy strategic emphasis on productivity increases through mechanization. Industries will exhibit a tendency for growth in the number of firms to peak before job growth, which in turn will peak before output expansion. Concentration of market power will also vary across the cycle, beginning with relatively high levels eroded by rapid entry but later reconstituted through firm failures and predatory practices of industry leaders. Occupational structure varies systematically across the cycle as well, with high proportions of professional and technical workers in innovative eras and of blue-collar production workers in later eras. A large managerial and sales work force will be relatively most prevalent in intermediate stages, as the tasks of organization building, mounting of an extensive sales network, cost cutting, and worker discipline become increasingly important.

Each of the profit cycle eras is marked by distinctive locational behavior on the part of industry members. Five parallel spatial patterns are hypothesized to correspond to profit cycle stages: concentration, agglomeration, dispersion, relocation, and abandonment. These spatial counterparts are the subject of chapter 4. Entrepreneurs in innovative sectors require proximity to each other and to particular pools of labor, which result in high rates of spatial concentration. Subsequently commodity standardization and the emergence of widespread competition force the twin disciplines of market penetration and cost cutting on surviving firms, which generally leads to dispersal from original sites of production. If an oligopoly is engineered in relatively early stages, however, this dispersal will be retarded; capacity will be underdeveloped in peripheral regions and overly concentrated in regions of origin. A profit-squeeze period will result in significant plant closings, most likely in the older sites, even to the extent of reconcentrating capacity in regions where labor costs are lower and the business climate more clement. If a highly spatially concentrated oligopoly enters an era of profit squeeze, the subsequent restructuring may have devastating consequences—from job loss and tax base erosion—for local communities.

Important distinctions can be made about the ways in which certain types of sectors react to profit cycle maturation. Sectors highly sensitive to natural resource costs are likely to display greater growth volatility. Their patterns of regional dispersion may show greater unevenness, both spatially and temporally. Similarly distinctions can be made between producer and consumer goods sectors. Since household consumers are more spatially dispersed than industrial customers, market-oriented spatial dispersion should be relatively more important to consumer goods sectors and may be responsible for a tendency to decentralize sooner in their evolution. Furthermore the possibilities for shaping consumer preferences and creating highly differentiated products suggest differential probabilities of longevity and success for oligopoly power in consumer goods industries. These distinctions among sectoral types are explored in chapter 5. For both theoretical and empirical reasons, the analysis in this book is confined to goods-producing sectors in the economy. Analogous work could be done on the service sectors, although the spatial dimension would be largely intrametropolitan and thus quite different in scale.

Every effort to generalize and codify behavior that operates on a relatively grand territorial scale is in danger of oversimplifying and belittling important aspects of reality. In this case the strength of the theoretical approach—its choice of corporate behavior as the analytical entry point and initiator of regional change—is also its weakness, for two reasons. First, it subordinates the historically evolved features of regions, which clearly condition and constrain profitability, to a relatively passive role in the analysis. This is defensible as an antidote to the overwhelming tendency in regional theory to do the reverse by assuming deterministic corporate responses to these same regional structures. But the industrial restructuring approach perhaps leads to an ahistorical assumption of the existence of regional differentials in wages, cultures, resources, and similar factors without adequately acknowledging the complementary role these have in regional development patterns. I have tackled this problem in a companion book, *The Politics of Regions.*

Second, the isolation of individual sectors from each other unnaturally abstracts from the more complex reality in which multiple sectors coexist spatially in client or competitive relationships. The compensating virtue is the model's focus on the conditions of competition and profitability among a group of competitors. Furthermore, the industry-by-industry approach permits the discovery of important eccentricities and historical accidents that explain the spatial tendencies of each and variations among them. Although I do not explicitly tackle this issue, the theory of profit cycles for individual industries is quite compatible with long-wave theories that predict the bunching up of innovations and the uneven temporal incidence of new sector formation. These conceptual issues are explored in chapter 6, which also addresses the ever-present problem of the sensitivity of the analysis to the regional scale to which it is applied.

1.2 Case Studies of the Changing Geography of U.S. Industries

The second half of the book presents an empirical investigation of the theory for fifteen sectors in the United States. Good data on industrial structure, particularly at the highly disaggregated level, are difficult to come by. The Censuses of Industry are the best source, being both more frequent and richer in detail than the decennial Census of Population. But there are formidable problems in creating reliable time series, due to reclassification, and in being assured of satisfactory spatial coverage, due to disclosure rules. As a result most past regional analyses have been confined to relatively large-grained studies, using two-digit or, more rarely, three-digit break-downs. As a result entirely noncompeting product lines are lumped together. Not only is this conceptually problematic, but the empirical result is that production looks much more evenly distributed spatially than it is actually. For this reason I chose to construct a time series from census data for fifteen four-digit manufacturing industries. Since these in most cases dated back only to 1947, I also examined case histories from secondary sources for each. The choice of sectors, which reflects a mix of ages and sector types, and the set of variables used to test the model, are described in chapter 7.

The empirical studies are quite rich. In order to do justice to at least one sector, I researched the steel industry throughout more than a century of activity. Steel proved to be an outstanding example, both of methodical tendencies toward sequential profit cycle stages and of the deformity in spatial diffusion engineered by oligopolistic practices in a youthful industry. The steel study is the subject of chapter 8.

Since similar detail could not be provided for the rest of the set studied, shorter case studies provide both temporal and cross-sectional evidence for the theory. Grouped by resource-sensitive, producer, and consumer goods categories, these are the subjects of chapters 9 through 12. In general all but one of the sectors could be characterized by successive profit cycle stages. The exception was wineries, whose history of multiple cycles can be explained by the short- and long-run effects of prohibition. In five cases (steel, autos, pharmaceuticals, aluminum, and soybean oil) no normal-profit competitive era ever emerged because market power was bred directly from an innovative environment. In several cases (textiles, lumber, and brewing), sectors oligopolized late, after a prolonged period of profit squeeze.

Employment growth rates proved a superior indicator of sectoral evolution. Furthermore in the large majority of cases, I was able to confirm the hypothesized sequential peaking of firm growth, employment, and output expansion. Similarly the tendencies toward greater competition and lower production-to-total workforce ratios in early stages were almost universally present, as were the symmetrical tendencies toward greater concentration and more homogeneous blue-collar work forces in later stages.

The spatial data produced somewhat less satisfactory results because of serious imperfections in the data base. Nevertheless I have been able to document extraordinary shifts in production and the prominence of dispersion as the major direction this movement takes. These shifts are not confined to an axis from the manufacturing belt southward and westward. The locus of lumber milling has most recently shifted from the Pacific Northwest to the Southeast, soybean oil mills from Iowa to states peripheral to the cornbelt, fish processing from both ocean coasts to the Gulf region, wineries from upstate New York to northern California, and brewing from Milwaukee to dispersed metropolitan areas. Furthermore not all older, competitive manufacturing sectors studied moved along the same north-south axis. The formerly northeastern shoe, textile, and apparel industries each gravitated toward entirely different low-cost regions of entry: to the Tennessee Valley states, the southeastern Piedmont, and Los Angeles and Florida, respectively.

The idiosyncrasies of individual industries come to the fore frequently in the interpretation of spatial outcomes, and for this reason I rely extensively on secondary sources to supplement the data series presented. The resource industries in particular turn out to be highly erratic. One sector, wineries, exhibits an inclination to disperse during eras of expanding markets and agglomerate during retrenchment. Three other resource sectors—fish processing, lumber mills, and soybean oil—have persistently moved, although their locational choices have been circumscribed by resource availability.

The belief that oligopolistic industry structures tend to retard decentralization of production in innovative eras and accelerate it during profit squeezes is strikingly supported for a number of sectors, including steel, autos, tobacco, pharmaceuticals, and, potentially in our own era, computers and electronics. In brewing, lumber, and textiles, where oligopolization has been imposed on previously troubled sectors, new locational patterns have emerged, combining interregional dispersion toward cheap labor regions with intraregional reconcentration of plants. The sectoral and spatial results of the case studies are summarized in chapter 13.

1.3 Regional Development Problems and Prospects

The profit cycle model of individual sectoral experience yields a fresh set of developmental concerns for regional economies. The final chapter sketches out the implications of the research findings for regional development prospects. First, I elaborate on the argument about the normalcy of regional boom-bust experiences. In most cases in the sectors studied, regional dispersion tendencies are a central feature of normal evolution. Eventually these result in job loss and abandonment of productive capacity in regions of origin. A central feature in this process is the maturation of capital-labor conflict in these older regions, manifested in high unionization rates, successful intervention in production decision making by workers through the winning of favorable work rules, and the development of a relatively strong set of state and local institutions, captured in the notions of the social wage and the closed shop. Corporate managers in post-superprofits eras will generally flee these fetters on profitability. Indeed they are given no choice by the competitive dynamic, especially when their previous oligopolistic power in a regional or national market is eroded by new international competitors or new substitute commodities. Other features of existing regional differentiation also play a role in this dispersal, particularly resource exhaustion and the opening up of new farflung markets.

Second, oligopolistic industry structures do tend to deform the interregional pattern of productive capacity. For several reasons, which I explore in chapter 3, industries that develop strong market power on the part of a few firms early in their lifetimes tend to overconcentrate production in initial locations. Examples are steel in Pittsburgh, autos in Detroit, tobacco in Virginia, and computers and microelectronics in California's so-called Silicon Valley. Outlying regions whose pools of productive factors and internal effective demands would otherwise attract new plants in these sectors do not benefit from such investments. Their residents enjoy fewer income-earning opportunities than they would in a more competitive situation. Examples are the underdevelopment of steel-producing capacity in both the South and the West, the retarded dispersal of tobacco toward Kentucky sources of supply, the failure of auto assembly to disperse until the postwar era, and the near-total absence of significant auto parts manufacture outside Detroit.

In the home regions this extraordinary concentration does not necessarily yield long-term developmental benefits. The oligopoly corporations heavily shape the structure of the local economy, including secondary linkages and the occupational and wage structure of the local labor force. Since they are relatively profitable due to market power, they tend to spawn strong unions whose compliance they are willing to buy off with relatively high wages. They come to dominate most local factor markets, thereby discouraging entrepreneurs in other sectors from setting up shop. The result is a relatively nondiversified economy that is very vulnerable to both short-term business cycles and an inevitable reversal in the fortunes of the oligopolized sector. Because they have considerable financial resources at their disposal, these industry leaders can respond rapidly and dramatically to changes in competitive conditions that require restructuring. Thus although the oligopolistic presence may have smoothed out and extended a long period of expansion, it imposes extraordinarily severe rationalizations in hard times.

The regional development consequences of this type of sectoral domination are grim. Regional economies topheavy with older capacity in a troubled sector suffer large-scale job losses. Few other sectors exist to draw on the resulting unemployed labor pool. Nor are the well-organized labor force and traditions of a high social wage and workers' rights attractive to new entrepreneurs in growing sectors, although in some cases the skills of the workers may be. Extraordinary job losses with few prospects for replacement activities become the fates of these regions, with widespread human suffering attached. This is what has happened in both Detroit and Pittsburgh and to many subregional steel centers, such as Youngstown and Buffalo.

The recent divergence in regional experience between the eastern seaboard and midwestern (including trans-Appalachia) areas of the manufacturing belt may be a product of the relative importance of oligopoly in their respective histories. Both New England and the Middle Atlantic coastal states experienced severe economic displacement in the 1970s, largely associated with the final demise of much of its textile, shoe, apparel, appliance, and related sectors, much of which are still highly competitive sectors with little market power. By the later 1970s these losses had begun to level off as other indigenous sectors took up the slack and some new innovative sectors expanded. But in the Midwest, in a swath from Pittsburgh to Milwaukee, a number of metropolitan areas built around one relatively old oligopolistic industry succumbed to dramatic restructuring from what may have permanent depressive consequences. Unlike its neighbors to the east, whose industrial origins lay in the small-scale, competitive economy of the mid-nineteenth century, this region experienced its greatest growth spurt during the turn-of-the-century explosion of trust building. As a result the Midwest may remain much more chronically troubled in the future.

A third implication of the research results is that the contemporary development potential of individual regions varies dramatically;

therefore entirely different strategies are appropriate for each. Regions with a preponderance of innovative sectors, such as Silicon Valley or the energy-rich intermountain West, have relatively golden short-term prospects, which must be monitored to prevent the curtailment of diversification or the despoliation of those resources that made them so attractive initially. Regions such as the Southeast, which have recently hosted in-migration of older industrial sectors seeking lower-cost locations, must confront the equally likely possibility that these same sectors may find overseas locations even more attractive. Regions such as the old manufacturing belt must confront their relative disadvantages for the profit calculus of private corporations. Each of these cases is complicated by the presence of oligopolists' headquarters within the region or by the absence of the relevant corporate decision makers from the regional discourse. These regional development consequences are addressed at length in chapter 14.

There is yet another use to which the profit cycle can be put in evaluating regional development prospects. The status of individual sectors in their cycles of industrial evolution implies the prevalence of a number of distinct features in the regional economy. First, regional labor force composition varies dramatically because labor needs at different developmental stages are so diverse. Regions dominated by high technology, innovative firms, such as California's Silicon Valley, will have a relatively bifurcated labor force with large proportions of professional and technical workers and relatively unskilled assembly workers. Regions dominated by mature oligopolistic industrial sectors will have large proportions of unionized, skilled blue-collar workers. Profit-squeezed sectors, oligopolized or not, will migrate to areas with low-cost, unorganized labor. In the first two cases the dynamics of the sector's evolution will most likely create labor pools over time, while only in the third is the growth pattern an outcome of response to an indigenous labor force.

Second, the structure of the business community will vary dramatically across the evolutionary stages. Innovative sectors will tend to produce large numbers of small competitors who constitute an active, indigenous entrepreneurial class. Oligopolistic sectors will create a sort of hegemonic indigenous capitalist class in the regions of origin and become absentee owners in regions of dispersed capacity. Mature sectors that have never become oligopolized will produce an indigenous class of small regional capitalists whose concerns will lean toward preservation of cheap production conditions rather than innovative activities. Thus the structure and concerns of regional entrepreneurship can be deduced from the stage status of dominant local sectors.

Similarly the major developmental planning issues of regions can be hypothesized from the evolutionary complexion of dominant industries, as can the major protagonists in planning politics. Those regions with an innovative industrial complex will exhibit pressures for land use planning, resource development, and infrastructure. Conflicts will arise principally within entrepreneurial sectors— between previous and incoming land users and between smaller and larger corporations in the innovative sectors. Regions with a preponderance of older, mature sectors will experience development problems associated with the out-migration of capital. If these regions have evolved a strong union movement, labor demands are likely to be a serious issue. If capital is headquartered outside the region, significant internal solidarity may develop around alternative approaches to development or controls on capital outflow. If capital is headquartered locally, conflict will develop over the transformation of metropolitan space toward finance, management, and service industries and away from basic production. On the other hand, in those regions where mature sectors have only recently arrived to take advantage of low-cost environments and where an organized labor force has not yet appeared, indigenous business leadership will dominate development planning. These differences in indigenous political posture are the subject of my book, *The Politics of Regions,* but are briefly sketched here in the last chapter.

These are my general arguments and findings. My intent is to pioneer an alternative approach to regional development studies that will enable us to cope with baffling changes in the contemporary economic viability of certain regions. The model offered suggests further research opportunities in testing a theory of industrial res- tructuring as the primary determinant of regional change. This new literature, which others have pioneered, promises to be the best means of reconciling the relatively moribund state of regional growth theory with the startling pace of contemporary regional change.

More generally the book's two arguments can be summarized as follows. First, dramatic long-run regional economic change is a nor- mal product of capitalist developmental dynamics. The competitive conditions within individual industries and regions dovetail to pro- duce generic tendencies toward rapid growth, followed by periods of normalcy and then periods of stagnation and decline. In some communities and regions this takes the form of a rapid boom-bust growth cycle, which can be as brief as a decade or less. In others it may be extended over several generations. Historical evidence on the prevalence of such patterns is compelling. Such longer-run dynamics caution mightily against the postwar optimism that industrial economic expansion, even when innovative, will lead to some guaranteed state of development that is the presumed standard against which all other regions are underdeveloped. We will soon have to accept a notion of overdevelopment or perhaps de-development into our lexicon if contemporary patterns of corporate competition and locational decision making prevail.

Second, the prevalence of market power, technically referred to as oligopoly, has been particularly harmful to the developmental patterns of both host and competitor regions in the United States. When oligopoly emerges quite early in the evolution of a sector—as in autos, steel, aluminum, tobacco, and more recently in computers and pharmaceuticals—pricing practices, restriction of output, and product differentiation strategies result in highly spatially concentrated industries at the expense of indigenous production in other regions. Although the centers of this activity may flourish during the period of expansion, they become top heavy with one type of production and squeeze out entrepreneurs in other sectors by dominating the supply of human, financial, and natural resources. Once the market power of the dominant oligopoly is eroded, either through the development of substitute products outside the sector or through new competition from more distant regions or countries, the lack of diversity in such economies becomes apparent. In this situation oligopolistic decision makers generally have the incentives, resources, and know-how to rationalize and restructure very rapidly, with devastating consequences for traditional centers.

In sum, then, I find that industrial development is no longer synonymous with community or regional development. In fact, what may be good for General Motors or Toyota may not be good for Detroit or Fremont, California, the site of a proposed joint venture. Incentives and enticements to firms in the form of free land, tax abatements, or capital subsidies may not be linked to job creation. Indeed these types of aid may increase their mobility or accelerate their movement through the profit cycle, with adverse longer-term consequences for the regional economies in question. This prospect raises challenging questions about our ability to plan at the regional and local level and about the adequacy of current economic development policy tools. Above all it suggests that aiding firms no longer guarantees aiding workers because boosting the profitability of a company is not necessarily linked to job creation in any particular sector, in any particular location. If jobs and a stable tax base are the goals of a regional economic development program, we must design better policy instruments than those we have relied on in the past.

2   The Sectoral Approach

The sectoral approach to regional development stresses the active agency of corporate and small business decision makers, amid the competitive environment in which they operate, as the central feature of the location and job creation process rather than the supply or demand characteristics of the region's economy. These decision makers can be studied by sectoral groupings. Regions, in turn, can be profiled by their industrial composition, a long-time acceptable practice in regional economics. This approach maintains that the study of innovative, expansive, and rationalizing behavior in those key industries that appear to drive a particular regional economy is the best method of projecting that region's future and differentiating it from its neighbors.

2.1 Traditional Regional Growth Approaches

Traditional theories of regional growth are preoccupied with the duality of demand- and supply-based growth forces. In their most elegant and abstract formulations, they deduce the spatial consequences of the behavior of household and firm decision makers. Indeed regional growth in the models of economists is so derivative that two of the most prominent could write the following: "Regional economics is the study of man's economic behavior in space"[1] and "Regional economics is the study of the neglected spatial order of the economy. It is the study of the geographic allocation of scarce resources."[2] In these theories individuals make decisions as consumers and resource owners about savings, consumption, and the supply of land and labor, in a presumed fully competitive and full information environment. Firms operate as resource allocators between resource owners and commodity consumers. Discretionary behavior on their part is severely restricted by the competitive discipline of the marketplace.

Supply-based theories locate the cause and promotion of regional growth with the availability within the region of factors of production: land, labor, capital, and entrepreneurship.[3] Supply-based theories can be illustrated by the literature on one factor: labor. Theories of development as a function of labor supply emphasize the characteristics of individual workers and the characteristics of the entire supply of workers in labor market areas. Workers are classified by age, race, sex, educational level, occupation, and other socioeconomic attributes. Then a theory of regional performance is built around deviations in these labor profiles from those of other regions. For low-income regions, for instance, attributes such as low rates of high school completion, high proportions of minorities, or high concentrations of dependent age groups are assumed to be associated with low marginal productivity of individual workers and even the area-wide labor force. This poor productivity is assumed to be the principal determinant of the region's underdevelopment. The policy implication is that upgrading workers' educational performance or preventing out-migration of prime age workers will make the region more attractive to potential employers.

Such a labor supply theory generally is accompanied by a research focus on the composition of the region's work force. Resulting empirical studies offer useful profiles for describing the contemporary possibilities for production yet do not tell much about the underlying causes that shape labor skills and attitudes. They generally do not link workers' handicaps or their poverty status to the characteristics of industries that have employed them in the past to the underlying dynamics of regional economic development.[4] The divorcing of labor supply characteristics from labor demand results in the implicit conclusion that workers' characteristics cause their unemployment and, by extension, the poverty of an entire region. Yet the characteristics have been shown merely to be correlated with such poverty. It can be argued instead that these characteristics reflect the distribution of unemployment—the determination of which individuals will fill the job slots in a regional economy and which will be unable to find paid work.[5] Unemployment itself is the product of problems of profitability in a dynamic economic system. The unemployment and poverty of indigenous groups may be caused by the erosion of prior sources of livelihood, decline in industrial sectors that previously shaped employment patterns, and certain features of contemporary sectors rather than by their own deficiencies.

Similar arguments could be made regarding resources, entrepreneurship, and local government behavior. Although each plays a role in the regional economy, each in turn has been and is now being shaped by corporate behavior and interactions with other factors. Furthermore growth theories that emphasize the role of comparative factor costs as dominant cases of business location decisions and therefore of regional growth prospects are not borne out by twentieth-century experience. High-wage regions continue to expand in and export high-wage, labor-intensive commodities, while imports to the same region may be more capital intensive. Factor supply theories are thus inadequate for explaining recent regional growth patterns in the aggregate, although they do offer accurate insights into the behavior of corporations within specific competitive and dynamic circumstances.

Demand-based theories emphasize the role of exogenously originated market bids for the output of the region: "At the root of changes in the economic geography of an advanced industrial society lies the evolution of its consumer demands."[6] Each region has an economic or export base that consists of one or more industries producing primarily for sale to external markets. Expansion of demand for products from that base will multiply through the local economy, which is often assumed to have perfectly elastic factor supplies to apply to expanded production for both export and local markets.[7] For short-run forecasting, economic base and input-output models constitute feasible tools. They remain, however, unduly tied to marginal changes in the existing composition of output in a region. Should technologies, relative prices, degree of monopoly power, or government oversight change, the forecasts will be inaccurate.

Both the supply and the demand approaches suffer from an artificially restrictive emphasis on qualities of the region as keys to growth. In demand-based theory, economic growth is a function of the static composition of the industrial base. In supply-based theory, it is a function of the existing array of factors of production. The treatment of the region in isolation from the larger economic system gives rise to misinterpretation similar to Massey and Meegan's criticism of much of urban analysis:

One unfortunate side-effect (of the concern with the decline of manufacturing in cities) has been the tendency for the problem to be defined in spatial terms, and consequently, for the causes of the

FACTOR MARKETS   PRODUCT MARKETS

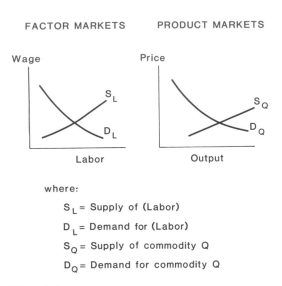

where:

S_L = Supply of (Labor)

D_L = Demand for (Labor)

S_Q = Supply of commodity Q

D_Q = Demand for commodity Q

Figure 2.1
Regional factor and product markets

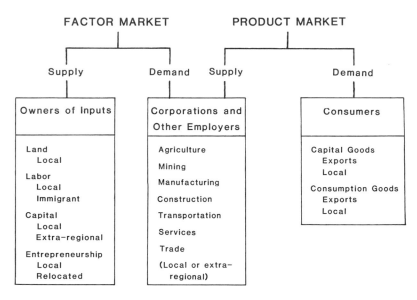

Figure 2.2
Participants in Regional Markets

problem to be sought within the same spatial area. This tendency to study the working of the city in economic and spatial isolation from the rest of the national economy has often seen emphasis being placed, for example, on assessment of the influence of such factors as the built-environment of the inner city areas (congestion, dereliction, site availability, etc.) or the personal characteristics of their residents (relating unemployment, say, to age, race or skill). The outcome of such research is often to blur and confuse the issue of causality.[8]

In the regional case, the problems we are concerned with arise mainly from changes in the industrial base and from in- and out-migration of workers and capital. The problem with neoclassical regional growth theory is that it has left the central agents in the development process out of its explicit analytical effort, assuming their behavior to be automatic given the array of regional and interregional production and market features. That is, it has collapsed two markets into one, ignoring the agents at the conjuncture of the forces of factor supply and market demand. In reality both factor markets and product markets are crucially and distinctly involved in the regional production process, as figure 2.1 demonstrates. Markets for both regional factor inputs and output are populated by two sets of buyers and sellers, as shown in figure 2.2.

The prominence of the factor supply and product demand dichotomy in regional growth theory, like its underpinning neoclassical theory, assumes that the corporate sector operates under a competitive discipline that permits it no power or leeway to behave differently from the imperatives imposed by the interaction of factor supply and consumer demand conditions. Therefore models built on this theoretical foundation eliminate any behavior or strategy of individual employers or corporations as causal elements in the development process beyond the perfunctory assumption of profit maximization. Instead they focus on factor supplies (SL) and product demand (DQ) as the causal forces.[9] Market power and political privilege may be reflected in market prices but are not explicitly examined in the model.

Yet in explaining regional employment and spatial change, the central agents are those who initiate the labor demands registered in a region, represented by DL. Employers normally invest in capital and hire additional workers when they can profitably employ them in production.[10] The key actors in the regional growth process, then, are the corporations and small businesses that choose to locate, expand, or contract in the various regions.[11] Because we cannot deal individually with each decision maker, we choose to study them in industrial sectors rather than by any other aggregation (employment size or category of business firm, for example) because the conditions affecting investment decisions are peculiar to the production and production process within each industry. This is especially true of the process of innovation, where new products and technologies emerge that can usefully characterize whole industries, provided the level of disaggregation is sufficiently small.

The terms *industry* and *sector* often are used interchangeably, although for our purposes the latter connotes greater precision and internal specificity than the former. A sector is defined as a set of corporations and firms that organizes the fabrication of a particular type of product (including services) using a common production process (employs a unique combination of labor and material inputs) and requiring a particular set of labor activities. In the vernacular of the business press, industries are generally conceptualized as steel, autos, chemicals, banking, real estate, and so forth.[12] Sectors are finer subdivisions of these industries, so, for instance, we can talk about the auto industry and its parts and assembly sectors.

The U.S. Standard Industrial Classification (SIC) divides all economic activity into four telescoped sets of increasingly differentiated subsectors. Although the system is vulnerable to classification problems, specifically the assignment of a multiproduct plant or operation to a specific category and the treatment of emerging new product lines, it offers an array of increasingly detailed data that relatively accurately reflect the quantitative dimensions of each sector. The SIC code permits analysis of corporate outcomes in the plant-by-plant allocation and location decision-making processes without sacrificing concern with the specifics of each commodity produced and competition across firms.

2.2 Theories of Sectoral Dynamics

A number of regional economists and geographers have pioneered in recent years a new inquiry into the consequences of corporate structure and decision making for individual regions. Beginning with Hymer's work (1972, 1979) on the division of labor within the firm, several other scholars have demonstrated how the separation of planning, management, and production activities has resulted in the tiering of regional space into distinct centers of each (Cohen, 1977; Noyelle, 1983). Bluestone and Harrison's (1982) work on deindustrialization contains an original argument about the role of conglomerate behavior in accelerating disinvestment. Massey and Meegan's (1982) work distinguishes among three types of corporate behavior that create potentially mobile employment: rationalization, intensification, and automation. Each of these theorists emphasizes the primacy of labor and the conflict between capital and labor as major locational forces.

A theory of sectoral dynamics must capture the tremendous dynamism in the development of capitalist economies. At certain historical moments the awareness of this developmental dynamic has been expressed in outbursts of theoretical work on it, such as Schumpeter's great treatise on innovation and entrepreneurial behavior and those of his successors, Chandler and Vernon.[13] But for the most part the investigation of this dynamic has been neglected. Economic theory concentrates on the comparative statics of competitive behavior, where the object is to describe concisely the ways in which competition produces an equilibrating process forcing prices down to a social optimum, toward the long-run average cost of production. The focus remains price, rather than the changing composition of commodities produced, and competitive behavior under free market conditions, rather than the existence of oligopoly at different stages.[14]

The field of macroeconomics has produced insightful models of the penchant for crisis in contemporary capitalist economies. But most macrotheorists are preoccupied with the notion of business cycles stressing the regularity of good times following bad rather than irreversible change in the sectoral structure of capitalist economies.[15] The permanent demise of certain sectors, the birth of others, and the evolution of new structural forms, such as the multinational corporation, are left unaddressed by business cycle models.

Yet what happens to the regional structure of these economies is clearly neither equilibrating nor merely cyclical.[16] Long-run disaster, registered in capital out-migration and job decline, may visit some, while others become first-time hosts of rapid capital accumulation and job expansion. The appropriate level of inquiry is sectoral, where irreversible dynamic patterns characterize at least large numbers of particular industries.

What drives the dynamics of these sectors? Three schools of thought offer elements for such a model: the institutionalist and Marxist work on capitalist dynamics, the product cycle model developed in U.S. business schools, and the theory of oligopoly, originating in theories of imperfect competition and surviving in the field of industrial organization.

The first element that must be embedded in the model's structure is the systematic existence of a competitive dynamic that stresses innovation as a dominant strategy of entrepreneurs. The unique quality of capitalist production is its drive toward the accumulation of capital, which, unlike the drive toward accumulation of wealth and the erection of monuments common in most previous class societies, constantly revolutionizes the production process. Rather than driving slaves harder to build pyramids, the successful modern corporation increases its profits by enhancing the productivity of retained labor through capital deepening.[17] This form of competition results in an institutionalized form of research and design behavior on the part of corporations (and inventive individuals) in which they constantly seek to improve machinery, to recast the organization of production, and to restructure the training of workers to increase profit margins. In times of crisis, such as the troughs of long waves, these activities tend to produce ensembles of new innovations, which lead the next round of investment and accumulation.[18]

A related requirement of the model is that it focus on one or more variables that capture this progressive experience of the sector in an empirically amenable manner. For this purpose, Mandel's notion of superprofits serves as a beginning.[19] Mandel argues that each new round of innovation results in short-term superprofits for the corporations involved. The new product or production process deployed either results in a new use value which is far superior to previously produced commodities (that is, the socially necessary labor time embodied in them is lower) or in a market price far below prevailing prices due to a labor-saving innovation in the production process. For a time other corporations are not permitted (by patent law) or are unable (lack of capital, lack of expertise) to follow suit. Eventually competition will increase and drive the rate of profit down toward the economy-wide prevailing rate. When this so-called normal rate is reached, the era of superprofits will end for the initiating corporation and its closest siblings.[20] This search for innovative opportunities which will yield short-term superprofits, is a continual and dominant dynamic within the international capitalist system. Mandel believes, too, that it will be most acute at times of deep crisis.

The product cycle literature offers a second set of insights into business behavior during the transition from innovation to mass production. Originated by Kuznets[21] and Burns,[22] the product cycle model envisioned a methodical, evolutionary development path for individual sectors. Output, after successful innovation, was expected to expand dramatically, to be followed by a slowdown as the market reached saturation. The expansion and contraction of the sector would be reflected in a bell-shaped curve for output over time. Since the 1970s, business school analysts have pioneered an updated version of the product cycle model. It also has been adopted to prescribe optimal management styles at successive junctures in sectoral evolution. It has been extended to distinguish between product innovations versus process innovations in early versus later stages.[23] The model of a profit cycle presented here has incorporated aspects of hypothesized product cycle behavior from the business literature; however, I treat it quite differently, for a number of reasons. First, the product cycle literature fastens on a secondary aspect of the production process as its focal point. It highlights the pattern of output rather than the motivation or behavior of the decision maker. Implicitly it holds a demand-based theory of production, which sees business decision making as an automatic response to market forces, particularly demand-side forces in the long run. It assumes that the rate of growth of demand for a product will exhibit a long-run rise and fall as its popularity waxes and wanes.[24] Yet there is no reason to believe that consumer demand will in fact behave this way; for some commodities, like wheat and coal, it clearly has not been true. The focus on sales or output as the key indicator is problematic as well. Most economic theorists, whether Marxist or neoclassical, agree that profit making is the primary goal of corporations and entrepreneurs.[25] While some of the more recent product cycle work incorporates adaptive managerial behavior, the empirical expressions of that behavior have not been worked out.[26]

Second, the product cycle model neglects the role of imperfect competition in its interpretation of corporate behavior, particularly in maturity. At two of the most crucial stages—the initiation of a new sector and its retrenchment after reaching market saturation—oligopoly is a pervasive quality of industry structure. The behavior of the industry is thus dramatically different at these junctures, yet the product cycle literature generally assumes that firms act throughout as nondominant market competitors and price takers.[27]

Finally, the empirical evidence for a long-run product cycle as originally proposed by Kuznets and Burns has simply not borne it out historically.[28] Physical output, and in cases where it is not measurable, real (constant dollar) value of output, has not followed a bell-shaped (sinusoidal) expansion and contraction path for many of the most significant industries in the United States. Other features associated with the profit cycle have much greater explanatory power than the output patterns hypothesized in the product life cycle.

The absence of explicit modeling of market power in the product cycle literature can be compensated for by drawing from the literature on oligopolistic behavior. Originally pioneered by Chamberlin[29] and Robinson,[30] the theory of imperfect competition addresses the behavior and outcome of firms selling commodities for which there are few sellers whose actions are visible and of concern to each other. In the case where only one company fabricates the product and controls the entire market, the theory predicts that the firm will restrict output and raise prices (if consumer demand is inelastic), thus realizing monopoly profit. With two or more producers the solution becomes more complex. If the competitors collude, they can set a price and allocate market shares so that they divide monopoly profits among themselves. Yet this outcome is unstable since any one of them has an incentive to cheat on the bargain and sell additional units to garner greater returns. Over time in sectors that are protected from new entrants, companies tend to adopt price leadership forms of market sharing and to compete on nonprice aspects, such as product differentiation.[31] Long-term oligopolies have been noted by industrial organization researchers to be relatively poor innovators, preoccupied with market management and competitive stability. Some of the strongest U.S. industries have atrophied under the weight of long-term oligopoly, ultimately vulnerable to competition from modernized, youthful counterparts in Europe, Japan, or developing countries.

Elements of each of these theoretical insights—Schumpeterian growth dynamics, Mandel's superprofits, product cycle theories of business economists, and oligopolistic models from industrial organization—are incorporated into the profit cycle framework. The theory argues that individual industrial sectors mature along a recognizable path in which profits and other economic features— employment, firm entry, market power, occupational structure— change in a predictable fashion. Distinct spatial tendencies also accompany each stage of a sector's passage through the profit cycle.[32]

The methodology employed to examine the model cannot be considered either neoclassical nor Marxist. Rather it fits most closely into the institutionalist tradition. Neoclassical interpretations of industrial geography suffer most from their inability to cope with long-run qualitative change. Their insights into marginal adjustments are quite powerful but generally flawed by reticence to explore the consequences of imperfect competition. Marxist models of industrial geography generally focus on the functional nature of uneven development for capitalist growth, without much effort to explain the precise orientations of individual capitalists at sequential moments in time. The institutionalist tradition has always been an acknowledged borrower from the various social science disciplines and paradigms. Generally it has been willing to take in orphans unwanted by the other traditions, such as oligopolistic behavior. It permits inductive as well as deductive thinking. The ability to synthesize within this tradition permits a superior interpretation of the existing locational array of various sectors.

3   The Profit Cycle Model

Each sector in the regional economic base can be located along the path of a long-term profit cycle. The profit cycle has five characteristic stages:

Zero profit: Corresponding to the initial birth and design stage of an industry.

Super profit: Corresponding to the era of excess profit from temporary monopoly and innovative edge.

Normal profit: Corresponding to the stage of open entry, movement toward market saturation, and absence of substantial market power.

Normal-plus or Normal-minus profit: Corresponding to the post-saturation stage, where either successful oligopolization boosts profits again or predatory and excessive competition squeezes profit.

Negative profit: Corresponding to the obsolescence stage of the sector.

These are hypothesized to constitute sequential temporal stages in the development of an industry and to correspond to different spatial behavior at each stage. The progression of profitability for an industry is represented schematically in figure 3.1. Individual firms within a sector may display profitability patterns that deviate from this profile because of location or corporate strategy; these variations are left to the case studies below. The differential between the two curves represents profit per unit output at each stage. The graph shows the growth of superprofit as a function of the difference between high (but falling) rates of growth in market demand and more rapidly falling unit cost as standardization takes place. Profit rates—return on capital—will depend as well on the magnitude of outlays. Profit rates are less straightforward to depict because the valuation of the capital stock used as the base often internalizes low

Cost, Revenue per Unit
(Constant $)

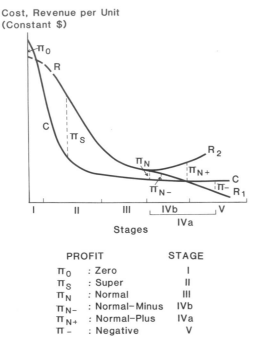

Figure 3.1
Profit cycle stages

returns by depreciation of the denominator.

The duration of a superprofit era will depend on the industry-specific evolution of both demand an cost structure during this period. Two possible paths are depicted in R_1 and R_2. In the first a competitive period is succeeded by a period of below-normal profits which ultimately (stage V) may become negative. In the second oligopolization may permit revenues to rise again, garnering monopoly profits for leading firms. Although the graph has been drawn to incorporate all stages, a sector can move directly from a superprofits stage to one of oligopoly, as in fact occurred in both pharmaceuticals and aluminum.

Profitability in this model refers to the classical notion of the ability to sustain a percentage margin between total revenue and total costs incurred directly in the production process, including maintenance of fixed capital. Generally profits are expressed for comparative purposes as a rate of return on capital, since this ratio expresses the attractive or repulsive power of a sector for investment funds. The magnitudes of profit rates used in the model reflect profit levels before reinvestment or expansion; they represent the receipts available to a corporation for stockholder dividends, profit tax payments, and retained earnings to finance internal growth.[1] Empirical verification of a particular sector's profit path is difficult due to the absence of profit data in the government industry census, to the inadequacy of alternative data sources, and to business accounting practices for recording profit. But conceptually, at least, the sources of superprofit and profit squeeze can be laid out, as well as the corresponding behavior of corporations at each juncture.

3.1 Stage 1: Zero Profit

Although the actual rate of return on capital may be volatile in this stage, the designation zero profit refers to the initial stage of development of a sector where conventional book profits are not recorded and no short-run profits are anticipated. Alternatively one could think of this as a period of negative profit, but this is less accurate since ordinary entrepreneurs in this stage do not think of their efforts as business outlays in the conventional sense. In this stage research, design, experimentation and prototype modeling take place, and the first commodities are fashioned in test runs. The inventive activity that dominates this stage may be carried out by the weekend basement tinkerer or the corporate lab researcher. Business organization and marketing for the projected product are nonexistent, and no mass production techniques are in place. Investment consists largely of inventive labor time; little or no investment in fixed plant takes place.

This is the stage of imaginative and risky scheming. Although the problem or use the inventive activity aims at addressing is frequently an articulated creature of social or corporate needs or bottlenecks that hamper the profitability of contemporary production, there is no existing market waiting to snap up the output.[2] This stage is pre-entrepreneurial. Because profit potential is least certain in this stage, new firms cannot garner large sums of venture capital unless they are attached to a diversified parent. Finance is provided either by internal corporate funds or from personal sources in the case of the independent inventor.

Output at this stage is low or nonexistent, although the rate of expansion may be rapid as prototypes proliferate. Employment of wage labor, too, is low or nonexistent. Prices, when the initial product is floated, are high due both to the high unit cost of its necessarily custom-made nature and to its use value to the purchaser. As the product proves its initial worth, prices may rise dramatically, depending on the difference between its use value and previous methods of satisfying that same need. The earliest generations of electronic computing equipment and calculators serve as good examples; prices for the original models were extraordinarily high, often ten times higher than eventual competitive prices. In general price can be expected to bear little relationship to cost throughout this stage.

The production process is necessarily highly customized at this point. Mechanization is rare, and the production process is relatively labor intensive because large numbers of engineers and specialists are needed to oversee development. Inventive skills and prototype modeling dominate the labor input. Few blue-collar production workers are needed. Any marketing, legal, or management functions may be subcontracted out, as well as some fabrication. As a result of the high unit costs associated with this type of process and of the fact that uncertainty about the marketability of a new product keeps prices close to cost, profits are nonexistent to low until the product takes off, which marks the beginning of the next stage.

No particular industry can be identified in the sector at this time.[3] Competition is generally absent or minor. No entry occurs. Concentration is thus potentially high, depending on how many firms or individuals are simultaneously pioneering the sector. Firms, to the extent they exist, are tiny, with the occasional exception of the large corporation pioneering an entirely new line. Ownership tends toward partnership and proprietorship. Manpower is focused on the design effort. Very little labor time goes into marketing and sales efforts.

3.2 Stage II: Superprofit

Once a new product or service is successfully innovated, it becomes a new sector. It then enters a dramatic growth stage in which profits rise well above the economy-wide level. These superprofits are a return that the entrepreneur or corporation is able to command in a market that it dominates in the short run, either through patent protection or through inability of potential competitors to respond in the short run. The degree of superprofits depends on the differential use value the new sector provides to its clients. It will be high if the commodity lowers the socially necessary labor time that other corporations require in their production processes (such as numerical control techniques and devices), lowers the time households must spend in reproducing labor power (washing machines are an example), or raises the quality of life for some group (such as birth control devices). Demand-led prices will dominate this stage, except in the case of the unsuccessfully innovated idea. Output will increase rapidly; investment in new capacity will tend to moderate price hikes. Recorded profit may not be high since revenues may be reinvested in large amounts in anticipation of future returns.

The production process will become more regular in this stage. The average cost of a unit of output will begin to fall as standardization takes place. Some mechanization will occur, raising the capital-to-labor ratio. Employment will grow rapidly, with occupations concentrated on the professional-technical end of the spectrum. Product design and improvement is still centrally important and the focus of firm strategy. Specialized types of engineers, scientists, designers, and craftworkers will be high in demand. Firms expanding will begin to do more of their own in house fabrication, marketing, and management.

Other firms will strive to enter the industry, but only those proficient in design and product innovation (or able to buy out those who are) will succeed. Much of this new firm formation will come from professionals splitting off from the parent firm and starting up their own companies.[4] Concentration in the industry will diminish in this stage, even though the size of firms will tend to grow rapidly. Some vertical integration may begin in this period, particularly if large buyers or suppliers believe they can successfully integrate forward or backward into this superprofit sector. An example was IBM's entry into the semiconductor manufacturing business. The marketing and sales effort is still only modestly developed at this stage; frequently the scientific and design staff themselves must approach potential customers because they are the only ones competent to explain the all-important new design features.

Large corporations may be the innovators, either because of inventions crafted in their own research labs or because they have bought out a firm. In general, industrial organization experts stress the record of a continual and remarkable stream of innovations from small firms, in part a result of conservatism on the part of larger corporations. In the last few decades, xerography, computer software, specialized computers, electronics, and scientific instruments have all been pioneered outside large corporate laboratories.[5] Others believe that the importance of large firms in the innovative process is increasing over time, citing as examples petroleum, coal, and steel in the United States.[6] If so, some of the pressures on infant industries are mitigated, particularly the capital famine, since large corporations can and do move funds around internally to subsidize new product lines. They may also establish sales and service networks that discourage new start-ups, and they may use their name recognition and reputation for service in other sectors to maintain a competitive edge. In cases where large corporations compete in innovative sectors, they will exhibit behavior similar to that of stage IV.

3.3 Stage III: Normal Profit

Eventually the entry of new firms into the market and the expansion of existing ones result in the chipping away of superprofits until an average rate of return is achieved. This is the situation most closely approximated by the models of competition presented in both standard microeconomics and Marxist economic theory. In the neoclassical model, such profits represent the price of capital—a combination of the price entrepreneurs must command in order to risk production and the price that holders of money capital must receive to forgo other uses of their capital. In the Marxist model this rate of profit represents the rate of surplus value appropriated from workers and redistributed across sectors with different organic compositions of capital.

In this stage output is still growing, but growth slows as market saturation is reached. Price competition may be intense, resulting in the lowering of price toward price of production. The strategy of the firm turns from product design and market outreach to more efficient management, greater mechanization, and possibly movement into new regional, national, or international markets. New capacity investment will be undertaken only if it promises significant scale economies or much higher labor productivity.

Mass production techniques are now fully in place. Production increasingly is mechanized, and in the interest of cost cutting, a large management team investigates ways of cutting costs through work discipline, reorganization of tasks, and more mechanization. A large production work force is now employed, although it may not be growing as fast as previously. Efforts at unionization may become widespread at this stage. The professional-technical occupations become less important as a percentage of the work force, while management and production workers grow in importance. Some deskilling of production jobs may occur as automation and task division take place. The firm engages in relatively less subcontracting than in earlier stages.

Industry structure is now in or past its most competitive stage. As more firms entered in the previous stage, horizontal integration also began as firms merged or were bought out by competitors. Average firm size has therefore risen dramatically, and some of the smaller firms have gone out of business. Vertical integration is also occurring. Increasingly firms are multiplant corporations. To the extent that price competition holds sway, corporate strategy concentrates on cutting costs and increasing productivity rather than on the marketing and sales effort.

3.4 Stage IV: Normal-Plus and Normal-Minus Profit

The normal profit stage may proceed as long as undue concentration does not occur, predatory competition does not enter the picture, or a new substitute product or process does not challenge the sector. One or another of these destabilizing factors eventually emerges in most industries. In the long run the innovative drive of capitalist economies ensures the obsolescence of most products, if not sectors. A sector's ability to weather this stage depends on its technical possibilities, financial resources, political power, and management acumen. Two paths are possible.

First, the industry may respond to its diminished growth prospects by oligopolizing. Indeed oligopoly is the most common form of contemporary industry structure and has been a major force in economic development since the turn of the century.[7] Domination of the market by a few sellers will permit these corporations to reinstate greater-than-normal profits by the classical maneuver of restricting output and raising price. Particularly if demand is highly inelastic, meaning that most buyers will continue to purchase the product despite the rise in price, profits can be substantially boosted in this manner (though not as high as during the superprofit stage). Corporate strategy will then aim at increasing and protecting market share, mainly by product differentiation and an extensive marketing and sales effort designed to persuade and woo new buyers.[8] Ancillary to this effort, the lead corporations will also lobby extensively for favorable policies such as lax antitrust enforcement, industry subsidies, and government contracts. In this case output may either rise or fall since oligopoly behavior restricts supply while the marketing effort expands it. Prices will rise, rapidly as oligopolization is occurring and moderately later on, to maintain the new monopoly price margin.[9] Profits will more than cover costs, although these costs now include a substantial increase in market analysis, advertising, and management budgets to engineer the oligopoly strategy.

Farsighted corporations may plow some excess profit back into research and development. But for the most part the era of innovation is over because markets are nearly saturated and because fixed plant, standardized techniques, and organizational habit render the corporation relatively inert; potential increases in market share only infrequently promise a profit margin high enough to warrant a costly retooling. New capacity investment in the sector will be modest and similar to that of the previous stage. Successful oligopolists in mature sectors are more prone to reinvest profit in unrelated sectors, in vertical integration, or in money markets than to expand capacity in the original sector.

Competition continues among few surviving corporations. Cost cutting is thus still important, and economies of scale will be pursued if they promise lower average unit cost. Mechanization will continue apace, increasing the capital-to-labor ratio. If output is not growing, rationalization of production may result in worker layoffs, sometimes quite substantially. Unions are likely to be strongest among production workers in successful oligopolies, threatening profit margins and requiring great corporate effort at work force discipline and control.

Industry structure will be highly concentrated, with a few large firms dominating the bulk of production. Firm sizes will be large, and firms may diversify into conglomerates (one use of normal-plus profit) or be bought out by one. New firm entry is nearly impossible if the oligopoly is successful. Yet a reversal in the practice of vertical integration may occur. More subcontracting may be undertaken as a means of disciplining workers in particular job categories (for example, maintenance workers). Subcontracting also may be designed to take advantage of scale economies of suppliers (such as dye makers that sell to all the auto companies) or of fierce competition among suppliers. Oligopoly profits may be used by management to diversify into entirely different sectors.

If oligopoly does not emerge from an era of normal profits, then the other likely fate of an industry is its decline in the face of competition from substitutes or imports. In the case of imports the loss of jobs may not be synonymous with corporate failure because domestic corporations may import from their own plants abroad while those in the home country are shut down. Or they may be harvesting profit by selling their production technology abroad. They may still make normal or higher profits by doing so. Aggressive marketing by foreign corporations (like the Japanese in the U.S. auto and semiconductor industries) may threaten the profitability of a national industry. More frequently a sector's demise comes about because a new product or process is introduced that serves as a substitute and undercuts its market, often because established firms refuse to meet the challenge. Examples are plastic for wood, aluminum for steel, synthetic fibers for cotton and wool, and synthetic rubber for natural rubber. If the use value of the new product is superior, then unless the existing sector can change over to produce the competing product, it will find its profits continually diminished as the cheaper substitute drives down the price of its product. If it can convert its physical capacity to the new product, it may find itself back in the superprofits stage or, more likely, the normal profits stage of expansion of the new product. Otherwise it will enter a period of protracted decline as its market dwindles.

In this stage of shrinkage the prevailing corporate strategy within the sector will be rationalization, severe cost cutting, and transfer of liquid capital into entirely new uses or production processes. Management will be trimmed to the bone and production workers laid off as each successive cutback takes place. No extensive marketing and sales effort will be pursued as corporations coast on their previous record. Trade associations will become vigorous and well heeled at this juncture, attempting to move government to bail out their industry by means of import restrictions, outright subsidies, and favorable regulatory rulings. Concentration may increase again as smaller firms fail and larger firms absorb competitors. No new entry will occur. In some cases conglomerates may take over operations in order to take advantage of short-term profit realization or pursue a cross-industry subsidization strategy.[10]

3.5 Stage V: Negative Profit

In the final stage corporate producers will be taking absolute losses on production and trying to liquidate plant as fast as possible. They may still take losses on their operating account to cover fixed charges (such as debt) that are still outstanding or sell physical capacity to some other user. Closings are numerous as output falls. Prices may

Table 3.1
Business behavior across the profit cycle

Profit cycle stage	Experimentation	Innovation	Competition	Maturity	Decline
Output, cost, price, profits, investment					
Output (physical)					
Level	Low	Moderate	Moderate/high	Moderate/high	Low
Growth	Slow to rapid+	Rapid++	Moderate+ to moderate−	Slow+ to rapid+	Rapid−
Price (real)					
Level	High	Moderate	Low	Low to moderate	Low
Growth	Rapid−	Moderate−	Moderate−	Moderate+ to moderate−	Stable to slow
Unit cost	High	Moderate	Low	Moderate to low	Moderate
Profitability	Low	High	Moderate	Low to moderate+	Low
Investment in new capacity	Low	High	Moderate	Moderate to negligible	Disinvestment
Production features					
Capital/labor ratio	Low	Moderate	High	High	High to moderate
Employment					

Level	Low	Moderate	High	Moderate to high	Moderate
Growth	Rapid +	Rapid ++	Slow + to slow –	Moderate –	Rapid –
Occupational composition					
Engineering/ technical (%)	High	High	Moderate	Low/ moderate	Low
Managerial (%)	Low	Moderate	High	Moderate	Low
Production (%)	Low	Moderate	High	High	High
Subcontracting	High	Moderate	Low	Moderate	Moderate to high
Advertising, Sales	Low	Moderate	High	High to moderate	Low
Industry Structure					
Entry	Low	High	Moderate	Low	Low
Concentration	High	Moderate	Low	Moderate	High
Size of firm	Low	Moderate	Moderate to high	High	High
Vertical integration	None	Modest	Extensive	Extensive	Moderate
Modal class of ownership	Partner/ proprietor	Corporate: Single plant	Corporate: Multiplant	Corporate/ conglomerate	Corporate/ conglomerate + small firm

or may not fall, depending on supply conditions. Disinvestment, or the net retirement of physical capacity, is ubiquitous.

Several forces operate on the capital-to-labor ratios. On the one hand the closing of the oldest plants raises the average degree of mechanization, which will show up as worker productivity increases. The layoff of workers at plants operating below capacity will also register as an increase in capital-to-labor ratio, although without any effect on productivity. On the other hand small labor-intensive operators may stay in business when the corporations step out because they are willing to settle for a lower rate of profit to keep their livelihood; examples are small sawmills, fishing, and artisans. This may register as a decrease in concentration, the size of firm, the capital labor proportions, and apparent labor productivity.

3.6 Key Variables across the Profit Cycle

The level and direction of change in each of the sectoral features hypothesized to be affected by the profit cycle are summarized in table 3.1. Designations such as "high" or "low" are relative to the average level or rate of the variable across the entire cycle. Some of them deserve additional graphic presentation to stress their variation across the profit cycle. Perhaps the most important of these are the relationships of investment, output, and employment, charted in figure 3.2.

Figure 3.2 shows how maturation of the profit cycle, the potential for oligopoly, and the tendency toward greater labor productivity through mechanization combine to shape levels and rates of change of output, employment, and investment. It shows how both employment and output rise through the initial stages of the profit cycle but how later, as the production process becomes standardized and mechanization more common, gains in labor productivity increase the ratio of output to jobs. In other words the number of workers required to produce a unit of output has fallen.[11] The inset shows the skewed evolutionary path of output and jobs gains under oligopoly. Since oligopolies by definition seek to restrict output and raise price, they will stunt the expansion during earlier stages, perhaps even producing a smoother growth path than the more exuberant competition of nonoligopolized sectors. If they succeed in product differentiation and consumer taste shaping, they may be able to extend output levels beyond what they would have been in the pure competition case. But once obsolescence or effective competition

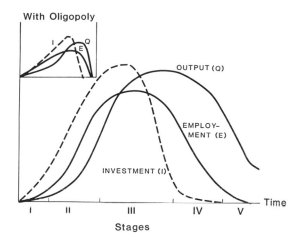

Figure 3.2
Production patterns across the profit cycle

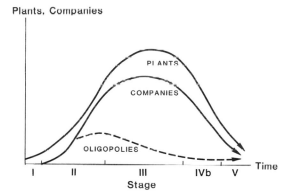

Figure 3.3
Plant and firm growth across the profit cycle

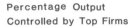

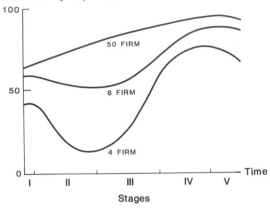

Figure 3.4
Concentration ratios across the profit cycle

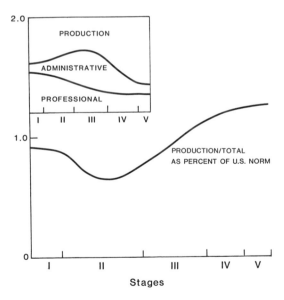

Figure 3.5
Profit cycle occupational composition

from abroad destroys market power, retrenchment may be much more severe and traumatic than in the competitive case, as the rapid down sides of the curves in the upper left-hand corner portray. Although in both portions, the graph shows output and employment rising and falling in a relatively regular manner, the hypothesis that employment exhibits a bell-shaped development path is much stronger than the output hypothesis.[12]

Figure 3.3 portrays the relationship between the numbers of plants and companies engaging in the sector over time. The curves reflect the growth from few firms and establishments at the outset, to substantial additions of both during the innovative stage, through a decline in both in the later stages. The flattening out and eventual decline of both curves results from increasing economies of scale and industry obsolescence. In the case of companies, the drop in numbers is also a result of consolidations. Thus the number of companies is expected to fall at a more rapid rate than the number of plants, reflected in the growing gap between the two in intermediate stages. The higher the degree of oligopoly, all else equal, the greater this divergence will be shown in the lower curve. The possibility that the larger firms will leave the market more quickly in later stages is incorporated by the diminishing gap between numbers of plants and firms on the right-hand portion of the graph

Change in concentration ratios over time is portrayed in figure 3.4. The curves represent the degree of output controlled by the top four, eight, and fifty companies over the cycle. In the initial stages, concentration of the innovators may be very high, followed by an era of vigorous entry, which pushes concentration ratios down. Ultimately both obsolescence (with its concomitant failure of smaller firms) and oligopolistic tendencies (smaller firms bought up by larger ones; larger firms expanding faster internally than small ones) will increase concentration ratios again. Only at the very end, if single firms demonstrate a willingness to produce at below-normal profit rates, will this trend be reversed. The model suggests that the largest corporations may lose market shares at two points: during the transition from innovation to competition and during the late decline stage. The second tier of firms may actually increase their shares during these same periods because their managements are more innovative.

Profit cycle occupational composition

The labor force composition at each stage is presented in figure 3.5. Three portrayals are used. The upper left graph presents the hypothesized percentages of employment accounted for by each broad occupational group at each period of time.[13] It shows the differential rates of expansion of each group, particularly the fact that while the production work force grows relatively slowly in early stages compared to other occupational categories, the managerial work force grows most rapidly in stages II and III and the initial high level of professional-technical labor declines rapidly as a proportion of total at first and then more modestly throughout. This technical form of labor is most prevalent at the initial stages, managerial employment is relatively greatest at the intermediate stages, and the production work force is relatively most prominent in the latter stages (even though it may be the largest group from stage II on).

These patterns reflect the relative importance of each group and its comparative growth over the profit cycle, not the actual magnitudes across all sectors, which may be expected to exhibit wide variation. Because the labor force composition of advanced industrial economies has exhibited a secular trend away from production workers, the interpretation of actual patterns is complicated by a strong tendency for this group to decline in share in all sectors. The lower right-hand graph shows the hypothesized relationship of production workers to all workers over the cycle, and the middle graph shows the normalization of this trend by expressing the ratio in any one sector to that of the norm for the United States.

4   Spatial Manifestations of the Profit Cycle

The changing regional array of plants and jobs in any sector reflects the priorities of corporations at each evolutionary point in the profit cycle. Profitability conditions place different pressures on business organizations at sequential historical moments. Corporate strategy varies dramatically over the profit cycle, ranging from an emphasis on innovation and product design in the initial stages, market saturation and efficient mass production at the intermediate stages, and creation of market power and/or rationalization of production in later stages. Each strategy places its own unique set of demands on factor inputs and renders the sector more or less sensitive to market pull. Both factor availability and market demand are unevenly distributed across regions, so that these distinct regions become more or less attractive to sectors in successive profit cycle stages. Thus we can derive the hypothetical spatial behavior of sectors and the consequent regional location patterns from the profit cycle behavior.[1]

4.1 Spatial Succession

Spatial Succession can be summarized by envisioning a sequence of locational tendencies in which a sector settles and concentrates in one or several regions at the outset and thereafter disperses outward, eventually abandoning its original centers. This pattern is shown in figure 4.1. Such a centrifugal impulse has always been an accepted image in the location theory literature. Hoover, for instance, summarized it and stressed the importance of labor as a determinant:

Changes in labor requirements, generally as a result of a modification of processes, exert profound effects on the locational patterns of industries. An industry requiring specialized or highly trained labor generally has a concentrated and rather stable pattern, clustering at points where such a labor supply has gradually developed. But eventually the processes of almost any industry become routinized, through technical and managerial improvements, so that ordinary labor without special training can be used. The normal result is that the industry spreads or moves to other areas, its dispersion from the original centers being sped by the relatively high wages and inflexible conditions that have become established there by the skilled elite.[2]

Recent industrial location studies have tried to determine which of several factors (wages, transportation costs, land costs, or market pull, among others) are most significant in explaining industry movement nationwide or within regions. Using cross-sectional techniques and aggregating across all sectors at given periods of time, their results have tended to be inconclusive.[3] The model offered here, by treating sectors individually and by modeling their behavior over time, is designed to return to the earlier interest of Hoover and others in broad historical tendencies. In addition, the profit cycle model's incorporation of recent work on innovation and the scarce evidence on spatial orientation of oligopoly permit greater detail in charting sequential regional choices.

The initial stages in a sector's evolution generally find it confined spatially to one or a very few locations. I call this pattern concentration.[4] The precise location is not specifiable theoretically. Initial locations of innovations like the automobile, and the semiconductor correspond to the somewhat arbitrary location of inventors or innovators.[5] Frequently they are not centrally located with respect to either ultimate markets or input availability. Yet once spawned,

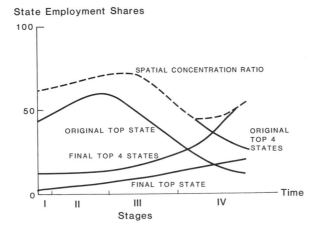

Figure 4.1
Geographical concentration across the profit cycle

their subsequent geographical diffusion is highly flavored by that initial historical accident. Not all new sectors settle at the point of invention.[6] Sometimes an important resource, such as water power in the case of aluminum, pulls the industry toward a region where that resource is ample.

In the superprofit stage the strategy of the rapidly growing firms will be on product design, professional expertise in research, development, and marketing, and flexibility. These needs emphasize the creation of a skilled labor pool, skewed heavily toward the professional-technical categories. Infant firms will tend to draw subcontracting firms and suppliers around them. The need to be near the center of ongoing innovative activity and to have ready access to new information results in the continued gravitation of new firms to the original location.[7] Indeed new firms frequently are formed from employees spinning off of older companies to found competitors. This spatial pattern I call agglomeration. It refers to the proliferation and growth in size of the innovating firms and their tendency to draw linked sectors, and a labor force, to them at the initial site. In this stage, production can be expected to continue to grow, pulling related growth with it, at the points where it first sprouted.

The third stage finds firms growing in size and beginning to diminish in numbers. Many become multiplant firms, where the size of the corporation exceeds the efficient economies of scale in production. Corporations in the stage approaching normal profits are concerned with reaching all corners of the market and maintaining market share. Thus a location closer to their markets becomes increasingly attractive, reinforced by the competitive dynamic among all firms. If other considerations permit—if resource tying is not overriding and sufficient labor is available at the market end—firms in this stage will tend to expand by dispersing their additional production units closer to markets. At the same time this dispersal may be linked to a search for cheaper labor and land, as cost cutting becomes more necessary to the performance and profitability of the firm.[8] If unionization has begun to appear at the original production sites, this search will include the desire to avoid unionized communities. Since the production process may be becoming more automated and thus require fewer skills, the search may lead corporations to locations with a smaller, less-skilled labor force.[9] This phenomenon I call dispersion, where for one or more reasons additional plants are sited in regions relatively remote from the core.

In the fourth stage spatial behavior of industries will depend on the relative degree of oligopoly present. By restricting the rate of growth of output, oligopoly behavior will truncate the dispersion process. We can call this effect retardation. If the industry becomes successfully oligopolized in an early stage, where firms are still heavily concentrated in one region, it will tend to overdevelop the sector there while slowing its development elsewhere.[10] If, as has been the case in several strategic industries, leading firms adopt a spatially based pricing system as the method of price collusion, these fetters on dispersion will be reinforced. Perhaps the most notorious historical example was the Pittsburgh plus system of pricing adopted by the steel companies. All steel companies based their delivered price quotes on the cost of shipping steel from Pittsburgh, thereby eliminating the advantage that any particular firm possessed due to its location closer to customers. The centripetal pull of oligopoly is also a function of the extraordinary demand for professional, technical, and managerial workers needed to fashion market strategy and the premium placed on being near competitors in a market situation where each watches the actions of the others.[11]

Oligopolies may shape regional sequences in two other ways. Those in the consumer goods sectors, where advertising can potentially raise the level of aggregate demand, eventually may be able to support more plants than they would have in the absence of market power. In this case the tendency toward retardation may be countervailed. In addition oligopolistic firms may cluster their plants in regional centers, as hypothesized by the Hotelling model.[12] Rather than be dispersed throughout the country at separate locations, firms will be found grouped together at the center of regional markets, maintaining a higher degree of spatial concentration than would have prevailed under more competitive conditions.

A final way in which oligopoly may affect location operates through political power. Oligopolies are more likely to have active trade associations, which lobby for import protection, loan guarantees, special procurement deals, leniency in the enforcement of environmental or other regulations, and patent protection. No clear bias in the locational process can be assumed across this portfolio of privileges. Yet in each individual sector these types of government aid may have substantial effects on the spatial pattern of economic activity. In general government actions intervene in the fortunes of regional economies, often through direct mechanisms like federal aid or military installations or indirectly through tax or expenditure patterns.[13]

But if oligopolies retard decentralization in earlier stages, they may accelerate the process in later periods. Oligopolized sectors as well as competitive ones will be intensely interested in cutting costs, increasing productivity, and tightening control over labor in a profit-squeeze situation. Successful unionization in mature industrial regions will tend to be associated with state and local welfare policies that boost the social wage, with some corresponding increase in local taxes to business. Corporations will thus continue to disperse production to regions where unions are absent and the business climate more favorable.[14]

If this occurs hand in hand with cuts in output or with significant new plant scale and technology, the aggregate spatial outcome will be relocation. In this phase industries may be observed to close plants in one region while expanding production in others. As Bluestone and Harrison point out, this process does not necessarily mean the closing of a particular plant and the transfer of its equipment and product line to another location; it may take place more slowly through the gradual retirement of plant in one region several years after new plants are built and running in others.[15] The phenomenon of regional relocation, where an industry increasingly shifts production to newer regions, will be true of highly competitive sectors as well as oligopolies, but since the latter have slowed the rate of relocation previously and presumably have greater resources to finance openings and closings, they may now make up for lost time with a vengeance. In other words dispersion may accelerate in later stages of oligopolized sectors' development.

The final stage, of negative profits, will find corporations retiring production as fast as it is operationally possible. Below-normal profits will have sent corporations scurrying to scrap capacity. At this stage the purpose will be to close plants or move to a cheaper site. The propensity to close plants seems to vary systematically across types of business organizations. Bluestone and Harrison found that conglomerates were most likely to close down or retire plants gradually, even when they were still operating in the range of normal profit; they do so because they are sometimes short of cash to make other, more promising superprofit ventures.[16] Milking a cash cow serves the purpose of supplying their money capital needs. On the other hand small businesses also tended to close plants more often than the corporate sector, which is lodged between the partnership-proprietorship form and the conglomerate form, mainly because their position is generally more precarious than corporate firms and they are thus first to go under. On the other hand one would expect that small businesses at a below-normal profit rate are likely to hang on longer in an established location than their corporate counterparts because they have greater personal stakes in the region and fewer means for moving their investment elsewhere. This final stage I refer to as abandonment.

4.2 Spatial Outcomes

The stages of sectoral succession can be charted by looking either at sectors themselves or at the experience of regions that host them. From the sector's point of view we should be able to observe the extent of spatial concentration or dispersion over time that corresponds to the movement of variables expressing the product cycle. The most likely candidate for this exercise is the level of employment. Figure 4.1 above shows the hypothesized evolution of spatial concentration, dispersion, and reconcentration of jobs.

Documenting the spatial behavior of sectors from the vantage point of the several regions is more difficult, particularly because gross regional income, employment, and output are the joint product of a number of basic sectors interacting. For a set of regions or subregions where one or more sectors in the same stage of evolution are dominant, we should be able to detect a growth, a leveling off, and a fall in total employment across the cycle as the specific sector(s) lead local growth rates. Alternatively we should be able to use cross-sectional data to detect these patterns. The current growth experience of each region is a function of the point at which it became an original host for an industry. Regions whose major industries are now in the fourth or fifth stages of the profit cycle should be experiencing slow or negative growth and unemployment, while regions that only recently have hosted first- or second-stage industries should be experiencing the opposite.

The profit cycle model enables two very different forms of sectoral growth in a region to be distinguished. A large increase in sector employment registered in a region may mean either the birth of a new sector or the dispersion or relocation of a more established sector from some other region. The local consequences of these two types of sectoral growth are dramatically different. In the former we might expect the generation of a highly skilled labor force and associated agglomerative activity, which can set off a major long growth spurt.[17] In the latter case long-term growth prospects may be an illusion because the relocation is due solely to the response of corporations to the relative underdevelopment of the regional economy.[18] As this new sectoral presence helps create a local labor market, pushes up wages, and encourages unionization, these benefits may choke off any further growth. The same cost-cutting insistence that encouraged the original relocation may lead to a further round of relocations to offshore sites, rendering the promise of sustained regional development even more ephemeral. These distinctions between stage status of incoming sectors have dramatic consequences for development potential. They suggest that the sunbelt boom, for instance, cannot be seen as a monolithic growth experience. The low-cost incentives to post-normal-profit stage corporations may result in very different futures for the Deep South region versus the electronics-induced growth of some subregions within the Southwest.

In addition to aggregate employment levels, the spatial behavior of sectors at different points of the product cycle will affect both the occupational composition and structures of the business community within regions. Firms in the initial zero and superprofit stages will tend to have relatively high proportions of professional-technical workers. As the production work force grows, a dual work force emerges in the region. Corporations in the normal-plus or normal-minus and negative profit stages will tend also to have a bifurcated class structure—managerial and production—but it is more likely to be spatially segregated interregionally or intraregionally. In the last stages production workers will predominate. The growth of employment, therefore, will result in very different occupational structures locally depending on which stage—agglomeration or relocation—of the profit cycle is involved. Regions specializing in certain sectors, such as nonrenewable resource extraction, will exhibit even greater tendencies than other regions toward pure working-class structure, especially when in otherwise rural settings, such as the solid working-class mining towns in Appalachia. Conflicts on the regional level may be a direct function of class structure and sectoral dynamics.

The entrepreneurial and unionization structures at the local or regional level also will be affected by sectoral type and dynamic. Regions with dominant sectors in the early stages of development will tend to have a large and robust entrepreneurial class composed of managers and proprietors of small firms. An example is the nineteenth-century agricultural Midwest, the basis of the birth of

Republicanism. Regions of origin with dominant sectors in the oligopolistic normal-plus profit stage will produce a resident owner and managerial class that has a discouraging effect on other entrepreneurial aspirants. Unionization will be advanced in these regions, with patent consequences for regional politics. Regions hosting new dispersals or relocations from existing corporations in other regions will complain of an absentee capitalist class, quite distinct from local small businesspeople in the tertiary sector. Unionization will not typically be extensive in these locations, although efforts to organize workers will develop eventually.

Within the product cycle we might expect variable stage length,
divergent magnitudes of profit differentials, and relative differences
in regularity, depending on the specific characteristics that shape
profitability in each sector. While appreciating such sectoral
specificity, we can also explore possible ways of aggregating sectors
so that hypothetical statements about the length, the intensity, and
the regularity of profit cycle experience can be made. Sectors have
long been clustered in groups useful to the economist and geographer. The first such schemas were fashioned by Fisher and Clark
with three basic sectoral groupings: primary or extractive industries
(agricultural, fishing forestry, mining), secondary industries
(manufacturing construction, utilities), and tertiary industries (commerce, transportation, communication, services). These categories
in turn were employed in stage theories of economic development.[1]
Contemporary macroeconomic models distinguish between producer
(investment) goods and consumer (consumption) goods. In this
chapter distinctions between producer and consumer goods sectors
and between resource-oriented and nonresource-based sectors are
explored.[2] Because their development strategies differ, these sub-
groups possess different regional orientations.

5.1 Resource-Dependent Sectors

Resource-dependent sectors are those whose dominant locational
concern is a spatially fixed or extensive resource, such as arable land,
mineable ore, or harvestable forest. The definition can be expanded
to include those activities commonly classified as manufacturing but
that are locationally tied to a resource base: sawmills (but not furniture manufacture), fish canneries, flour milling, ore processing (but
not steel making or coking). Generally this proximity reflects high

transportation costs of the preprocessed raw material compared to the processed commodity. The classification of an industry or sector as resource oriented does not mean that labor is not central to the production process. It does mean that labor must be brought to the resource region rather than the reverse. Examples of resource-oriented industries in which labor historically has been vigorously recruited (and where procurement of labor remains an important problem) are agriculture, particularly California fruit and vegetable production, and mining. Changes in resource dependency are possible over time. Utilities, for instance, were once dependent on waterfalls and then became increasingly market oriented. More recently the popular repugnance for pollution and the potential for interregional electricity transmission across high-power long-distance lines are rendering utilities resource oriented once again, this time toward sparsely populated, clean air locations.

A number of important differences may be hypothesized about the profit cycle experience between resource-based and other sectors. In the former we might expect fewer substitutes. If so, profit cycles will tend to be stretched out over longer periods of time (coal, oil). In addition resource-based industries tend to produce raw materials for sale to other producers. Generally the product is highly homogeneous so that the type of oligopoly associated with product differentiation is less likely to prevail in the mature stages.[3] These industries will engage in less advertising and exhibit relatively greater price competition. Oligopoly will succeed only to the extent that ownership of resources is concentrated (oil, for instance) or economies of scale dominate. The accumulative urge will tend to be manifested in continual improvements in process (rather than in product or in marketing), resulting in severe employment declines in later stages even when output is rising rapidly. Because of their competitive nature, these sectors will employ large proportions of production workers with relatively fewer managerial and sales workers. Since the product is standardized, the work force will tend to be less internally differentiated than in other sectors. As in oil, the emergence of market power will countervail these tendencies.

These features will be reflected in the baseline variables in several ways. The profit cycle will tend to be longer on average than for other types of sectors. The differential between numbers of establishments and numbers of companies will be much smaller since concentration is less characteristic. Mechanization in the face of competition in the later stages will tend to force employment levels down more rapidly. And the proportion of production workers to total work force will be relatively higher throughout. In contrast, nonresource-based sectors may exhibit output and job cycles that end more abruptly because substitution across sectors is more likely. Product differentiation will be a more common growth strategy, creating more oligopoly power and supporting a larger proportion of professional and technical labor. Greater stress on innovation may increase possibilities for recycling through the profit cycle, resulting in bumpier expansion paths.[4] These distinctions affect the spatial behavior of the sectors involved. They are explored in subsequent chapters by choosing a subset of clearly resource-based sectors as candidates for case studies.[5]

5.2 Producer and Consumer Goods Industries

A second distinction among sectors is the difference between client types.[6] Producer goods sectors sell the bulk of their output to other industries. Examples are industrial chemicals, heavy machinery, process plant construction steel, and textiles. The buyers are corporations that transform these materials further or use the machinery and plant to produce consumer goods (or more producer goods). In these sectors product differentiation is less prominent. On the other hand, oligopoly is frequently prevalent due to the existence of significant economies of scale.[7] Producer goods are more vulnerable than other sectors to sharp falls in price that may represent the obsolescence of their product due to substitution from an alternative. Such substitutes are not as likely to be produced within the sector as in the previous cases. The substitution of aluminum for steel, for instance, required such different production technology and resources that it was pioneered by and evolved into a completely separate sector. Producer goods sectors may also suffer sharp reversals due to poor prospects in client sectors. When the auto industry faced sagging demand in the late 1970s, the steel, paint, glass, and machine tool sectors stagnated as well. Those producer goods sectors that sell capital equipment are particularly subject to lean times induced by client retrenchment. Thus the profit cycle for this group may be subject to dramatic declines in later stages.

Consumer industries may act quite differently. The potential for product differentiation is much greater in this sector because advertising can achieve greater success in selling consumer-perceived qualities.[8] Oligopoly may be built on this form of market power even when economies of scale are not necessarily present. Consumers also exhibit greater inertia in buying patterns than do corporations, so the growth and decline cycle may be stretched out, with less dramatic temporal changes.[9] Substitutes are more likely to be reproduced within the sector, so that recycling through the stages of the profit cycle is possible (as in the auto and clothing industries), although successful market penetration by products manufactured abroad by either domestic or foreign firms may tend to produce declines in both output and employment domestically, even while profit and/or sales are rising.

The consumer goods sectors, then, are characterized by more regular employment and output growth and decline patterns than for producer goods sectors. The profit cycle is likely to be longer and flatter (superprofits may not rise as high). Concentration will occur at a slower pace. Employment declines in later stages will tend to be more moderate than in producer goods sectors.

5.3 Spatial Sensitivity of Sectoral Types

Just as the sectoral orientations denote different corporate development strategies, they also temper spatial behavior. For instance, resource-oriented sectors by definition are less spatially responsive than other sectors. Coal seams and taconite deposits are spatially fixed and cannot be moved to locations where labor is cheaper during later profit cycle stages. On the other hand mines can be opened and closed across regions and between regions, especially in response to labor militancy; we would expect to see more of this type of behavior in later stages of the sector's evolution. Some spatially sensitive behavior should still be detectable in the resource sectors.

Concentration, agglomeration, dispersion, and relocation are more likely to occur in an abrupt and uneven manner, partly because severe short- and intermediate-term price fluctuations are so common in these sectors and partly because these sectors rely more on new discoveries and relatively discontinuous technological breakthroughs than do others. We would, for instance, be less surprised to find substantial regional shifts and even erratic reversals in industry concentration early on in the profit cycle for these sectors since new discoveries could substantially reorder spatial patterns. The history of gold and silver mining in the nineteenth-century West displays just such an erratic locational pattern.

Producer goods industries may be more vulnerable to resource supply or demand constraints than consumer goods industries, especially if heavy raw materials and/or heavy, bulky commodity output constrain locational choices. Heavy machinery producers, for instance, probably will continue to locate near their clients even in later stages of the profit cycle because of special design features and the tailor-made nature of each machine. Steel cannot move too far from least-cost transportation modes for coal, iron ore, and steel. Still, here too, a relative tendency for regional shifts as the profit cycle matures should be detectable.

Consumer goods will approximate the spatial model of the profit cycle most closely. Some are also dependent on particular supply factors or on specialized marketing styles. The extraordinary product differentiation that we might expect in the normal-plus profit stage will tend to produce the need for a larger managerial and sales staff and more face-to-face informational contacts available chiefly in large cities.[10] However, large corporations in this stage have perfected means of divorcing production from control and market research functions. Production employment can still be relocated to new regions even if headquarters and market research remain at the home base.[11]

6 Conceptual Problems with the Profit Cycle Model

6.1 Interindustry Linkages

The major drawback to the profit cycle theory is its singular focus on individual sectoral experience. Thus what is arguably the model's strength is also its weakness. The theory presents a model for long-run industry evolution, based on a developmental rule for capitalist competition, which includes stages of market power. Interactions among sectors and the aggregate consequences of corporate behavior registered in the business cycle are subordinate to the sector's individual dynamics. Yet both profoundly affect profitability patterns and may result in significant irregularities in the empirical evidence. Certainly the peaks and troughs of the business cycle, particularly those associated with long waves of economic activity, will show up in the profitability profiles of most sectors in the economy. Empirically this problem can be dealt with by adjusting the data cyclically or by taking longer-run averages across such cycles.

Another aspect of this macroeconomic pattern, which is obscured by the sector-by-sector product cycle argument, is the way in which the initiation and demise of sectors tend to bunch up at certain points in time. Clearly dramatic restructuring and abandonment of existing plant are most common during severe recessionary setbacks. The long-wave literature, and Mensch in particular, provides a plausible argument that the crisis-prone nature of capitalist economies as a whole results in a dynamic where basic innovations are forthcoming at critical historical junctures—severe troughs in long-run cycles.[1] During the times of prosperity corporations are preoccupied with retaining market share, product differentiation, and pseudo innovation. Only during times of economy-wide stagnation are corporate resources directed toward basic innovation. Mensch's empirical documentation of the bunching of inventions around troughs in the long-wave cycle is compelling. It suggests that the timing of profit cycle initiations is predictable and that sectoral debuts will be historically discontinuous. The long-wave argument supplements the profit cycle theory by hypothesizing specific historical conjunctions of new sectors. Here, however, we are more interested in the existence and sequencing, rather than the mutual timing, of profit cycles.

The effects of interaction among sectors are harder to detect and account for in the product cycle model. The innovation of a new product in one industry or irregular changes in price or technique of production may reverberate through a number of associated sectors, changing their short- to intermediate-run profitability picture. Four types of interactive effects can be enumerated: changes in technology, changes in factor prices, changes in class struggle, and changes in demand.

Changes in technology external to particular sectors but with dramatic applications across sectors have frequently emerged in capitalist economies. Contemporary examples are the airplane, telex, satellite, and computer with its ability to introduce numerical control into many assembly-line manufacturing processes. This innovation has the potential for increasing labor productivity dramatically, but it may not affect the long-run profit cycle significantly. Unless one or a few firms can move into a position to monopolize the innovation within their sector, competition, even among oligopolies, will tend to push the profit rate down to the preceding normal profit rate (for competitive sectors) or to the oligopolistic profit rate (for sectors with some degree of monopoly). The innovation is more likely to affect market shares of individual firms in the short run than to affect long-term profitability of the sector. It will, however, affect both quantity of output, which will expand as the market price is driven down, and employment, which may fall if the labor-saving nature of the innovation overrides employment gains from increased output.

Changes in factor prices (materials, machinery, labor, credit) will affect short-run profit directly and will result in changes in output as well. A price increase may be a result of monopolization of the supplier industry; if the purchasing sector in question is also monopolized, the supplier may be able to transfer normal-plus profit backward into its own coffers. If the purchasing sector is competitive, it will have to cut output and employment as profits fall below normal.

This seems to have happened to marginal producers in agriculture over the last century, as seed, feed, fertilizer, farm machinery, and credit suppliers became increasingly monopolistic. If a factor price rises or falls due to depletion of resources or newly found sources, respectively, output will respond in the opposite direction. Employment will tend to do so as well, although if labor is a close substitute for the scarce factor, then employment losses will be mitigated through the substitution effect. A technological improvement that lowers the price or raises the quality of a factor input will boost output in the purchasing sector; its effect on employment will depend on which factor embodies that technological change. The price or quality of labor itself may change, due to labor force participation behavior, labor migration, unionization, or education, with resulting adjustments by the employing sector.

Changes in the degree of class struggle will also affect the fortunes of one sector, frequently inducing growth in others. Militant unionism often encourages the development of highly automated substitutes, as it did in the historic shift from cigars to cigarettes around the turn of the century. Persistently high wage rates won by a well-organized union may engender the success of competing commodities produced in sectors without unions or with weak ones. Companies marketing security equipment and services have prospered in areas where high unemployment or worker sabotage have threatened the safety of property.

Fourth, an adverse change in demand for a sector's output may reflect the success of a newly innovated product substitute or the misfortunes of a closely-related complementary good. For instance, the U.S. auto industry has been suffering from both the high price of gasoline, a complement, and the availability of gas-efficient, lightweight front-wheel-drive imports. Profits, as well as output and employment, will be cut back. Consumer tastes may also change abruptly, or buyers may become monopsonized, both adversely affecting demand.

All of these events will affect the pace, if not the shape, of the profit cycle for individual industries. Some of them were built into the theory of the profit cycle, such as the ultimate emergence of better substitutes that dislodge older sectors from market position. The interindustry effects are likely to be most potent in the later stages of the profit cycle, where profits are near normal at the minimum acceptable rate. Thus the employment and output experience of sectors may be more variable at this end of the cycle. New technological applications, factor price decreases, or increases in demand that evolve from events in other sectors will tend to lengthen output expansion. The employment path may also grow, or it may diverge faster from output, if cost savings are embodied in factor substitutes or in labor-saving techniques. Factor price increases or sagging demand will hasten the diminution of both output and employment.

Paradoxically interindustry effects underscore the universal tendency toward profit cycle paths. If the dynamic of capitalist growth forces firms to innovate continually, then sequentially new sectors emerge with promise of excess profits. These new sectors bid up the price for labor and other inputs on the market. Older established sectors will experience supply adversities reflected through this price competition for inputs.[2] This process will ensure the truncation of a normal profits era unless that sector can compensate with internal product and process innovations or cost-saving efforts of its own. Thus interindustry effects ultimately will guarantee the operation of the product cycle in the long run, as well as complicating its shorter-term movements. Proof of the importance of the profit cycle for explaining the experience of each sector is an empirical rather than a logical question.

6.2 The Problem of Spatial Aggregation

A second conceptual problem that merits examination is that the empirical manifestations of the profit cycle are quite sensitive to territorial scale.[3] While the profit cycle can be viewed as a universal aspect of capitalist dynamics, its observed length will vary directly with the geographical boundaries of the economies to which it is applied. For instance, using U.S. figures, we will detect the beginning of the later stages of the profit cycle in a sector such as autos or steel somewhat earlier than their commencement on a worldwide scale. This is because of the relocation effect hypothesized to correspond to these stages. When a U.S.-originated sector begins to disperse internationally, it will appear to be relocating or abandoning production at home (and thus passing through later stages of the profit cycle). Similarly if we studied a subnational regional economy, such as New England or Detroit, an industry like textiles or autos might appear to be in the last stage of its profit cycle while for the country as a whole it is still in the third or fourth stage.

Output

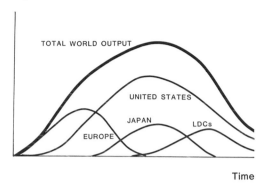

Time

Figure 6.1
Hypothetical succession of output cycles among nations in one industry

This scale effect will vary in the direction of more truncated cycles the smaller the territorial unit. A hypothetical view of this scale relationship is shown in figure 6.1. Thus the profit cycle for the U.S. auto industry, for instance, will progress through its stages faster than will the international auto industry. This lag will be particularly evident in domestic employment patterns, although it may not be true of the profitability of the U.S. corporations, especially those with significant international operations.[4]

The existence of this scale variation may be the key to resolving the differences between Mensch (1979) and Burns (1934) on the tendency toward a shortening of long-run cycles. Burns argued that the empirical record through the early 1930s suggested that product (not profit) cycles were becoming shorter in length, although he did not venture a deductive argument why this might be occurring. Mensch argues that long waves, which he sees as individual product cycles bunched together with common starting and ending points, have not changed appreciably in length. But Mensch is working with international data, while Burns was looking at strictly U.S. sectoral change. It may be that what was apparently the shortening of output cycles to Burns reflected the growing internationalization of the economy, where production in successive eras is more quickly transferred to overseas facilities.

More rapid penetration of domestic markets by imports would hasten this decline in domestic output and employment. That this experience within the United States may continue is suggested by the rapidity with which the semiconductor industry has internationalized certain production activities and the Japanese have penetrated the U.S. market. Differential in the duration of cycles among individual countries can still be consistent with the historical regularity in long-wave length that Mensch and others have postulated. But the concern within national economies over the abruptness of industrial mobility may soon result in one of two types of intervention. Capital controls could reverse the regional employment consequences of the later stages of the profit cycle by prohibiting or at least hampering the pace of capacity retrenchment. Or state promotion of R&D and other stimuli to innovations could result in a disastrous quickening of the product cycle worldwide whose disruptive regional consequences would snowball.

7   The Case Studies

Empirical support for the profit cycle model is sought in fifteen case studies. Each case focuses on a sector's structural and locational changes over time in the United States. In contrast to the cross-sectional shift-share method of inquiry, these studies attempt to explain regional shifts on the basis of longitudinal profiles of individual sectors.[1] The focus, then, as in the theory, is on sectors first, with regional consequences derived or inferred from sectoral imperatives.

The case studies seek to confirm or reject the following sets of hypotheses: (1) that profit cycle stages are discernible and sequential; (2) that the structural characteristics of new firm formation, concentration, and ownership form vary systematically through stages of the profit cycle; and (3) that methodical agglomeration, dispersion, and reconcentration tendencies accompany passage through the profit cycle stages. The case studies are arranged in groups according to their identification as resource-oriented, producer-oriented, and consumer-oriented sectors to detect variation across these three basic types.

Indirectly the case studies probe the degree of spatial singularity of sectors — that is, whether the aggregate treatment of large regions as manufacturing belts does violence to the finer-grained individuality of regions and their sectoral mainstays. They also shed light on changes in concentration of market power and corporate structure over time. For instance, the precocious emergence of oligopoly in newer sectors can be contrasted with its comparatively slow pace of development in the past. At the same time they offer an opportunity to investigate the permanence or insubstantiality of individual corporations' leadership in regions and the economy at large. Finally the case studies of innovating sectors offer a chance to test theories of innovation diffusion in systems of cities.

Evidence that can be marshaled to study the profit cycle behavior of sectors is available from three basic sources. First is the data base available from the Census of Manufacturers. Because of comparability problems, this source was relied on only for the period since 1947. Despite longitudinal discontinuities and gaps from disclosure provisions, it provides structural and geographical data on a highly disaggregated set of sectors. Second are the locational studies carried out in the past by geographers and regional economists. The geographers' work offers evidence on factor costs and market differentials and tends to be rich with detail on original and subsequent locations.[2] The economists' contributions lie in the development of empirical techniques that describe and explain urban and regional variation and shifts in industrial structure, relying on nationwide data bases.[3] Third are the studies of individual sectors carried out by industrial organization specialists, which offer detailed accounts of the trends toward or away from oligopoly in important sectors and the reasons for these movements.[4] The studies rely on all three of these sources, supplemented by business press accounts of the most recent developments in innovative sectors.[5]

7.1 Stage Identification

Profitability is a fundamental variable for entrepreneurs and managers, signaling the competitive status of their plants and guiding their future comportment. The magnitude and sources of profitability have been argued to vary systematically across time, and a series of business priorities, including specific locational decisions, have been hypothesized to be associated with each epoch; however, it proved impossible to use data on profits over time as the empirical discriminator among profit cycle stages for individual sectors, for several reasons.

Time-series data on business income by industry are available from two sources: the Internal Revenue Service's *Source Book, Statistics of Income,* published since 1916, and the Federal Trade Commission's *Quarterly Financial Report for Manufacturing, Mining and Trade Corporations,* published since 1947.[6] Both sources include both total net income (and deficits) and various aggregates that can be used to compute different variations of profit rates: total revenues, stockholder's equity, and (in the case of FTC data) total assets. Three major problems render these data unusable for present purposes.

First, because of legal provisions respecting corporate privacy, profit data are collected not on an establishment or plant basis but by corporate or unincorporated business unit. Each corporation and reporting unit is allocated to what is called an Enterprise Standard Industrial classification (ESIC), which corresponds roughly to an SIC category, at least down to the three-digit level. A corporation is assigned to whatever ESIC division accounts for more of its output than any other ESIC, first at the one-digit level, then at the two- and three-digit levels. As the FTC cautions, "These procedures may lead to a conglomerate corporation being assigned to an industry group from which only a small proportion of its receipts are obtained."

Although the same classification problem occurs in the Census of Manufactures data, it is much more serious when entire corporate operations are being allocated instead of individual plants. For instance, when a merger joins two disparate types of corporate activities, the new entity will be reclassified and profits from the less dominant portion now included with those of the other sector. This source of bias has been especially problematic in recent decades as conglomerate mergers have become more commonplace. In the census, by comparison, such mergers have no effect on the classification of individual plants, which remain identified by the sector that accounts for the largest portion of their output. Since 1947, cautions the FTC, there have been fourteen discontinuities in the corporate income series, only two of which have been changes in SIC categories (which also affect the census data) and nine of which have been industry reclassifications of this sort.

Second, the business income statistics are not collected on a census basis but rather indirectly through the reporting requirements to the IRS. Both the IRS and the FTC (which draws a sample from the IRS files) note that the statistics are strongly biased toward the largest corporations. The FTC's sample includes virtually all corporations with assets in excess of $1 million, yet its sample covers fewer than 9,000 of the 260,000 manufacturing corporations in the nation. This is problematic because profitability has been hypothesized to vary with the size and resources of corporations at different points in the profit cycle. Yet large corporations are those that may be expected to be highly diversified so that large differences in rates of return to individual plants and sectors will wash out in the corporation's overall profit performance record.

Third, both sources present data only down to ESIC levels comparable to the SIC two- and three-digit level. (Although the *Source*

Book has a set of four-digit designations, they are equivalent to the three-digit level in the SIC.) It is impossible, for instance, to distinguish semiconductors from computers, basic steel from steel fabrications, and auto parts manufacture from auto assembly with this level of disaggregation. To use the available profit data would have required abandoning the decision to operate at the four-digit level and thus to forego the opportunity to test the theory that individual sectors have much more disruptive and severe historical growth patterns than are apparent from aggregate industry groupings.

As a result of these three problems, available data on profit sales are inadequate for use as stage delineators. They are too highly aggregated to be reliable estimates of individual sector profit profiles over time. Each source of error—reporting at the corporate rather than the establishment level, disproportionate weight given to large diversified corporations, and disaggregation down to only the three-digit level—obscures much greater variation on an individual plant and industry basis, tending to overestimate profitability in profit-squeezed sectors and underestimate it in superprofits sectors.

The decision not to use profit data to delineate stages does not mean that empirical evidence on profitability has not been worked into the case studies. The case studies do draw on profit rate series in cases where they are good proxies for actual profitability over time. Profit data problems are less severe in industries dominated by single-plant corporations (such as pharmaceuticals) and in those in which multiplant corporations are not significantly diversified (such as basic steel up to the mid-1970s). In these and similar cases, I have included profit data to complement the census data.

The use of other delineators rather than profit rates does not mean that the results are not a test of the profit cycle theory. Concern for profitability operates in this model much like utility maximization operates in neoclassical economics—as the underlying behavioral postulate. Just as economists do not have to document empirically the actual composition of a utility function in order to test hypotheses about consumer behavior, one does not have to document empirically profit functions or profit levels in order to test hypotheses about corporate behavior. The empirical research that follows tests the inferences about corporate decisions expected to accompany sequential areas of profit-motivated behavior: the conjunction of systematic patterns of firm formation, employment generation, consolidation of market power, occupational composition, and locational orientation.

Unable to use time series on profit rates as a means of distinguishing profit cycle stages, I have relied on the next best—expansion patterns in employment levels and concentration ratios. The model predicts that when superprofit exists, employment will grow at dramatic rates; that when a period of normal profits is reached, employment growth will begin to slow, level off, and even contract, as process innovations overtake product innovations; and that a period of less-than-normal profits will be responded to by absolute decline in employment. Concentration ratios have been used to distinguish sectors that have oligopolistic sources of profit rather than simply normal profits in a freely competitive market. Boundaries between stages II, III, and IV are conceptually identical to the first and second derivatives of the slope of the sinosoidal employment growth curve. However, since the data series are discontinuous, I have used the absolute values presented in table 7.1.[7] Distinctions between stages III and IVb in cases where annual growth rates fell between 0.0 and −2.0 were made by looking at firm formation rates.[8]

Sectors in this classification were permitted to pass directly from stage II to stage IVa, if high degrees of concentration warranted it. Sectors were also permitted to recycle back to stage II if an unusual reversal pushed employment growth rates up dramatically for a sustained period. Sectors could move from stage III to either IVa or IVb. Although cyclical trends in the economy at large complicate the strict interpretation of data, the use of broad historical series permitted the neutralization of temporal downturns such as the depression. Myopia about our present location in the cycle lends the interpretation of data from the 1970s a more tentative tone.[9]

Table 7.1
Numerical values delineating profit cycle stages

Stage	Average annual employment growth rate	Concentration ratio[a]
II	+2.0 or more	Not applicable
III	+2.0 to -2.0	Less than 50 percent
IVa	+2.0 to -2.0	Greater than 50 percent
IVb	0.0 or less	Less than 50 percent

Source: *Census of Manufactures.*
a. Value of shipments or value added accounted for by largest four firms at close of stage.

7.2 Sectoral Variables

Four sets of variables are used to exercise the model. The first documents output, employment, plant, and company growth.[10] The second set covers industry structure in two dimensions. First, changes in degree of concentration of output accounted for by the top four, top eight, and top twenty firms are investigated.[11] Second, the changing proportions of both establishments and employment accounted for by multiplant corporations as opposed to either single-plant corporations or nonincorporated businesses are probed.[12] All data are drawn from the Census of Manufactures, which offers consistency of collection techniques across time. Unless otherwise noted, the Census is the source of data for all tables and figures in the chapters which follow.[13]

A third set of indicators tests propositions about the composition of the labor force in different stages. The census disaggregates data only on the basis of production workers to total employment.[14] This was the only variable recomputed after the initial case study results were reviewed. It turned out that consistently, regardless of profit cycle stage, the ratio of production to total workers fell in every sector. Further investigation showed that a dramatic secular trend in this ratio has characterized manufacturing nationally since World War II (figure 7.1).

Figure 7.1
Production workers as a percentage of total manufacturing employment, 1889-1980

Therefore the ratio for individual sectors is normalized by expressing it as a percentage of the national ratio. This is the meaning of "relative ratio of production workers total" found on the vertical axes of the occupational structure figures in the chapters to come. Relative ratios of greater than 1.0 are expected for later stages of the profit cycle and less than 1.0 for initial stages. Declines in the relative ratio are expected in initial stages, and increases in later stages.

The normalization does not imply that secular decline in the aggregate ratio is independent of changes in each of the component sectors. Rather, the intention is to reformulate the hypothesis about occupational composition to predict that more mature profit-squeezed industries will experience relatively higher levels and a slower than average decline in the proportion of production workers to total, while superprofit sectors will exhibit relatively lower levels and a greater than average decline. Although similar normalizations could have been employed with variables such as ownership patterns and concentration ratios, the strong results on these variables despite similar trends made such normalization unnecessary.

7.3 Geographical Variables

The final set of indicators tracks the locational orientation of sectors. I have chosen to use states rather than regions or Standard Metropolitan Statistical Areas as the basic geographical unit for several reasons. The 1977 census does not publish the regional total for four-digit industries in printed form. State-level data permit full geographical coverage of establishments and, at minimum, intervals for employment.[15] State-level data offer the best chance to detect both intraregional and interregional dispersion.

Two types of indicators are constructed for gauging interregional shifting from the state-level data. The spatial concentration ratio is analogous to industry concentration ratios. It registers the share of plants and/or employment accounted for by the largest one, four, and eight states. These ratios are expected to increase in early stages and decrease in later stages.[16] A second measure is the proportion of plants or jobs accounted for by the initial four leading states. If this shift measure is equal to the four-state dispersion measure over time, then no significant changeover in the identity of leading states has occurred. If, however, the rates diverge, new locations are replacing older ones in the top ranks. State definitions, fortunately, remain the same over time, with two exceptions. Up to 1958 the territories of Alaska and Hawaii were not included in the statistics. This proved to be problematic for the case of fish processing, so it was necessary to reconstruct the series using other sources for the earlier periods.

7.4 Choice of Sectors

Perhaps the most difficult decision of the research design concerned the sectors chosen for case studies. It was impossible to cover all four-digit sectors, given the commitment to substantive research on historical development for more mature sectors and intractable problems of disclosure and sectoral redefinition in the Census. The use of as highly disaggregated data as possible seemed essential; indeed even four-digit breakdowns are inadequate to detect true profit cycles in some cases. The problem was complicated by the need to choose cases at the outset by some initial criterion, such as apparent contemporary position in the profit cycle, which might prove deceptive on further investigation.

Cases were chosen, therefore, on the basis of their recent divergent employment experience and with the requirement that each of the intermediate stages (II, III, IV) of the profit cycle for each of the three sectoral types be covered. At minimum this mandated nine case studies. But because a range of competitive versus oligopolistic experience was desired, the number was expanded to fifteen—five in each of the three sectoral types. After the initial selection, several of the choices turned out to contain highly differentiated subsectors, specifically fish (frozen versus canned), women's apparel (dresses versus suits and coats), and textiles (cottons versus knitwear). Altogether eighteen four-digit sectors were selected. These are listed in table 7.2, along with their employment growth rates for 1967 through 1977.

Resource-oriented industries were proxied by those manufacturing sectors that process their raw materials at or near the source. Thus relatively low employment figures in some of these sectors (winemaking, fish processing) should be considered indicative of larger job totals in the extractive industries associated. Resource-oriented industries are not always clearly distinguishable from ones in which labor orientation predominates, for several reasons. The relative significance of each factor may alter over time. More than one resource may figure in locational decisions; a steel site midway between coal and iron ore, for instance, may not clearly appear as

Table 7.2
Case study four-digit sectors, by SIC, type and job growth rates 1967-1977

Stage	Resource-oriented			Producer-oriented			Consumer-oriented		
	SIC	Type	Job growth rate	SIC	Type	Job growth rate	SIC	Type	Job growth rate
II	2092	Fish, frozen	+60%	3674	Semiconductors	+95%			
	2084	Wineries	+35%	3573	Computers	+85%			
				3334	Aluminum	+30%	2834	Pharmaceuticals	+25%
III	2075	Soybeans	+18%				2335	Women's suits	+12%
	2111	Cigarettes	+6%				3717	Automobiles	+7%
	2091	Fish, canned	+1%	2253	Textiles/knit	0%			
IV	2421	Sawmills	-16%	3111	Steel	-20%	2337	Women's dresses	-20%
							2082	Brewing	-28%
				2211	Textiles/cotton	-45%	3144	Shoes	-45%

Source: *Census of Manufacturers.*

resource oriented. And as in the case of aluminum, a nonmaterial resource such as cheap power may be dominant.[17]

If the distinction between resource- and labor-oriented industries is dropped, the sample still contains about equal numbers of producer and consumer sections.[18] The boundary between producer and consumer commodities is straightforward conceptually. Empirically most SICs cover commodities that are sold to both markets, but generally one or the other predominates.[19]

The actual sectors chosen offer known regional contrasts and are not designed to constitute a totally representative sample.[20] I have deliberately avoided local-market-oriented sectors, although these constitute only about 12 percent of all manufacturing employment and a similar segment of four-digit SICs.[21] Nonrenewable resource sectors such as copper, coal, gold, and molybdenum were eliminated from consideration because preliminary inquiries showed that their locational patterns were completely dominated by resource availability and exhaustion. This amounts to an admission that the profit cycle model's spatial hypotheses probably are not valid for these types of sectors.

Sectors chosen were not necessarily the most mobile in their categories. Many agricultural commodities, for instance, have been more mobile over time than soybeans. Rubber has been more mobile than automobiles. Pulp and paper production has shifted more prominently than lumber production. Industrial chemical plants have changed spatial orientation more than pharmaceuticals. Thus, although the suitability of the profit cycle model to other sectors awaits the test of further research, there is no reason to believe that the overall behavioral pattern will be strikingly different from what this set reveals.

8 Profit Cycles, Oligopoly, and the Geography of Steel

The study of steel reveals that the early emergence of oligopoly had profound impacts on subsequent regional development. Because the leading steel companies engineered successful variants of monopoly pricing, overall growth was retarded and plants overly concentrated in the innovative core region of Pittsburgh and neighboring valleys. Furthermore the economies of the original steel-producing centers became top heavy with steel plants and steel-using activities, discouraging other users of labor, land, and entrepreneurship from locating there. Pittsburgh and Youngstown became overly specialized in steel and underdeveloped in other manufacturing sectors.

In contrast steel capacity in other regions was underdeveloped up to World War II. The large firms chose to serve southern and West Coast markets from northeastern mills rather than build up competing capacity. To ensure control of those markets, U.S. Steel and Bethlehem bought up all significant independents. During World War II the federal government added substantial new capacity to the industry, but although several of the new integrated works were built in the underserved West, they were located poorly for postwar profitability. Thus the government's actions further crippled the West Coast steel sector, leaving that market wide open for import penetration.

Poor prospects, then, for steel jobs and communities in the present period can be attributed to the deformities in geographical siting of steel plants throughout the twentieth century by both private and public sectors. Abrupt and devastating restructuring ensued when oligopolistic control of the domestic market collapsed in the 1970s. The largest steel corporations closed many northeastern plants and spent existing cash reserves and incoming profits on diversification into entirely new commodity lines, largely through buy-outs. At the same time West Coast steel capacity was inadequate and poorly sited,

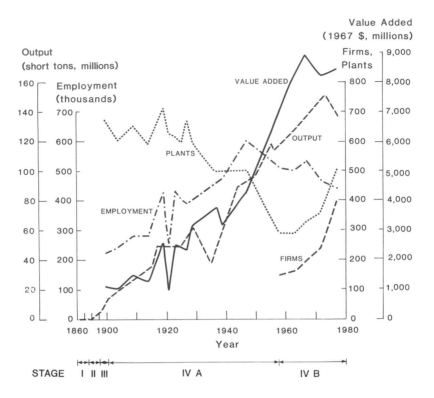

Figure 8.1
Steel industry growth, 1860-1977. Data for 1899-1947 may not be strictly comparable with data for 1958-1977 for value added and plants.

enabling the Japanese to compete effectively with steel shipped from their home ports. The extraordinary adjustment costs borne by steel communities in the late 1970s reflect both the vulnerability of an oligopolized sector to new challenges from abroad and the rapidity of corporate response when diversification is an option.

A century of employment, output, occupational composition, and firm and plant populations in steel is portrayed in figure 8.1. The steel industry is narrowly defined here as steel mills and blast furnaces (SIC 3312), to avoid the inclusion of other downstream steel-making activities such as fabrication. The output path of the U.S. steel industry appears to approximate a bell-shaped curve, with the peak occurring in the early 1970s.[1] Relatively steady output expansion accompanied oligopoly structure until recently, consistent with the notion that dominant corporations focus on orderly market management. Possibly the expansion path for steel might have risen

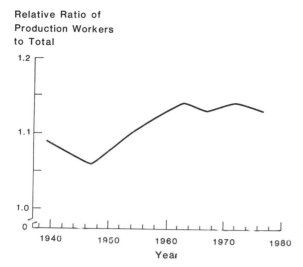

Figure 8.2
Occupational structure in steel, 1939-1977

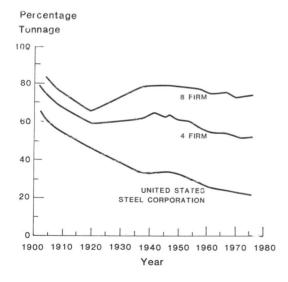

Figure 8.3
Concentration ratios in steel, 1902-1977. (Source: Duke et al., 1977:53. Data from *Iron Age.*)

more dramatically in the early decades of this century had not oligopoly prevailed. Thus the peaking in the current period may be much sharper than it would have been under a more competitive climate.

Steel exhibits predictable relationships between output, value added, and jobs. Value added since World War II has grown faster than output, reflecting a switch toward higher-quality, more labor-intensive specialty steels. Employment has been dropping steadily since the war, reflecting stepped-up efforts toward rationalization in a renewed competitive climate. In addition the ratio of production workers to all workers has been consistently higher than the national average and is rising, confirming the occupational hypothesis of the model (figure 8.2).

The presence of oligopoly can be charted by the shares of output accounted for by the top four and eight corporations (figure 8.3). The share of U.S. Steel Corporation fell from over 65 percent in 1902 to 22 percent in 1977, stunning testimony to the difficulty of maintaining a monopoly. The share of the top eight firms, however, has fallen only modestly, from 84 percent to 74 percent, and corporate multiplant firms have maintained a tight hold on the job market (figure 8.4). Recent mergers have reinforced domestic market power in basic steel production, although a new form of competition—the minimill—has emerged in limited product lines.

In the world context, steel production is still expanding. The industry has not reached the peak of its profit cycle worldwide, if output is any measure. Three major producers—the United States, Europe and Japan—began to lose market shares in the 1970s, and Europe and the United States experienced an absolute fall in output (figure 8.5). The steel industry appears to be sequentially profitable in disparate portions of the world economy, entering low profitability stages earlier in the original host countries. This confirms the notion of shorter, more peaked profit cycles for individual regions nested in a longer-term worldwide cycle.

8.1 Innovation and Competition

Steel's predecessor, the iron industry, was highly resource oriented and clustered around small deposits of ore and coal. After 1830, as scale economies in the production of both coal and ore increased and railroads moved inputs and outputs over greater distances, the production of iron began to gravitate toward coal sources. In this presteel era, four states—Pennsylvania, Ohio, New York, and New

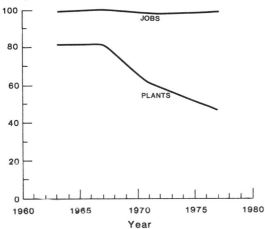

Figure 8.4
Ownership patterns in steel, 1963-1977

Figure 8.5
Major shares of world steel output, 1870-1980. (Source: Adams and Mueller, 1982:74)

Jersey—accounted for 75 percent of pig iron output, with Pennsylvania alone contributing more than half of the nation's output.[2]

The era of rapid growth and excess profits in steel began when the first Bessemer steel furnace was built in Pittsburgh in 1875. Bessemer steel production required proximity to good coking coal. Pittsburgh offered the nearby Connelsville deposits and was well situated to serve emerging midwestern markets.[3] Tremendous spatial concentration in the production of steel took place in this stage, as entrepreneurs like Andrew Carnegie erected mill after mill. Agglomeration began, too, as fabricators and other users of steel set up shop in the Pittsburgh area. As late as 1894 Pittsburgh mills produced 44 percent of all steel ingot in the United States.[4]

By 1890 the steel industry had entered a period of intense competition. Superprofits to the original innovators were eroded by the rapid diffusion of technology and numerous start-ups. By 1890 dispersion westward along the Great Lakes axis had begun. The competitive era drove steel makers to least-cost locations amid the contemporary sites of ore, coal, and markets. The discovery of high-quality iron ore in northern Michigan and Minnesota in the latter half of the century enhanced the advantages of Great Lakes shore locations once the Soo Canal was built. Moreover steel buyers—the railroads, agricultural machinery companies, and construction firms—were moving westward with the population. Lakeshore sites permitted relatively cheap assembly of coal and iron ore.[5] A rival southern industry, begun during the Civil War by Confederates at Birmingham, Alabama, near coal and ore deposits, was rebuilt during the 1880s with northern capital, serving a spatially distinct market.

By 1900 these competitive pressures resulted in Illinois, displacing the easternmost states as the number three steel producer behind Pennsylvania and Ohio. Chicago had become a major market center; its first major steel works had been built in the 1880s. New York and New Jersey were declining in importance, while steel production in states like Wisconsin, West Virginia, and Indiana was growing rapidly. Even Pittsburgh had lost its magnetism as the center of an agglomerative steel industry. Pittsburgh's location was relatively poor with respect to markets, and as coal mining activity shifted to the southwest down the Appalachians and the significance of input costs was diminished by large gains in productivity, Pittsburgh's growth rate slowed. Pittsburgh's share of output peaked in the year 1900; the last major new mill to be constructed in Pittsburgh went up in 1911.[6]

8.2 The Long Era of Successful Oligopoly

This competitive impulse toward dispersion was short-lived. During the period of intense competition in the late 1890s, prices for steel products fell and price wars were common. A number of attempts at temporary pools failed, until in 1897 an intense merger movement began. In just three years enough monopoly power was concentrated in the hands of a few corporations; virtual market control prevailed for the next quarter-century. The new trust was led by U.S. Steel, which controlled 65 percent of output and was the world's largest corporation. The effect of this monopoly on location was dramatic.

Around 1900 the steel industry adopted a simple procedure for fixing prices, called the Pittsburgh plus or, more generally, the basing point system. All suppliers quoted clients the Pittsburgh rate on a product plus the cost from Pittsburgh to the client's plant. The system eliminated any advantage of market proximity for a plant located nearer the buyer than Pittsburgh. While internally recorded profits might be higher if a customer were to be supplied by a nearby plant, the buyer had no particular incentive to purchase from the nearest or least-cost producer. This system of oligopolistic price fixing retarded the decentralization of the industry during this era and favored the continued prominence of Pittsburgh as a production site.[7] The regional effects operated through three mechanisms: elimination of transportation cost differentials in delivered prices, the restriction of output through successful oligopolization, and parallel location decisions made by steel fabricators and users.

The Pittsburgh plus system protected the initial advantage of Pittsburgh plants by eliminating any market advantage that decentralized locations could realize from their proximity to distant markets. Thus the general westward trend toward the Ohio and Chicago-area Great Lakes locations was retarded. The big steel corporations themselves had an incentive to locate plants in the more westerly areas if real transportation cost savings existed, since internally they would be able to boost profits by saving freight costs without disturbing the pricing system. And indeed some capacity expansion occurred. U.S. Steel built its huge Gary, Indiana, plant, the world's largest, in 1906. But the balance of ore, coal, and market freight rates seems not to have offered the highly profitable big corporations enough incentive to move. The enjoyment of substantial normal-plus profits diminished the importance of potential cost savings.

The retardation of decentralization can be documented in several ways. First, despite the tremendous growth in auto production and its appetite for steel, no steel plant was built in Detroit until 1922. That plant was constructed by a relatively small steel company, which was subsequently bought out by Republic Steel in 1929. Prior to that date, all steel was supplied to Detroit by plants from Chicago to Pittsburgh. Some suggest that the major steel firms colluded in keeping out of the Detroit area to avoid too keen competition. Even to the present day, Detroit-area autos are heavily dependent on steel from outside the immediate area. Second, costly cross-hauling was apparent in many of the northeastern Great Lakes markets. Third, the natural southern market, which should have been served by Birmingham, was consistently penetrated by shipments from Pittsburgh and Maryland, resulting in substantial retardation of industrialization in the Alabama steel-making area. Finally, one can cite the fact that no major new "greenfield" (one not in an already built-up steel area) plant was built in the United States between 1906 and 1952, except under the extraordinary circumstances of political pressure or government intervention. The Duluth plant of U.S. Steel, erected in 1915, was a concession to political demands from the ore-producing state of Minnesota.[8] World War II plants were built to serve strategic needs. In both instances profitability was below normal in the long run.

The retardation of industrial decentralization was enhanced by the pure monopoly results of steel price fixing. Since excess profits at this stage of the profit cycle are achieved through the restriction of output in a relatively inelastic market, the rate of new capacity additions lagged what it would have been in a competitive climate. Since cost and market considerations would have dictated that those capacity expansions be at the new decentralized locations—the Chicago area, Detroit, Birmingham—industrialization at those locations was retarded disproportionately by the monopoly effect. An enlarged market would have induced greater capacity and employment opportunities at those sites in the early twentieth century. This would have been the case even in the absence of the Pittsburgh plus system. This effect was exacerbated during slump periods of overcapacity. Instead of closing down plants that were older and more remote from markets, such as those in Pittsburgh, the big steel corporations protected their capacity by inefficiently serving outlaying customers from these plants. If competition had prevailed, they would not have been able to do so. The fact that U.S. Steel had bought out smaller companies—among them the largest Birmingham mills—in the panic of 1907 aided them in this action.

Finally, the location of steel users was distorted by the effects of the Pittsburgh plus system. Fabricators tended to locate around Pittsburgh and other historic locations because the pricing system and concentration of capacity encouraged it. Stocking (1954) shows how this operated in the South. Birmingham producers in shipbuilding, wire products, steel structures, agricultural implements, and boilers had to pay higher than normal prices for steel because of the Pittsburgh plus system, thus cutting their advantage in supplying their southern market. The net effect was to favor Pittsburgh area and northern suppliers in southern markets, reflected in the locational decisions of fabricators in the long run. This downstream effect shored up the developmental advantage of Pittsburgh even after its locational advantages had begun to erode. Because of the interactive effect, both steel producers and customers continued to expand capacity in Pittsburgh, although at a somewhat lower rate than farther west.[9]

The locational effects are shown in table 8.1. Alternative Great Lakes sites like Cleveland, Buffalo, and Chicago grew but only modestly. Pennsylvania's share of steel output fell from 50.6 percent in

Table 8.1
State shares of raw steel output, 1910-1972
Percentage share of total U.S. production

State	1910	1920	1930	1940	1950	1960	1970
Illinois-Indiana	15	22	21	21	20	22	25
Pennsylvania	51	42	35	30	28	24	23
Ohio	19	24	23	21	20	24	18
Subtotal	85	84	79	72	68	63	66
Michigan	0	0	1	5	6	7	7
Maryland	1	5	4	6	6	7	5
New York	5	5	4	6	5	5	3
California	0	1	1	1	3	3	3
Total	92	96	89	90	88	85	84

Source: AISI, Annual Statistical Report, 1912-1972, compiled by Hekman (1978).

1910 to 41.9 percent in 1920, while the Illinois-Indiana and Ohio locations increased their shares moderately. Small increments of regional capacity began to appear in this area in places like Colorado (where Rockefeller's older Colorado Fuel and Iron Corporation supplied steel for the railroads) and in California, where a small competitive industry, depending wholly on scrap supplies, served the canning, oil and gas, railroad, lumbering, and mining industries.[10]

The long-term locational consequences of this pattern laid down during the Pittsburgh plus period were exacerbated by the fact that this era encompassed the fastest-growing demand for steel. Consumption grew 6 percent a year from 1900 to 1916; from 1916 to 1929 it remained constant; and it was depressed, or negative, from 1929 to 1939. Even in the war and postwar period (1941−1970) demand for steel grew at an annual rate less than 2 percent.[11] Thus the century's major expansions in new plant and furnace construction occurred under the Pittsburgh Plus regime.

Through World War II the maintenance of oligopolistic pricing and the decline in depression demand for steel continued to retard the dispersion of steel-making capacity in the United States; however, a major change in the basing point system diminished the degree of distortion in locational advantage that had prevailed previously. Despite the steel cartel's successful weathering of a trust-busting court case, the industry was forced in 1924, and again in 1938, to expand the number of basing points by an FTC investigation. The investigation was a tardy response to irate Chicago area fabricators who in 1919 formed the Western Association of Rolled Steel Consumers for the Abolition of the Pittsburgh Plus and who resented paying the artificially high prices produced by the Pittsburgh plus system. The new basing points were Chicago, Birmingham, and Bethlehem. Immediately monopoly profits were diminished proportionately though not eliminated. A further expansion of basic points occurred in 1938.[12]

Locationally the modified basing point system still restricted output, although it favored expansion at the new basing points. Any dramatic spatial restructuring, however, was curtailed by the depression, which sent output plunging (see figure 8.1) and cut short investment plans. The modest westward shift in state output continued throughout the era (see table 8.1). Pennsylvania's share fell from 42 percent in 1920 to just over 30 percent in 1940, and the Chicago area climbed from 15.4 percent to 20.6 percent of output. Large numbers of small plants closed during the depression (see figure 8.4). States like Virginia and Tennessee, which had only small producers, lost most of their capacity. Virginia, for instance, lost seven of eight of its blast furnaces, closing down over 90 percent of state capacity.[13]

In some cases the elimination of the locational bias in the pricing system came too late for decentralized locations to catch up. Birmingham, for instance, lost its labor and materials cost advantages from the depression on. Its previously tractable workers had unionized in both steel making and mining, and out-migration had cut into the ranks of the cheap local labor force. Both coal and ore deposits near Birmingham had become relatively more expensive to mine than more northerly or international sources. Thus Birmingham was not able to catch up in building the industrial complex around steel that might have been engendered earlier. Although the same cost problems would have occurred later, Birmingham undoubtedly would have had larger, more modern mills and a larger more complex local fabrication sector that might have generated its own growth dynamic.[14] Alabama never had a tin plate mill or high-quality steel capacity (perhaps reflecting as well retarded industrialization and low productivity in southern agriculture) because U.S. Steel had preferred to meet southern demand from its northern mills. By World War II the Alabama steel industry was too far behind in these areas to catch up.[15]

8.3 The Role of Government in New Wartime Capacity

The relocation incentives arising from this round of basing point changes paled in comparison to the direct investment decisions of the federal government during World War II. The War Assets Administration spent $770 million on steel plants during the war. The biggest changes involved the building with government financing of four large new integrated plants, one in California, one in Utah, and two in Texas, chiefly for producing plates and structural steel for ship building. The percentage change in output in the West was far above that of any other region; the seven westernmost states increased their capacity by 250 percent during the war. Prewar basing prices had favored steel shipments by both Bethlehem and U.S. Steel to the West Coast from their Sparrows Point, Maryland, and Birmingham, Alabama, plants. These seven states had consumed 2.3 million tons of steel in 1939; more was supplied by the Alabama and Sparrows Point plants than by all local plants combined.[16]

Wartime steel plants were not sited optimally. For strategic reasons the government avoided cost-minimizing coastal locations. Both the Geneva (Utah) and the Fontana (Los Angeles area) works were located inland where their profitability subsequently was handicapped by high transportation costs. Nor were their product lines well matched to postwar demand. Producing chiefly plate for a wartime shipbuilding industry that more than doubled its prewar capacity, neither of the California plants faced the postwar economy with profitability assured. Both plants were to suffer ongoing difficulties from these war-related characteristics.[17]

It would be a mistake to conclude that the government radically altered the regional pattern of the steel industry during the war period. The Northeast, because it had an available labor supply and management and because in-place expansions were quicker than new plant start-ups, received 74 percent of capacity growth during the war. Its share of total capacity fell only slightly—from 93 percent to 91 percent—in the war era. In fact the distribution of wartime aid temporarily halted the movement westward toward Chicago and toward eastern tidewater sites.[18] The wartime choices of the federal government may have retarded long-run West Coast production at tidewater sites by saddling the region with two large inefficiently located producers. The extraordinary recent success of Japanese penetration in West Coast markets from their own coastal plants suggests this possibility.

8.4 Postwar Expansion

In 1948 the industry abandoned multiple basing point pricing, replacing it with a system of price leadership where all firms automatically and covertly would follow U.S. Steel's lead in pricing. This system worked well to guarantee short-term normal-plus profits. Prices rose steadily as the industry leader aimed at a target rate of return; price increases bore little relation to the excess of demand over supply.[19] Profit rates were as good as or better than in U.S. manufacturing in general (table 8.2), even though the industry was undertaking substantial capital investments in this period.

In the postwar prosperity of the 1950s, steel corporations made large investments on new and expanded plants without much alteration in the regional status quo. Although the abandonment of the locationally biased basing point system was a potential incentive to decentralization, the tremendous scale and fixity of existing steel

Table 8.2
Steel industry profits and rates of return, 1950-1977

Year	Steel[a]	Primary Iron & Steel[b]	All U.S. Manufacturing[b]
1950		14.3	15.4
1951		12.3	12.1
1952		8.5	10.3
1953		10.7	10.5
1954		8.1	9.9
1955		13.5	12.6
1956		12.7	12.2
1957		11.4	11.0
1958		7.2	8.6
1959		8.0	10.4
1960		7.2	9.2
1961		6.2	8.8
1962		5.5	9.8
1963		7.0	10.3
1964		8.8	11.6
1965		9.8	13.0
1966		10.3	13.5
1967		7.7	11.7
1968	5.3	7.6	12.1
1969	4.6	7.6	11.5
1970	2.8	4.3	9.3
1971	2.8	4.5	9.7
1972	3.4	6.0	10.6
1973	4.4	9.5	12.8
1974	6.5	16.9	14.9
1975	4.7	10.9	11.6
1976	3.7	9.0	14.0
1977	0.06		
1978	2.6		
1978	2.6		
1979	2.1		
1980	3.3		
1981	4.2		

Sources:
a. Income as a percentage of revenues, from AISI *Annual Report* (1977, 1978, 1980, 1981).
b. Return on stockholders' equity after taxes, from Duke et al. (1977:68). This figure is not net of reinvestment.

mills that was the result of fifty years of protection seems to have outweighed it. The first three columns of table 8.3 show the distribution of new plant and the most important types of equipment in basic steel making from 1945 on. New open hearth furnaces (now considered to have been a mistake because they do not compare efficiently with other steel-making furnaces) were concentrated in Pennsylvania, New York (the Buffalo area), Ohio, and Indiana. New blast furnaces were shared among states in percentage rates close to their shares of output and value added (columns 7 and 8). Even the basic oxygen furnace (BOF), which was not adopted in this country until 1954, has been introduced largely in the older steel-making centers, including California and Alabama. As a result the proportions of output accounted for by each state did not change more than 4 percentage points from 1950 to 1960 (table 8.1). What shifts did occur replicated the earlier pattern. Pennsylvania dropped again from 28.2 percent to 24.0 percent, the Chicago area rose from 20.1 percent to 22.2 percent, and smaller gains were made in Michigan, Maryland, New York, and California. But the major producing states accounted for almost as much of total output in 1960 as they had in 1950.

But new investment was not synonymous with new job growth in these regions. Automation resulted in a historic reversal in employment growth (see figure 8.1). The persistent elimination of jobs in the postwar era was also a response to the degree of organization and militance of the United Steel Workers of America (USWA), which by 1942, had organized 90 percent of the basic steel industry and won substantial wage increases and work rule gains. From 1949 to 1959 they engaged in at least one major strike per year. In 1959, as collusion in the industry began to break down, they struck for 116 days, refusing to accept greater productivity at constant real wages.[20] Postwar restructuring rendered much steel capacity obsolete before its natural life span—its use value—had been expended. Workers, too, found their skills redundant before their working lives had been completed.

8.5 The Internationalization of Steel Markets

Beginning in the late 1950s, effective oligopoly power in the steel industry was destroyed. While U.S. production remained concentrated in a few firms, several developments eroded the ability of the large corporations to practice oligopolistic behavior. The national

Table 8.3
State shares of postwar steel capacity added, 1945-1970

State	New blast furnace 1945-1970[a]	New open hearth furnaces, 1945-1970[b]	Basic oxygen furnaces, 1954-1970[c]	Continuous casting mills 1970[d]	Mini mill capacity, 1954-1970[e]	Integrated specialty output 1977[f]	Percentage total value added, 1977[g]	Percentage total output, 1977
Pennsylvania	26.9%	b	24.2%	14.0%	2.9%	33.0%	30.0%	20.5%
New York		b	6.0	2.0	2.9	4.9	3.0	3.2
Connecticut						2.9		
New Jersey						4.9		
Delaware				2.0		1.0		
Maryland	7.6		3.0			1.9		
West Virginia	3.8		3.0	2.0	3.1			
Ohio	15.4	b	18.1	12.0	2.6	15.5	19.8	17.2
Indiana	15.4	b	12.1	6.0		2.9	12.6	17.2
Illinois	7.6		12.1	12.0	10.7	5.8	12.6	8.6
Michigan	9.6		9.0	6.0		5.8	6.3	8.1
Wisconsin						1.9		
Missouri				4.0	5.0			
Virginia				4.0	5.5			
North Carolina					2.1			
South Carolina				8.0	8.3	1.0		
Georgia						1.0		
Florida				4.0	6.0	1.0		

Table 8.3 (continued)

State	New blast furnace 1945-1970[a]	New open hearth furnaces, 1945-1970[b]	Basic oxygen furnaces, 1954-1970[c]	Continuous casting mills 1970[d]	Mini mill capacity, 1954-1970[e]	Integrated specialty output 1977[f]	Percentage total value added, 1977[g]	Percentage total output, 1977
Mississippi					1.7			
Kentucky	1.9		3.0	2.0	2.7			
Tennessee				4.0	2.7			
Alabama	3.8		3.0	2.0	6.2	1.0	2.2	
Louisiana					2.1			
Arkansas				2.0	1.7			
Nebraska[h]								
Colorado			3.0					
Texas				4.0	9.9	4.9	3.4	
Oklahoma				2.0				
Arizona					3.1			
Utah					1.0			
California	5.8		3.0	6.0	11.2	7.8	2.2	1.6
Oregon				2.0	6.7			
Washington					1.8	1.0		
Hawaii					1.0			
Total	52 furnaces	43 furnaces	33 plants	50 plants	4,812 K tons	103 plants	15,331.9 ($ million)	125.3 (million tons)

Sources: Calculated from Hogan (1971:1544, 1518-1519, 152., 1564, 1567, 2067-2073, AISI); *Annual Statistics* (1969, 1977); *Census of Manufacturers, 1977.*

a. Plants with new enlarged blast furnace capacity, 1945-1971.

b. States with new open hearth capacity added, postwar.

c. Sites of basic oxygen process installations. Each site has between one and three furnaces, most having two.

d. Plants with continuous casting mills, 1970.

e. Total capacity of thirty-eight new plants with capacity under 200,000 tons per year built by 1970.

f. Plants for thirty-eight integrated (possessing melting furnaces) specialty steel producers.

g. Addition of small nonintegrated firms would increase apparent dispersion.

h. Nebraska in the 1970s became the site of the largest new min. mill.

competitiveness and international viability of the big steel corporations began to wane. The percentage of world output accounted for by U.S. steel declined from 47 percent in 1950 to 17 percent in 1977. Imports (in tonnage terms) since the early 1960s have increased more than 1000 percent while exports have fallen in volume. By 1977 imports of steel accounted for 17.8 percent of U.S. consumption, up from 2.9 percent in 1958.[21] Import penetration is a result of both lower labor costs and/or superior degrees of modernization, especially in Japanese steel. This international competition placed new pressures on the U.S. steel oligopoly.

The development of new low-cost materials substitutes, particularly aluminum and plastic, began to erode the demand for steel, cutting the price inelasticity of demand. For most years from 1955 on, steel shipments lagged behind the rate of growth in output for many of its user industries. Apparently the consistently high and rising prices of steel encouraged users to begin substituting plastics, aluminum, glass, timber, cement, paperboard, and plywood for steel inputs. Plastics began to substitute in a massive way for steel in the auto, container, and domestic appliances industries. The American Iron and Steel Institute complained in 1961 that this penetration by substitutes accounted for 2 million tons of lost U.S. steel output per year. The European Economic Community estimated that world losses in steel to competitive products had reached 5 percent and would grow to at least 7.5 percent in the short run.[22] In the larger sense these substitutions represent the inevitable technical progress inherent in capitalist dynamics.

The discipline of emergent competition in the 1960s and 1970s resulted in clear relocational tendencies in space. Although a series of process innovations had mixed effects on spatial reorganization, the search for lower labor, materials, and energy costs resulted in the systematic closing or running down of plants in older locations and the construction of new ones at decentralized locations. Three types of decentralization can be distinguished: greenfield plants proposed and/or built within the steel belt but in relatively nonurban locations, dozens of new small-sized, small town minimills scattered throughout the United States, and a general locational shift of production capacity toward the sunbelt, mainly Texas. From the point of view of U.S. steel consumers, the location of production has decentralized internationally as well, with Japanese plants now supplying a significant share of the U.S. steel market.

Table 8.4
State steel employment shares, 1958-1977

State	Jobs (000)					Jobs change	Percentage change
	1958	1962	1967	1972	1977		
New York	27.3	27.4	28.4	22.4	19.4	− 7.9	− 29
Pennsylvania	163.9	150.3	164.9	134.1	120.7	− 43.2	− 26
Ohio	82.7	79.6	76.7	73.3	67.8	− 14.9	− 22
Indiana	56.3	57.0	62.8	62.6	63.3	+ 7.0	+ 12
Illinois	38.3	41.6	43.9	39.8	38.4	+ 0.1	0
Michigan	17.3	21.3	22.3	19.7	20.7	+ 3.4	+ 20
Alabama	20.1	18.9	20.9	17.8	14.9	− 5.2	− 26
Texas	8.9	7.5	11.1	11.7	13.4	+ 4.5	+ 51
California	15.6	15.8	18.3	15.4	13.5	− 2.1	− 13
United States	511.4	500.6	553.1	469.1	441.9	− 69.5	− 14

Source: *Census of Manufactures.*

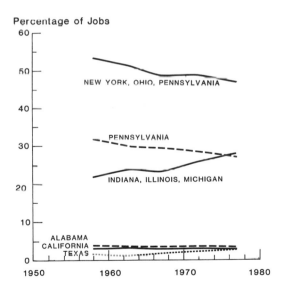

Figure 8.6
State shares of steel employment, 1958-1977

Changes in the shares of national employment for the biggest steel-producing states are shown in table 8.4 and figure 8.6.[23] (Due to disclosure requirements, the Census of Manufacturing does not publish state-by-state figures for the states with one or a few large plants, such as Colorado.) Employment share fell more or less consistently in the states that represent the old centers of their markets: Pennsylvania, Ohio, New York, Alabama, and California. Employment share increased modestly in Illinois, significantly in Indiana and Michigan, and dramatically in Texas. The disparity in absolute numbers is striking; while Pennsylvania lost 4,700 jobs from 1958 to 1977, Indiana gained 3,300 and Texas 1,300.

Three investment features contribute to these shifts: new steel-making technologies, the minimill, and specialty steel.[24] New technology generally has taken the shape of process improvements, which have had mixed effects on location. Scale-enhancing improvements like the giant blast furnace have reinforced the advantage of older centers; they still rely heavily on ore and pellet inputs and coking coal. Both new blast furnaces and the basic oxygen furnace, as table 8.3 shows, have been concentrated in the steel-belt states. But at least one researcher predicts that the BOF will redistribute output to the southern and western regions.[25] Regional employment shifts will lag behind output shifts, however, because a BOF furnace needs only 17 men and women on the furnace floor compared to 131 for an open hearth furnace. Furthermore, the work is less difficult, so that steelworkers on a BOF are paid less.[26]

The tremendous boom in minimills seems to have had the greatest impact on the decentralization process. Figure 8.7 shows the national distribution of minimills. A minimill is a relatively small, scrap-based steel plant, usually specializing in concrete-reinforcing bars and other simple products, highly automated, and almost universally nonunion. Minimills are particularly responsive to the lower labor costs and easier labor discipline available in small town locations outside the sunbelt. More than half of all minimills built before the 1970s were located in urban areas with populations of less than 30,000.[27] Fully 63.3 percent is located in the sunbelt, defined as Virginia through California, while only 36.7 percent is located in the frostbelt, defined as Maryland, West Virginia through Oregon and above. Within these broad regions minimill capacity is more often than not located outside traditional steel-making states. Only 43 percent of sunbelt capacity, for instance, is in the traditional steel-producing states of California, Texas, Alabama, and Colorado. In

Figure 8.7
National distribution of minimills. (Source: Adams and Mueller, 1982:84)

frostbelt, some 42 percent of minimill capacity is located in the non-steel states of Minnesota, Oregon, and Washington. This trend toward interregional and intraregional decentralization appears to have continued into the 1980s.

The rise of specialty steel had a countervailing role in spatial reorganization. Table 8.4 shows that frostbelt states account for over 80 percent of specialty steel capacity, which is only slightly below the frostbelt's share of total value added and output. Within the frostbelt the shares of Pennsylvania, Ohio, and the Chicago area in specialty steel are also only modestly below their overall position in the industry. Within the sunbelt, too, specialty steel is concentrated in the older manufacturing states; California, Alabama, and Texas account for more than two-thirds of specialty steels output in the sunbelt. The lower degree of independence of this new sector from older steel-making and urban centers is a result of their closer association with spatially concentrated industries like aircraft and of their need for relatively high numbers of engineers and technical workers to work on the product design, quality control, customer service, and marketing stages of their output. Large numbers of specialty steel plants surround Pittsburgh, where they take advantage of corporate headquarters-related facilities.[28] Thus specialty steels operate as a new innovative sector, agglomerating at the old core steel sites where corporate research labs and marketing operations still exist. Minimills, on the other hand, represent much more the deskilling of work,[29] the propulsion of the industry toward low-cost locations, and the market orientation of minimills (in large part toward the decentralized construction industry), all of which characterize the competitive and normal-profit-minus stages of the profit cycle.

8.6 Abandonment and Restructuring

What appears to be a permanent decline in the growth of steel demand within advanced capitalist countries has ushered in a new era. Output and shipments of domestic manufacturers are down, employment has fallen even more dramatically, and massive plant closings have occurred. The closings are unevenly distributed, with the Pittsburgh and Youngstown areas hit hardest, following by significant cuts in the work force in New York, Alabama, and California. One large integrated steel corporation—Kaiser—publicly pondered liquidation in late 1980.[30]

Since the mid-1970s registered profits of steel corporations have been about half those of manufacturing firms in the economy as a whole (see table 8.2), and there is reason to believe that they are greater than zero only because of nonsteel portions of their business such as freight charges on Great Lakes shipping. U.S. Steel Corporation averaged a zero profit rate (profits as a percentage of equity) from 1974 to 1980.[31] In response U.S. steel makers closed down 8 million tons of capacity from 1977 to 1980, 2 million in 1980 alone. Not only have capital expenditures been low, despite the need for modernization, but the biggest corporations have drastically slashed their capital budgets in response to the profit crisis. Sacrificing market share for short-term profit, they have been willing to shut down plants even if it means reducing overall capacity.[32] By the early 1980s, this strategy appeared to have paid off modestly, as profit rates rose from nearly zero in 1977 to a still insufficient 4.2 percent in 1981.

The causes of this profit crunch are the continuation of problems: the slippage of the U.S. steel competitiveness due to earlier oligopolistic failure to innovate rapidly enough, the comparatively superior performance of Japanese corporations, and the adaptation by clients of new materials that substitute for steel. Imports are estimated to have cost steelworkers about 50,000 jobs in 1977 and 12,700 in 1978.[33] Materials substitutes appear to account for another 5 percent of the fall in demand for steel. Steel corporations also blame two other causes for their troubles: high labor costs (including wages, pensions, and work rules, which impede productivity) and antipollution control requirements. Both of these can be seen as the culmination of successful class and community-environmentalist efforts to win concessions from the steel corporations. Whether these battles have made significant inroads on profitability, the steel industry is now trying to roll back each set of gains to improve its troubled status.

The industry's response to its prolonged profit squeeze has assumed the form of wholesale plant abandonment. The scale of plant closings in the United States has been devastating.[34] In October 1977 Bethlehem cut its capacity 10 percent, eliminating 7,300 jobs. Hardest hit were the Lackawanna, New York, plant (at Buffalo) and the Johnstown, Pennsylvania, plant. Smaller companies have closed shops too. Armco permanently laid off 6,500 workers at its Middletown, Ohio, plant. The Alan Wood Corporation, in eastern Pennsylvania at Conshohocken, closed a mill with 3,000 jobs. In a dramatic attempt to restore profitability, U.S. Steel announced in November 1979 that it would permanently close twelve facilities, eliminating 13,000 of its 165,000 jobs in the United States. The mills closed were concentrated in the states of Pennsylvania, Ohio, California, and Alabama. The closings cost U.S. Steel more than $780 million, mostly in supplemental unemployment benefits and pensions, but they would permit the corporation to write off a tremendous amount of physical capacity in hope of raising rates of return on mills in operation.[35] In 1984 U.S. Steel undertook a further set of closings of about the same magnitude.

Both the Pittsburgh and Youngstown regions have been hard hit. Pittsburgh, while absorbing more job losses, has a larger steel-making base to survive on; in addition it has many corporate-management-related jobs because most of the largest firms are still headquartered there. Pittsburgh lost 2,100 employees of U.S. Steel at seven area plants in early 1980. In 1981 Jones and Laughlin, now a subsidiary of the conglomerate LTV, laid off 1,000 employees permanently at a forty-three-year-old strip mill.[36] Experts predict more Pittsburgh-area closings in the mid-1980s. In late 1982 only one blast furnace was operating in the Monongahela Valley.

Youngstown's economic base is more dependent on steel production than any other region. In 1977 Lykes Corporation, a conglomerate that had bought out Youngstown Sheet and Tube, closed two of its area plants, the Campbell and Struthers Works, putting out of work more than 5,500 workers. In 1979 U.S. Steel announced that it was closing two major area works, its Ohio Works and McDonald Works, casting another 5,000 out of work. In 1979 as well LTV Corporation bought out Lykes Steel interest and closed its third and final Youngstown plant, the Brier Hills Works. The estimates of employment loss range from around 12,000 to 25,000 for this city of 500,000 people, which was once second only to Pittsburgh as a steel-making center. The nonsteel conglomerate buyers of Youngstown Sheet and Tube seem to have been more interested in pumping the steel operation for cash to pay off the acquisition debt than in upgrading plant and equipment in the area.[37]

Closings in Alabama and California have been marked as well. In Alabama U.S. Steel's Fairfield Works had been unprofitable for three and a half years before it was closed in 1980, laying off 7,000 workers in that area. In California the Kaiser Fontana plant, which had been built to government specifications in World War II, closed most of its operations, as did a fabricating plant with 400 workers near Los Angeles and a Torrance, California, works, with 670 workers.[38]

While workers suffer the unemployment from closure in steel-making, steel corporations are investing what capital they do have in nonsteel ventures. Most steel corporations are remarkably nondiversified. Most still earn between 70 and 80 percent of their receipts in steel sales. Most do not engage in foreign production of steel. But diversification is increasing and drastically restructuring the industry. U.S. Steel produces iron ore, coal, timber, and chemicals and is seeking new manufacturing operations. Its American Bridge Division is a large builder of bridges, office buildings, and plants. U.S. Steel is also one of the nation's largest real estate developers. Steel capacity is predicted to drop to 48 percent of U.S. Steel's assets in 1990, down from 61 percent in 1980. Similar diversification is occurring among other steel corporations. Armco's steel assets will fall from 73 percent of total in 1976 to 49 percent in 1983. Most steel corporations diversify into supply substitutes or customer activities rather than unrelated products. National Steel, for instance, has branched into magnesium (a steel input), aluminum (a competitor), and construction containers and oil and gas equipment (steel users).[39] These moves have been exacerbating the adjustment problems of older steel centers.

8.7 Steel Sector Summary

The steel industry affords an unusually clear case of the retarding effect of oligopoly on decentralization on the one hand and the accelerating effect of conglomerate diversification on the other. The long-run effects of this phase of oligopolistic normal-plus profits have been far from beneficial for either the host areas or the country as a whole. One can argue, as Stocking did (1954), that the undue concentration of employment in the Pittsburgh and Youngstown areas came at the expense of healthy steel-based regional development in other centers like Birmingham. For the first part of this century, the agglomerative effect worked in the Pittsburgh-Youngstown areas' favor, as fabricators and users located nearby in greater numbers than they would have with competition. But Chinitz (1960) argues that the regional dominance of steel in the Pittsburgh area curtailed the availability of land, labor, entrepreneurship, and capital to other potential regional employers and stunted regional development in successive eras. Thus steel-dependent spin-offs were engendered while resource-competing, independent industries were discouraged. Core regions, then, became bloated with steel-related activities but underdeveloped as diversified urban economies.

Whatever the net effect of these two forces, the evolution of the spatial structure in steel resulted in the increased vulnerability of both favored and unfavored regions to conditions in the 1970s. The older regions have had to cope with the devastating effects of rapid readjustments that were suppressed during the oligopolistic era. The smaller steel sectors in places like Birmingham and California have been underdeveloped as the core regions were overdeveloped and are incapable of meeting the competitive challenge from abroad. The size of the giant steel corporations permits them to transfer money capital rapidly from their ailing steel operations into more promising diversified product lines. The steel study shows, then, that the oligopolistic phase of the steel industry profit cycle exacerbated spatial adjustments in the sector. In the current period high unemployment rates are being borne by workers in the old core areas; production in all other areas, except perhaps Texas and Indiana, where the most modern large-scale facilities exist, cannot meet international competition.

The spatial dislocation process in steel is not a function of oligopoly in steel alone. In a larger sense it is the product of capitalist dynamics in general and productivity-enhancing innovation in particular. Even without the oligopolistic period, regional unemployment would have followed in the wake of a westward-moving sector and a generalized decline in the late profit stages. One can argue that the process might have been more gradual and might have left the U.S. industry better balanced interregionally and thus better able to withstand competition, especially on the West Coast. One could argue too that the adjustment to competitive disadvantage for workers and cities in the steel belt would have been eased by a more gradual history of dispersion.

But even without the distorting influence of oligopoly, the industry would have been victim in the longer run to imports based on cheaper foreign labor and to substitutes in its product market.[40] The case of the steel industry suggests that sectoral relocation is a vital companion to the evolution of any industry rather than a historical aberration or accident. It remains to future research to demonstrate if this is indeed the case for all sectors.

8.8 The Profit Cycle versus Neoclassical Views of Steel

The steel industry case study demonstrates how a model that posits changing sensitivity to levels and sources of profitability over time can better predict the regional location and development impacts of individual sectors throughout their evolution than can neoclassical economics. Past empirical efforts to test locational models of steel industry geography have been built on the black box competitive model. A brief comparison of the two models and methods underscores the strengths of the profit cycle approach.

Four problems characterize these past efforts. First, they are not fundamentally historical but use contemporary cross-sectional comparisons of cost and demand features to infer recent and future locational orientations. Hekman, for instance, notes that almost all growth in steel output has taken place at sites already established by 1900 and seeks only to explain why output has grown faster at some of these (mainly Chicago-area mills) than others. He assumes away, in other words, the most important set of locational decisions: why to locate plants at precisely those sites. Isard and Capron argue that resource transport costs account for these previous location decisions, yet they do not directly test the changing comparative cost structure of all potential locational sites during that historical period. Indeed, all of these articles are conspicuous for the absence of longitudinal data on regional comparative costs.

A second and related problem is the reliance on marginal change as a method of analysis and prediction. Isard and Capron, writing in 1949 and using data from the late 1930s and early 1940s, argue that comparative transport costs suggest a future dispersion of production toward the Detroit, Pacific Coast, eastern seaboard, and even Birmingham locations. Yet their data are consistent with my interpretation that production should have dispersed toward these locations long before the 1940s.

A third problem is that each of these models assumes that the location decisions of steel-consuming industries are independent of the locations of steel plants. Yet the evidence presented in this chapter suggests that the curtailment of steel production in places like Birmingham, Detroit, and the Pacific Coast, which was part of a deliberate, market-controlling strategy of the major steel corporations, operated as a disincentive to steel users to locate and produce within those regions. Furthermore my argument (and Chinitz's, 1960) that early steel-using industries like machining tended to cluster around the original oligopolistic steel centers but that domination of regional resources in those areas tended to discourage new generations of steel-using entrepreneurs is not inconsistent with Hekman's (1978) findings that growth in steel-consuming sectors explains the Chicago-area steel mill's relatively faster growth over the Pittsburgh-area mills in the twentieth century.

A fourth problem is that these research efforts, which assume competitive behavior, employ only cost and demand factors as geographic explanatory variables. Although Isard and Capron (1949) acknowledge the possible role of basing point pricing and Karlson (1983) alludes briefly to the possibility of spatial collusion among interdependent firms, neither research effort models these behavioral aspects directly. Indeed the fact that the three empirical efforts at issue here arrive at contradictory conclusions regarding the relative importance of transport costs versus market demand suggests that the models are misspecified and that missing variables capturing oligopolistic interdependencies may be the missing link.

Profitability is a function of techniques of realization as well as production. Especially in oligopolistic industries, where greater-than-normal profits are achievable through market management, there are strong reasons for concentrating production in certain sites despite strictly production inefficiencies. The clear failure of the Isard and Capron predictions about future decentralization of steel production toward Detroit, the Pacific Coast, Birmingham, and the eastern seaboard is additional indirect evidence of the argument embodied in the profit cycle model. Karlson's (1983:49) evidence that "firms choose the locations of integrated steel plants without perceiving the responses of consumers to price changes as differing by industry group or region" leads him to conclude rather weakly that location decisions are not inconsistent with a model in which firms choose a location that minimizes input transportation costs. But his findings suggest even more strongly that oligopolistic behavior, past and present, could be the dominant factor, especially given Isard and Capron's evidence that, as of 1949, transport costs did not (nor presumably now do not) favor these existing locations.

9   The Producer Goods Sectors

The five producer goods sectors chosen for investigation of profit cycle behavior—electronics, computers, aluminum, steel, and textiles—run the gamut from the most dramatically expanding to the most rapidly rationalizing and profit-squeezed sectors. Each comprises a major employment cluster in the economy, and each has played a central role in the evolution and economic structure of host regions.

9.1 The Computer Industry

The computer industry is wholly a postwar phenomenon, an industry that, with semiconductors, has formed the backbone of the so-called high tech revolution. Some analysts believe that these sectors will lead a contemporary capitalist revival, constituting another round of Menschian innovations restructuring production and restoring profitability.[1] Computers are also a leading-edge industry for the United States in the world market. Computer manufacturing is so new an industry segment that census data have been collected on it only since 1967, when the industry already employed 100,000 workers.[2] Since then, in the ten years covered by the census, output and employment doubled, indicating that the industry is still squarely in an innovative phase.

Profit Cycle Stages, Output, and Jobs

The successful commercial innovation of computers was preceded by research efforts, often government and military funded, at several private and nonprofit institutions.[3] The transition from this inventive activity to stage II superprofits occurred in the late 1950s.[4] By 1967, when it was accorded status as a new four-digit SIC, the industry was

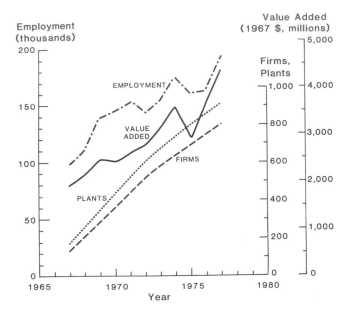

Figure 9.1
Computer industry growth, 1967-1977

booming commercially. The industry is still heavily engaged in product innovation and research activities. At least thirteen new technologies have proved successful as mass-marketed commodities since the late 1970s.[5]

The growth experience in computers confirms an innovative pattern. Firm numbers grew dramatically (over 400 percent) and faster than either jobs or output (figure 9.1). Output of computers, as measured by value added, has risen by 120 percent since 1967, and employment has risen by 92 percent; 200,000 workers now work in computer manufacturing operations, and many other jobs have been created in computer programming and in business consulting services that are primarily computer related.

The stunning pace of technical change has led some in the industry to claim that innovation will be continual and job growth thus sustained. Yet the age of expansive profits and gargantuan growth may be drawing to a close. The computer industry, typical of a stage II sector, has experienced falling product prices every year since its emergence. Profit margins are falling, and pressures to automate and streamline production are intensifying.

Within the industry there are distinct subsegments with different growth paths: the mainframe, mini, and personal computer markets.[6] Product definition and market segments are constantly changing in response to technological breakthroughs. Recently a semiconductor manufacturer produced a three-chip system, dubbed the micromainframe. With the capability of a mainframe computer "on a desk-top," this new device could blur the distinction between mainframe and minicomputers and even between computers and semiconductors. The new microprocessor, as the system is also called, could sell within a few years at 20 percent of the cost of today's minicomputer. This case illustrates the difficulties in classifying sectors in their youth. It also underscores the vulnerability of individual companies in the industry to rampant innovation, which can restructure products and prices in a year's time.

Industry Structure

The computer industry remains quite competitive, although the size and market power of companies vary across segments. The industry is modestly concentrated; four firms account for almost 44 percent of shipments. A steady increase in the number of both plants and companies has occurred since the 1960s (figure 9.1). Concentration ratios confirm the hypothesized tendency for a stage II industry to decline in concentration as industry leaders are joined by new entrants during a superprofits era (figure 9.2).

Ownership form data show active industry entry (figure 9.3) but reveal underlying tendencies toward larger and more established firms. Multiplant firms accounted for a smaller share of plants by 1977, falling from almost 60 percent to less than 40 percent. But during the same period three big firms increased their share of jobs, which remains at nearly 90 percent.

Concentration among mainframe makers is more pronounced than in other segments. One corporation, IBM, dominates both the U.S. and world markets, with 71 percent of total world sales in 1977. One firm, RCA, dropped out in the 1970s. The other major mainframe makers—Sperry Rand, Honeywell, Burroughs, Control Data, and NCR—all have less than 10 percent of the market apiece. Competition in product quality has remained vigorous until recently. IBM has led the market with successive generations of new and better mainframes. In 1978, however, its newest generation was too innovative and competitively priced; after a decade of superprofits, IBM's earnings declined 3 percent. Some customers decided not to buy and preferred to lease, anticipating that new breakthroughs would make

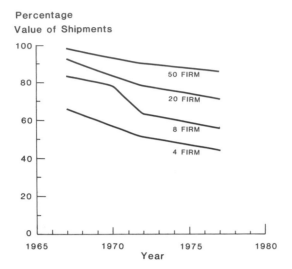

Figure 9.2
Concentration ratios in computers, 1967-1977

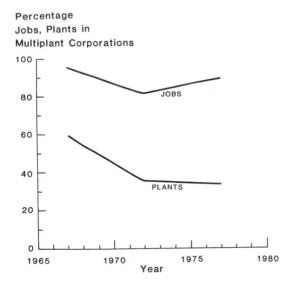

Figure 9.3
Ownership patterns in computers, 1967-1977

current models obsolete rapidly. As a result IBM priced its 1980 model significantly higher than previous models without improving the quality sufficiently to render the latter obsolete. This behavioral change and the increased certainty that it has introduced into the market presages the beginning of a successful transition in main-frames from stage II to a stage IV oligopoly. Computer industry analysts believe that it is headed for a settled oligopoly form, perhaps a "big 10," internationally in the next twenty years.[7]

In the minicomputer and personal markets, several new small firms were dramatically successful in the late 1970s. The most phenomenal, Apple Computers, grew from a garage operation to a $100 million public corporation in four years. Yet even in the mini-computer market, market power is persuasive. IBM controls 29.2 percent of output and Digital Computers 14.6 percent, and five firms account for almost 60 percent. The bigger corporations are able to build market share by establishing retail outlets in many locations, a practice that their enormous financial resources permit them to do at the expense of smaller firms.

The computer industry has an extraordinarily low proportion of its workers in production activities, a finding consistent with the model's hypothesis for an innovative sector (figure 9.4). Only 40 to 45 percent of the work force consists of blue-collar workers, about 60 percent of the U.S. norm. Several factors account for this difference. First, because there are so many small firms, unusually

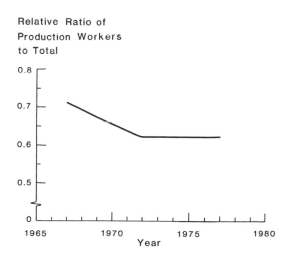

Figure 9.4
Occupational structure in computers, 1967-1977

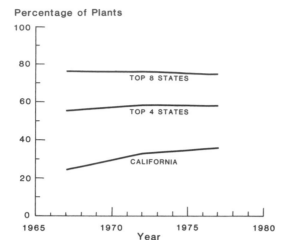

Figure 9.5
Geographical concentration in computers, 1967-1977

Table 9.1
State shares of computer jobs and plants, 1967-1977

State	Number of Plants[b]			Plant change	Percentage change	Number of jobs, 1977[c]
	1967[a]	1972	1977			
Massachusetts	13	37	43	+ 30	+ 231	22.0
Connecticut	1	6	11	+ 10	+1000	2.8
New York	19	34	34	+ 15	+ 79	16.7
New Jersey	9	22	23	+ 14	+ 155	5.6
Pennsylvania	11	15	18	+ 7	+ 64	5.7
Michigan	5	12	9	+ 7	+ 80	3.4
Minnesota	10	22	23	+ 13	+ 130	23.1
Maryland	2	4	10	+ 8	+ 400	1.1
North Carolina	3	5	5	+ 2	+ 67	2.5
Florida	5	15	17	+ 12	+ 240	6.7
Texas	4	8	14	+ 10	+ 250	6.5
Colorado	6	11	9	+ 3	+ 50	3.0
Arizona	2	8	9	+ 7	+ 350	7.6
California	34	113	154	+120	+ 353	58.5
United States	140	354	434	+294	+ 210	192.6

Source: *Census of Manufactures.*
a. 1967 was the first census year for SIC 3573.
b. Plants with more than twenty workers.
c. In 1967 and 1972 disclosure miles limited severely state job data published.

large numbers of managers and proprietors populate the sector. Second, large numbers of professional workers are required for the design and experimental stages of computer manufacturing. Third, an extraordinarily large sales and service force advertises and sells equipment, educates and informs users, and services machines. Finally, a large clerical force is attached to the administrative end of the business. Workers tend to be young and better educated, except in the assembly and clerical operations, where low-paid, frequently Third World women predominate.

Geography

The original centers of commercial innovation in computers have become the major production sites. Four states—California, Massachusetts, New York, and Minnesota—control over 58 percent of plants and have increased their share over the period (figure 9.5). The entire increase is due to the disproportionate growth of plants in California, the largest state in the industry. This confirms the agglomerating tendencies attributed to stage II industries.

The job figures for the latest census year show that the distribution of jobs closely approximates plant shares (see the last two columns of table 9.1). California has almost 59,000 workers, 30 percent of the U.S. total, and close to 35 percent of all U.S. establishments. The top eight states account for 76 percent of jobs and 75 percent of plants, which suggests that the industry is still so new that standardized production lines have not been moved far from the centers of innovation.

Minnesota, a state generally not found among leading U.S. manufacturers, makes an unusual appearance among these states. Minnesota's share is due to innovative activity by two major Minneapolis-based corporations—Control Data and Honeywell. As a result of its early start, the state accounts for 12 percent of computer jobs, largely in the mainframe segment, making it more specialized per capita in computers than California, New York, or Massachusetts, the other major producing states.[8]

While continued innovative ferment may keep plants wed to these centers of agglomeration, tendencies toward decentralization have already appeared. As the industry's structure becomes more settled, the same centrifugal forces that disperse most sectors have come into play. As the industry matures and grows, a substantial portion of sales and service jobs move closer to users, resulting in a more decentralized pattern. In New England branch plants increasingly are located outside the Boston area.[9] Some assembly operations are already dispersed to low-wage locations such as Ireland and Latin America. But for the present the need to be close to other innovators, the formation and drawing on a large pool of technical labor, and the sharing of related services (such as market research firms) keep the bulk of industry jobs tied to their original centers, particularly California. New firms are still being formed as spin-offs of older ones, and whole new suburban areas (Santa Clara County, California; Route 128 in Boston; Roseville, north of St. Paul) are industrializing as these new agglomerations grow.

Summary

The computer industry has posted job gains of almost 5 percent per year for the decades since its statistical birth. A perfect illustration of profit cycle innovative behavior, the numbers of both firms and plants have risen steadily, with new entrepreneurs entering the highly profitable competition. Concentration has declined, although it remains at a level strikingly high for an innovative sector (44 percent for the top four firms; 71 percent for the top twenty). In certain subsectors, such as mainframe computers, concentration is considerably higher, sufficient to constitute oligopoly. Innovative behavior changes under such circumstances as firms like IBM try to control price cutting and tame the pace of new product offerings. Production workers form a relatively low (40 percent) and falling proportion of the computer work force, as the ranks of research and design, managerial, sales, and clerical workers swell and as assembly jobs are exported to developing countries.

Regionally the computer industry has centralized about 35 percent of plants and 30 percent of jobs in California, a leadership role the state has been able to increase by 46 percent over the decade. Massachusetts has also increased its share, and the next three leading states—New York, Minnesota, and New Jersey—have gained both plants and jobs but lost relative shares. Florida, Maryland, Texas, and Arizona have gained plants at a rate greater than the national average. Thus decentralization has begun to take place, especially in the manufacturing stage, while innovation and marketing activities continue to cluster around the two growth poles of Boston and Santa Clara Valley. The computer industry confirms the spatial arguments of the profit cycle model.

9.2 The Semiconductor Industry

The semiconductor is an electronic device that has revolutionized computing and control mechanisms in the postwar period. It has replaced the vacuum tube as the predominant electronic technology, propelling more than two dozen new firms into national prominence. By 1979 semiconductor manufacture had become a $13 billion industry worldwide. Semiconductor firms demonstrate the classic features of an industry in a superprofits stage.[10] The new electronics industry is conspicuously agglomerated at sites different from the older electronics centers: Santa Clara Valley in California, the Route 128 ring around Boston, and areas in and around Houston and Dallas, Texas.

Profit Cycle Stages, Output, and Jobs

Semiconductors were first marketed commercially in the early 1950s, almost entirely to military users.[11] By late in that decade the industry had entered its innovative superprofits period. Over the next twenty years this momentum was sustained through three dramatic changes, each corresponding to the prominence of a single product and a major user market. During the first era (1956-1964) a few firms developed the planar process for imprinting silicon chips, which were custom made and marketed to a relatively small market of two dozen aerospace and communication firms. During this period the Pentagon consumed over 70 percent of the industry's output, particularly in the Minuteman missile and the Apollo spacecraft programs. In the mid-1960s, the development of the integrated circuit extended the market to computers, and a large number of merchant firms entered the fray. Since 1972 the third generation of technology, the very large scale integrated circuit (VLSI), has permitted the penetration of consumer markets and new industrial applications.[12]

Characteristic of an innovating industry, prices plunged at the same time that sales soared. Price declines of 30 percent per year are not uncommon. A memory bit that cost $50 in the mid-1960s cost $0.0005 by 1979. In 1975 the combination of price competition with slack demand caused total sales receipts to fall as well. But in most years electronics firms have been highly profitable. Fairchild, for instance, earned more than 10 percent every year from 1974 through 1979, and in three of those years it posted returns in excess of 25 percent. Innovating firms frequently employ a dual pricing strategy to keep profits up. On new, leading-edge or small batch items they practice creaming—high prices that cannot be undersold by competitors. For older and more mass marketed chips, they resort to penetration pricing, designed to undercut rivals and increase market share.[13]

High levels of research and development activity have typified firm behavior, consistent with the model's innovative stage. The semiconductor is a silicon chip on which is implanted an elaborate set of carefully designed impurities to impede and guide electrical current across it for signaling purposes. The original chip had only one circuit on it; now companies market chips that handle 70,000 circuits, and the device with a capability of 250,000 is not far off. In the tremendous growth stages in the late 1950s, R&D spending was as high as 27 percent of sales. In the 1970s it remained high, at 8 to 10 percent. Much of this research activity, however, is concentrated in the largest firms, with about 50 percent in IBM and ATT alone.[14]

Throughout the innovative era sales boomed; in the 1970s they increased by 19 percent per year. Both employment and value added grew dramatically (figure 9.6). Once computers emerged as a major

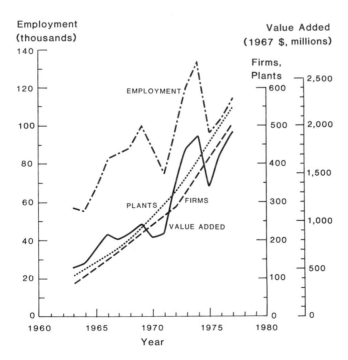

Figure 9.6
Semiconductor industry growth, 1967-1977

application, the number of firms and establishments grew even more rapidly than previously. The rate of new firm formation has exceeded job growth rates, as predicted.

Industry Structure

The new electronics sector contains some of the most dramatic success stories of small-to-large business growth in contemporary capitalism. William Shockley, a former Bell Labs researcher, set up the first commercial firm in Palo Alto in 1954, with financing from an established instruments firms. In 1957 eight of his employees left to form Fairchild Semiconductor, with financial help from Fairchild Camera and Instruments. In almost methodical fashion, engineers continued to desert Fairchild to set up their own companies in the years that followed; by 1971 twenty-one of the twenty-three semiconductor manufacturers in the Bay Area were direct offshoots of Fairchild. As recently as 1980 five new custom chip firms spun off the biggest electronics companies.[15]

Through the mid-1970s, this phenomenon of new firm formation produced measures of concentration that confirm the innovation stage hypothesis of the model. Concentration ratios fell across the period, except for the short period from 1967 to 1972 for the largest four and eight companies (figure 9.7). Multiplant corporations' share of all establishments has actually declined (figure 9.8). The share of employment accounted for by these plants fell as well, although 90 percent of all workers were still employed by multiplant corporations in 1977. These were typically buy-outs of semiconductor independents by large corporations, of U.S., European, and Japanese origin, that wished to ensure and internalize their own supply.[16] Of thirty-six new independents formed between 1966 and 1979, only seven remained independent by 1979. On the other hand the number of captive plants rose from less than a dozen to forty-three by 1977.

New entry appears increasingly difficult due to prohibitive capital costs and marketing requirements. In 1980 $50 million was needed to start a semiconductor firm compared to $1 million in 1965. Those who do succeed, such as Zilog, which spun off of Intel in the mid-1970s, rely on capital from corporations such as Exxon. Many believe that by the mid-1980s, ten giant firms will come to dominate the industry. At least several of these will be international; Japanese

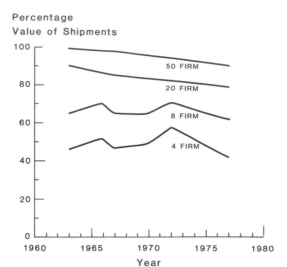

Figure 9.7
Concentration ratios in semiconductors, 1963-1977

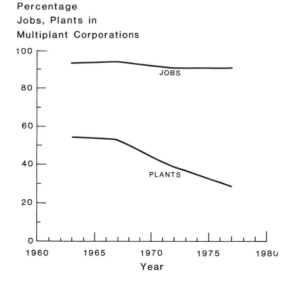

Figure 9.8
Ownership patterns in semiconductors, 1963-1977

firms have already won 23 percent of the U.S. market.[17]

The work force in electronics is bifurcated between highly skilled professional and technical workers and unskilled assembly workers. Research, design, experimental, and testing activities are dependent on skilled engineering labor. The percentage of production workers dropped precipitously over the period from over 72 percent to less than 54 percent of the total work force. Compared to the manufacturing average, the ratio fell from the norm in 1958 to more than 20 percent below the norm in 1977 (figure 9.9). In 1971 40 percent of chip firms' workers were professional, technical, managerial, and marketing employees, 48 percent production and maintenance workers, and 12 percent clerical. Workers were largely nonunionized; only 27 percent belonged to unions, and 96 percent of these were concentrated in northeastern locations. Despite high capital intensity, wages in production work were almost 20 percent below that of the average manufacturing wage in the United States.[18] On the other hand professionals in electronics firms received wages significantly higher than their counterparts in other manufacturing sectors.

Geography

The semiconductor industry has centered in Santa Clara Valley in California, although two other hubs—one in southeastern Texas and

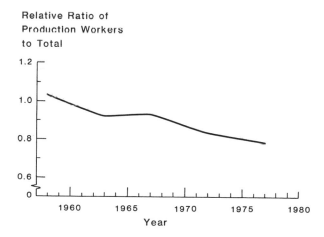

Figure 9.9
Occupational structure in semiconductors, 1963-1977

Table 9.2
State shares of semiconductor plants, 1963-1977

State	Number of Plants[a]				Plant change	Percentage change
	1963	1967	1972	1977		
Massachusetts	15	15	22	23	+ 8	+ 53
Connecticut	6	6	5	6	+ 0	+ 0
New York	11	10	23	22	+ 11	+100
New Jersey	8	10	18	11	+ 3	+ 38
Pennsylvania	9	12	12	16	+ 7	+ 78
Ohio	1	2	5	5	+ 4	+400
Florida	1	2	7	9	+ 8	+800
Texas	2	2	8	16	+ 14	+700
Arizona	4	5	5	9	+ 5	+125
California	22	33	65	80	+ 58	+264
United States	87	117	196	219	+132	+152

Source: *Census of Manufactures.*
a.   Plants with more than twenty workers.

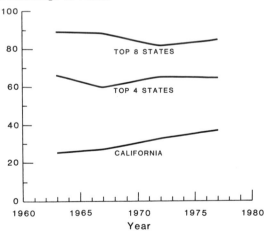

Percentage of Plants

Figure 9.10
Geographical concentration in computers, 1967-1977

another in the Boston area—have remained competitive. The initial
anchoring of the industry in the San Francisco Bay area can be attributed to several factors; Shockley was a native of Palo Alto, Stanford
University provided an ongoing source of engineering talent, as well
as basic research at Stanford Research Institute, and the aerospace
industry, Lockheed in particular, was located nearby. Shockley and
Fairchild spawned dozens of firms that agglomerated in the valley
and provided tremendous employment growth in the area—some
150,000 direct jobs by 1980.[19] Consistent with the model's predictions, California, the lead state in 1963, increased its plant share
dramatically (table 9.2). The top four states maintained their plant
share, while the top eight experienced only a minor loss (figure
9.10).

Nevertheless impulses toward dispersal can already be detected.
The limited data on job growth suggest that Texas and Florida have
posted larger percentage gains than California. In addition assembly
functions have been relocated to overseas sites for nearly twenty
years. During this period production jobs grew at a miniscule rate in
the United States while they grew by more than 100,000 abroad. By
1974 U.S. companies profited from eighty-nine facilities in Mexico,
Korea, Singapore, Malaysia, and Thailand. The major attraction for
relocating this phase of production is low wages—on the average only
10 percent of those in the United States—lowering total integrated
circuit manufacturing costs to less than 50 percent of domestic costs.
The lure of low wages in Third World countries is enhanced by tax
breaks and subsidies, often as part of an export platform package and
by friendly governments that prohibit labor organizing.[20]

Assembly operations and wafer fabrication have begun to be
decentralized within the United States. Table 9.3 shows that Santa
Clara County firms have distinct concentration and dispersion patterns according to stage of the production process. Seventy-nine percent of their research and development facilities are in the valley,
but only 33 percent of advanced manufacturing and 3 percent of
assembly plants are located there. Dispersion is directly related to
labor requirements. Research and management functions, demanding largely skilled white-collar workers, remain spatially concentrated.
Wafer fabrication requires one highly skilled engineer to every two
unskilled workers, and 80 percent of these plants remain in the
United States. Advanced manufacturing plants increasingly are
located outside Silicon Valley, mostly in the nonunion West within a
three-hour plane ride from headquarters. Workers in Third World

Table 9.3
Plant sites of San Jose-based firms, by phase of production, 1980

	Control	Advanced R & D	Manufacturing	Assembly
Santa Clara County	100%	79%	36%	3%
Pacific Northwest and Southwest	0	0	35	9
Rest of United States	0	0	13	0
Europe and Japan	0	21	16	0
Third World	0	0	0	88

Source: Saxenian (1980:142a).

countries form more than 80 percent of U.S. corporations' assembly work force.[21]

These tendencies may be reversed in the future as the movement of assembly jobs abroad reverses and research functions decentralize. Military contract provisions and ongoing experimental efforts keep about 20 percent of assembly jobs in the United States. Semiconductor manufacture may be completely mechanized (IBM has reputedly achieved it in one lab) and repatriated, although few new jobs would be created because robots would replace hand assembly.[22] Although headquarters activities seem firmly anchored in existing locations, even research is not permanently attached to the founding centers.[23] Recently Intel, National Semiconductor, AVX, Motorola, and Control Data set up research and development centers in Israel, attracted by pools of trained personnel, particularly engineers, and support from local universities. Salaries for Israeli skilled personnel are only 40 percent of what they are in the United States and, in tandem with government subsidies, result in lowering research costs to only 30 percent of what they would be in the United States. Thus the hegemony of the Silicon Valley may be waning as even skilled labor becomes cheaper elsewhere.[24]

Summary

The semiconductor sector, closely linked to computers but distinct in entrepreneurship and origins, has created jobs at a rate of 3.6 percent per year since its birth in the census in 1963. In the same period the number of plants jumped by almost 500 percent and the number of competing companies by 400 percent. Highly profitable, the sector's originators, initially engendered by government military-related research and procurement, have faced stiff competition from these new entrants, however, the sector appears headed for oligopoly, as the top twenty firms, many newly acquired by computer corporations, have increased their sales share to 79 percent. Only 54 percent of jobs are classified as production work, down 72 percent from fourteen years previously, relatively greater than the economy-wide shift away from blue-collar workers. Clearly the sector exhibits behavior characteristics of an innovative superprofits stage.

The U.S. semiconductor industry is centered in California, which claims 37 percent of plants and has increased its share by 44 percent since 1963. The other top states—Massachusetts, New York, and Pennsylvania—have lost relative shares to fast-growing states like Florida and Texas. This combination of agglomeration and dispersal reflects the dissociation of research, design, and management from manufacturing operations. As this sector matures, the prominence of Santa Clara Valley will probably decline as production becomes more highly standardized, innovation winds down, and some research and design operations are spun off to places like Boulder, Tucson, and Israel.

9.3 Basic Aluminum Industry

The aluminum industry is a producer goods sector that is no longer innovative yet is still expanding.[25] Aluminum proves to be a sector in which innovation and growth are fused with market power so that it displays characteristics generally associated with later profit cycle stages, even during expansionary eras. Geographically aluminum is unique. Aluminum reduction consumes enormous amounts of electricity and is thus highly sensitive to cheap power sites. Access to skilled labor, however, is also an important factor and continues to favor sites in developed countries even as unexploited hydroelectric power becomes increasingly attractive overseas. Thus the sector is grouped with the labor-oriented sectors rather than the resource industries.

Profit Cycle Stages, Output, and Jobs

A uniquely successful monopoly fused the superprofit and oligopolistic stages in the aluminum industry's developmental path. The

Aluminum Company of America monopoly reshaped the expansion path of the industry dramatically.[26] Until World War II, a more rapid expansion, followed by a competitive slackening, undoubtedly would have ensued had not the monopoly power of the company permitted it to restrain capacity growth.

The monopoly and its superprofits were the product of strict patent protection for the first twenty years, up until 1909. By the time competition was legally permitted, the corporation had seventy-five subsidiaries in the aluminum business and wielded such strong control of every stage of the process, including resources, that no new entrants appeared. In subsequent years numerous antitrust cases were ineffective at reinstating competition, even though economies of scale, while large, clearly did not justify Alcoa's monopoly. To keep prices up, Alcoa built plants at a rate that substantially lagged demand, realizing continual profits even during the Great Depression.[27]

Government willingness to challenge the aluminum monopoly, coupled with the extraordinary demand for aluminum, especially for aircraft, changed the face of the industry during World War II. The federal government contracted with Alcoa for construction of eight new aluminum plants between 1940 and 1942, at a public cost of $674 million. Four of these were located at high-cost sites—Long Island, Los Angeles, Modesto, and Burlington, New Jersey—and were scrapped at the war's end. The others became permanent additions to aluminum capacity, some sold to competitors, creating profitability problems for Alcoa at the war's end. The prolonged period of low growth in output prior to the war, compared with the rapid postwar expansion, confirms a hypothesis of oligopolistic retardation (figure 9.11).

Anxious to find new markets, the industry pioneered new domestic applications to absorb swollen capacity. In addition, the Defense Production Act of the Korean war era showered the sector with favors such as rapid amortization, loan guarantees, subsidies for costly power, and guaranteed markets for output. From 1947 to 1958 the number of plants doubled from ten to twenty, and output grew steadily. But heightened competition began to take a predictable toll on jobs. The aluminum companies adopted cost-cutting and productivity-enhancing practices, which began to displace workers in the mid-1950s and mid-1960s (figure 9.11). Not until the 1970s, when successful oligopoly pricing was restored, did value added, output, and employment climb in tandem again.

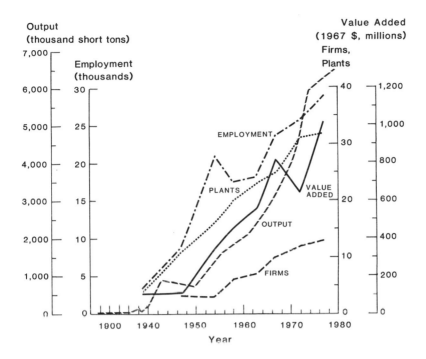

Figure 9.11
Aluminum industry growth, 1890-1977

Industry specialists foresee an end to three decades of postwar growth in aluminum. They expect demand to grow very slowly—less than 4 percent per year—during the 1980s. Two of the largest corporations have shut down potlines capable of producing some 88,000 tons a year and representing approximately 400 jobs. These closings may be countered by new potlines opening up elsewhere, but only one new plant was constructed in the United States in the 1970s. Extraordinarily high domestic costs of power, including hydro and coal, have influenced the locational pull of sites in developing countries, so that global expansion by the large aluminum companies, now multinational, no longer registers as an increase in U.S. jobs.[28]

Industry Structure

From its inception the aluminum industry had an extraordinarily concentrated structure for a growth industry. Alcoa's total monopoly lasted until World War II. At that point the government sold its wartime plants to three corporations—Alcoa, Reynolds, and Kaiser—in a lame attempt to introduce competition into the indus-

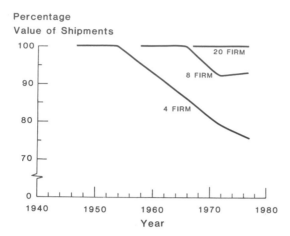

Percentage
Value of Shipments

Figure 9.12
Concentration ratios in aluminum, 1947-1977

try.[29] It thus created a three-way oligopoly, which has continued to dominate the industry. In 1977 the largest four corporations still controlled 75 percent of industry shipments (figure 9.12). Worldwide, six corporations, including the U.S. triumvirate, dominate noncommunist production.

Yet the big three have not been entirely successful in preventing new entrants from eroding their power and profit levels. Up to 1954 the big three still owned all operating aluminum plants, for an average of 5.3 plants apiece. Since the mid-1950s, ten new corporations have built aluminum plants. By 1977 thirteen companies owned thirty-two plants between them, an average of 2.5 apiece. Some of these remain single-plant corporations in that they generate only one aluminum facility, although they are immense, diversified corporations with plants in other, often related, industries. Although the newcomers have been more innovative, the multiplant corporations still control almost 95 percent of all employment (figure 9.13).

The ratio of production workers in aluminum rose unsteadily from an average rate at wartime to well above that for U.S. manufacturing as a whole (figure 9.14). This is not the pattern hypothesized for an innovative industry and indicates that such an era is long past. The technology for aluminum reduction is fairly straightforward and has been relatively unchanged for a long time. Managerial requirements are few, and marketing is not very important because aluminum is a standardized commodity sold to other industrial users. The rise in the ratio suggests, too, that postwar competitive pressure is resulting in successful efforts to cut labor requirements. Workers tend to be

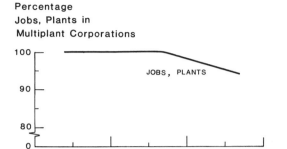

Figure 9.13
Ownership patterns in alumninum, 1954-1977

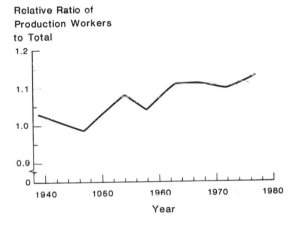

Figure 9.14
Occupational structure in aluminum, 1939-1977

highly skilled and unionized.[30]

The leaders of the aluminum industry have a clear strategy for the 1980s. As their domestic markets level off, the biggest corporations have decided to expand overseas, where both markets and resources, including cheap power, exist. Particularly attractive are Brazil and Australia. The multinationalization of the industry is facilitated by the huge size and internal resources of the corporations involved. Alcoa has invested nearly $1 billion in Brazilian production facilities, and four companies (Kaiser, Reynolds, Alcoa, and Alumax) have committed $4 billion to expansion in Australia. Aluminum production in Australia and New Zealand, largely as a result of U.S. ventures, will increase by 1 million tons by 1985, while U.S. capacity will increase by only one-tenth that amount. Low domestic capacity expansion is part of a strategy to keep prices up.[31]

Geography

Aluminum, at least until recently, has been severely tied to fuel supplies because its reduction requires immense amounts of intense heat. Power costs comprise between 20 and 30 percent of final market price. Since there are fewer than three dozen plants, it is relatively easy to document the complete set of spatial shifts in the industry's center of gravity over time.

The first center was the New York-Pennsylvania region. Alcoa located its first plant in Pittsburgh in 1888, using steam power. Six years later it was moved to New Kensington, outside Pittsburgh, to take advantage of cheap natural gas. The next year the decision was made to migrate to Niagara Falls to take advantage of hydroelectric power. A second center appeared in the Tennessee Valley in the 1930s, where TVA power projects offered cheap energy supplies.

The third, and perhaps most significant, move was the shift to the Northwest, where the Bonneville Power Project offered cut-rate hydroelectric power. Five of seven surviving wartime plants were built in Washington and Oregon, the other two in Alabama and Arkansas. Yet a fourth shift was tied to cheap natural gas and lignite resources in the Southwest. Five new plants were built in Louisiana, Texas, and Arkansas in the immediate postwar period. A fifth shift, after hydroelectric and natural gas prices rose, was linked to coal and centered on the Ohio River Valley, which was also adjacent to two-thirds of the U.S. aluminum market.[32]

Since the early 1960s two more shifts can be discerned (table 9.4). Between 1954 and 1967 three new plants were built in the Pacific Northwest, reinforcing its specialization and prominence. Beginning in 1958 four new plants were built in the Tennessee Valley, boosting the East-South Central region to renewed importance. Since then aluminum plant closings have occurred wholly in the Pacific Northwest region, where both Alcoa and Reynolds have shut down capacity amounting to about 5.5 percent of the region's output. The closings were due to a sudden escalation in hydroelectric prices as Bonneville doubled its prices after many years of taxpayer-subsidized cheap power, and alternative sources ran as much as ten times as high as this public power. The only new plant in the 1970s was added by Alumax at Mt. Holly, South Carolina; one other producer, Alcoa, expanded capacity at its North Carolina plant by 50 percent.[33]

Overall the aluminum industry has been quite mobile, not the pattern hypothesized to accompany a rapid-growth stage. Methodical decentralization in the industry, indicated by the clear diminution of state shares in table 9.4, corresponds appropriately to behavior associated with later stages in the profit cycle, though obscured by the retarded and elongated output and employment growth patterns. Even if this sector's decentralization can be considered consistent with the model, however, no similar argument can be made about an agglomerative tendency after the turn of the century. Oligopoly tendencies to retard dispersion were clearly overridden by the pull of cheap power. As resource exhaustion and profit cycles in energy sectors change the geographic centers of cheap power, the aluminum sector will follow.

The pattern does not constitute a smooth decentralization. The aggregate figures do suggest a decentralizing impulse, except for a short reversal in the mid-1960s led by a second round of additions to Pacific Northwest capacity. More accurately the trend consists of a series of shifts to other regional power centers as relative fuel prices change. This can be clearly seen in figure 9.15, which shows discontinuous additions to capacity occurring in one region after another. Nevertheless the dominance of the Pacific Northwest, once the location of half of all aluminum plants, is still clear, if eroding. In 1977 Oregon and Washington still accounted for 28 percent of the plants and in 1980 for 30 percent of aluminum output.

Table 9.4
State shares of aluminum plants

State	Number of Plants[a]							Plant change
	1947	1954	1958	1963	1967	1972	1977	
New York	1	1	1	2	2	2	2	+ 1
Ohio	0	0	1	1	1	0	1	+ 1
Indiana	0	0	0	1	1	1	1	+ 1
Missouri	0	0	0	0	0	1	1	+ 1
Maryland	0	0	0	0	0	1	1	+ 1
West Virginia	0	0	1	1	1	1	1	+ 1
North Carolina	1	1	1	1	1	1	1	0
Kentucky	0	0	0	0	0	2	2	+ 2
Tennessee	1	1	1	2	2	2	2	+ 1
Alabama	1	1	1	1	1	2	2	+ 1
Arkansas	1	2	2	2	2	2	2	+ 1
Louisiana	0	1	1	1	1	3	2	+ 2
Texas	0	3	3	3	3	3	3	+ 3
Montana	0	0	1	1	1	1	1	+ 1
Washington	4	5	5	5	7	7	7	+ 3
Oregon	1	1	2	2	2	2	2	+ 1
United States	10	16	20	23	25	31	32	+22

Sources: Perloff et al. (1960); *Census of Manufactures.*
a. Used "all establishments" because all 1977 establishments had more than twenty employees, averaging 894 each.

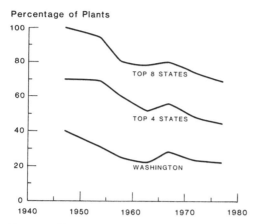

Figure 9.15
Geographical concentration in aluminum, 1947-1977

Summary

The aluminum sector displays an abnormal expansion path because patent protection permitted the creation of a monopoly that prevailed for fifty years. Rather than following a bell-shaped employment curve, job growth steadily climbed throughout the twentieth century because the dominant aluminum corporations were able to restrict output growth to keep profits above the economy-wide average. Monopoly power averted a rapid expansion of capacity, which would have created more jobs sooner. Aluminum thus appears to be a rapid-growth sector long past the time when truly innovative behavior characterized investment and design practices. The direct link between the sector's birth and market power make it difficult to identify the point of passage of the sector from stage II to stage IVa, placed here as 1972.

Concentration has fallen relatively in the postwar period as large metals and chemicals firms have diversified into aluminum production, challenging the sector's leaders, consistent with behavioral predictions for stage IVa. Yet four firms still control 79 percent of the market in aluminum, and fewer than ten firms produce all domestic supply. Aluminum has a relatively high proportion of production to total work force, a result of its standardized commodity output. This ratio has risen over time, consonant with predictions for a maturing sector.

Spatially the aluminum industry has moved irregularly, favoring a new location each decade as the sites of cheap power change.

Although it has consistently decentralized, this industry's locational pattern is not closely profit cycle related since in its earliest years it did not agglomerate appreciably, at least not at its initial sites. In retrospect the aluminum industry might better be classified with resource-oriented sectors since it shows a sensitivity to an often land-based input that overrides other spatial impulses.

9.4 Cotton and Knitwear Textile Industries

The textile industry is a quintessential mature, mobile industry. It is the sector that most readily comes to mind when capital flight in the United States is discussed. A highly labor-oriented industry, domestic producers have moved both interregionally and internationally. While competition from foreign firms has increased, the United States in 1977 was still the world's foremost supplier. Textiles are classified as a producer good since 70 percent of output is sold to intermediate markets, about half of this to the apparel sector.

Wholly new materials and novel fabric construction techniques are currently being innovated in this industry. In order to detect differences between two basic types of textile production—weaving and knitting—one subsector was chosen from each of two three-digit textile SICs: cotton weaving mills (SIC 2211) and knit outerwear mills (SIC 2253).[34] The latter, which sells the bulk of its output to consumer markets, combines both the fabric-making and clothing construction phases under one roof. The relative youthfulness of production techniques and the preponderance of the use of synthetic fibers place this subsector in an earlier phase of the profit cycle than its cotton weaving counterpart.

Profit Cycle Stages, Output, and Jobs

The textile industry has perhaps the longest history under capitalism of any other major commodity. Indeed it initiated the industrial revolution. During its experimental manufacturing stage, between 1760 and 1790, several important discoveries permitted the mechanization of both spinning and weaving. Agglomeration occurred in this era around the center of innovation, Lancashire in England, and by the early nineteenth century, English production dominated the world market from this region.

The U.S. textile industry began in 1790 as an import-substituting activity. Its innovative stage lasted until about 1880, when expansion slowed and fierce competition set in. By this date technology in the industry had become fairly standardized, and the industry had settled into a long era of relatively labor-intensive production. Textile making required almost totally unskilled and semiskilled labor since machinery was light and easy to operate and repair. Operatives comprised more than 50 percent of the work force. From an early date mill owners thus placed great stock in securing and maintaining low-skilled labor. Employment peaked in 1942 at 1,342,000. The normal profit competitive stage lasted until World War II when cheap imported textiles and a slowdown in market demand combined to push the industry into a period of less-than-normal profits. Value added fell, employment declined, and many firms failed (figure 9.16).

In the postwar period the U.S. textile industry suffered a long less-than-normal profit era. Job loss amounted to 340,000 from 1942 to 1957 and several hundred thousand more in the next twenty

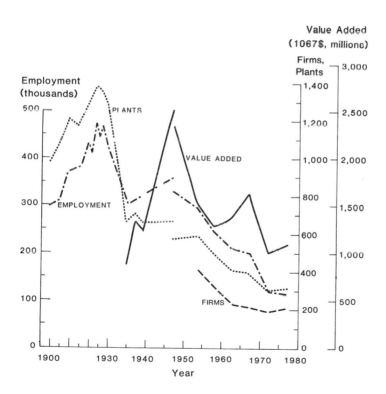

In 1947, the industry was redefined in the Census, which accounts for the discontinuity in the series.

Figure 9.16
Cotton textile industry growth, 1900-1977

years. Yet because of substitutions, the two subsectors endured different experiences. Cotton textiles lost 250,000 workers over the period, down 69 percent. Value added fell proportionally, although the growing divergence between the two curves reflects productivity increases realized since the mid-1960s. Knitwear employment, on the other hand, more than doubled since the war, up 40,000 workers.[35]

Job loss has been caused by the dual adversities of very slow market growth—on the order of 1.5 to 2.0 percent per year—and rising imports from Hong Kong, Taiwan, India, Pakistan, and, more recently, Latin America and China. Although productivity is estimated to be one-third to one-fifth lower in Hong Kong and India than in the United States, wages of U.S. workers are seven times those in Hong Kong and ten times those in India. Third World mills also run twenty-four hours a day to lower amortization costs. Imports into the United States increased over 400 percent from 1958 to 1968.[36] Furthermore basic research and long-range investment have been discouraged by severely cyclical business patterns, competition from paper and plastics, low profit margins, and a conservative attitude toward long-term development.[37]

An exception to this general pattern is the synthetic fabrics industry, stimulated by the chemical possibilities innovated in the postwar period. Knitwear, a largely synthetic subsector, enjoyed an innovative stage through the late 1950s, aided by the introduction of highly automated machinery. This subsector has been competitive since the 1950s but has not yet reached less-than-normal profits, so it falls sequentially one stage behind the cotton weaving sector (figure 9.17).

Industry Structure

The textile sector's competitive structure has been ensured by the fact that entry has always been easy since not much capital is required. As late as 1950 a study of North Carolina found that no corporation accounted for more than 7 percent of the state's textile work force, and most mills employed fewer than 100 workers. Economists have concluded that there have been no significant economies of scale through most of the sector's history. Furthermore little in the way of product differentiation was possible since fabrics were woven or knit to standard specifications and sold on a commodity market where prices were set competitively. However,

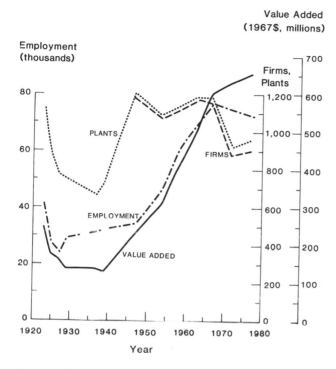

Figure 9.17
Knitwear industry growth, 1923-1977

some companies did become multiplant firms, particularly under the duress of the Great Depression.[38]

Symptoms of oligopoly structure have begun to appear in the postwar era. Between 1951 and 1968 1,100 mergers took place in the industry. Once acquired, 80 percent of the assets involved in these mergers belonged to eleven large corporations.[39] The results of generally low profitability and consolidation can be seen in the attrition of firms in figures 9.16 and 9.17. Almost half of all cotton mills that existed at the war's end had disappeared by 1977; some 200 firms had failed or been bought out. On the other hand, innovation in knitwear, a function of the introduction of synthetics and new machinery, resulted in marked growth of plants and firms until 1967; concentration in this industry actually fell until the early 1960s.

Concentration ratios also show the trend toward larger firms. In cotton mills concentration more than doubled since the war, if measured by the market share controlled by the top four or eight firms (figure 9.18). Although the ratio is much lower in knitwear, it also

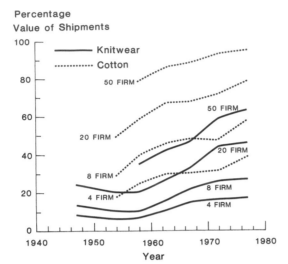

Figure 9.18
Concentration ratios in cotton and textiles and knitwear, 1947-1977

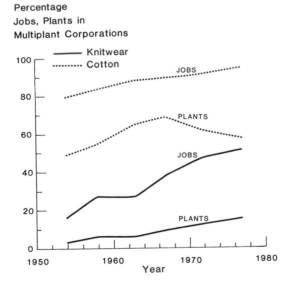

Figure 9.19
Ownership patterns in cotton textiles and knitwear, 1947-1977

increased from 1958 on. Ownership patterns confirm that employment is much more concentrated than establishments are in multiplant firms for both types of mills (figure 9.19). In the most recent period, however, multiplant corporations have lost their share of cotton mills, suggesting that they may be closing down cotton mills faster than the smaller firms as they automate, concentrate employment in larger mills, and switch to synthetics.

Profit rates, jobs, and headquarters for the largest textile mill companies are shown in Table 9.5. These fifteen companies controlled almost half of all employment in 1968.[40] Headquarters are about evenly divided between New York and the South. Profit rates are low for a majority of firms, although five did better than the average. The differences in profitability among corporations reflect their attitudes toward mechanization and new product innovation, two strategies that have helped stave off import competition in the 1970s. New automated machines can cut labor costs from 40 to 80 percent, but rapid adoption is impeded by low profit rates. New investments have been made by only a few companies, which then recoup superprofits at their competitors' expense. The faster-growing corporations are also selectively choosing product lines that they can dominate to garner normal-plus profits.[41]

Labor remains relatively unskilled and low paid. Figure 9.20 shows that the proportion of production workers is high for both subsectors. It increased relatively up until the early 1960s but since then has leveled off, maintaining a margin of more than 20 percent above all other manufacturing. Within the production work force, automation has amplified the ranks of skilled mechanics and has taken its greatest toll on the semiskilled occupations.[42] The production labor force increasingly is composed of women and blacks—those who have the most difficult time finding remunerative work elsewhere. Women, who are paid lower wages and are expected to absorb seasonal swings in employment, comprise 70 percent of knitting mill employees and 40 percent of weaving mill workers. Blacks are found largely in the laborer and service worker jobs, cleaning the mills and lifting bales of cotton, though more are becoming operatives each year. Textiles recorded one of the lowest payrolls for its employment size of any other U.S. industry.

Geography

The U.S. textile industry had its start in New England, where three

Table 9.5
The fifteen largest textile mill products companies, 1968

Company	Rank[a]	Headquarters	Sales (000)	Employees	Net income as percentage of	
					Sales	Invested capital
Burlington Industries	52	Greensboro, N.C.	1,619,253	83,000	4.9	12.5
J.P. Stevens	106	New York	963,163	49,300	3.3	8.6
United Merchants & Manufacturers	155	New York	651,968	35,000	3.2	9.4
Kayser-Roth	226	New York	425,997	29,500	3.6	12.2
Indian Head	252	New York	369,531	19,100	3.3	14.8
West Point-Pepperell	262	West Point, Ga.	347,075	20,380	4.3	8.0
M. Lowenstein & Sons	270	New York	338,267	18,106	2.4	6.6
Cannon Mills	289	Kannapolis, N.C.	308,075	18,00	5.8	8.5
Dan River Mills	298	Danville, Va.	285,099	19,000	2.6	5.5
Cone Mills	320	Greensboro, N.C.	261,854	14,000	1.3	2.5
Spring Mills	331	Fort Mill, S.C.	253,089	19,000	0.8	0.8
Kendall	378	Boston	209,827	10,800	4.4	9.7
Fieldcrest Mills	384	Eden, N.C.	203,732	11,652	4.7	13.4
Collins and Aikman	437	New York	167,545	5,600	3.8	12.9
Riegel Textile	450	New York	160,953	9,022	2.8	7.0

Source: Rowan (1970:15).
a. *Fortune* ranking among top U.S. industrial corporations.

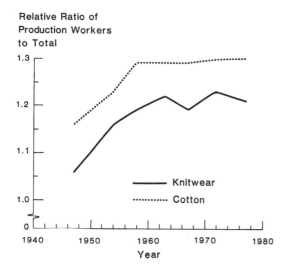

Figure 9.20
Occupational structure in cotton textiles and knitwear, 1947-1977

sequential locational patterns dominated. Although the United States imported most of its textiles well into the nineteenth century, aspiring Yankee entrepreneurs with profits from whaling and shipping began to set up small shops employing low-paid agricultural workers, especially farm girls, as early as 1790. The first mill was set up in Pawtucket, Rhode Island, in 1790, and its early competitors were dispersed around waterfalls in the countryside. Subsequently larger mills appeared at the more ample waterfalls, especially along the Merrimack River towns of Manchester, Lowell, and Lawrence, all in Massachusetts.

With the shift to steam power in the 1830s, factories began to gravitate toward coastal sites for both resource and labor reasons. Mill owners desired to escape militant organizations of mill girls whose protests of working and living conditions won community support in the smaller towns. Cheap immigrant workers began to be substituted for the indigenous New Englanders.[43] The competitive advantage of the port towns was also ensured by ample supplies of coal and cotton shipped in from other regions. By 1920 the two Massachusetts towns of Fall River and New Bedford accounted for two-thirds of all New England capacity.

By the 1880s competitive pressure in the industry initiated the migration of production to the South. The industry was mobile because machinery and entrepreneurship could be moved cheaply, and ready supplies of cotton and power were available at the new sites.[44] All analysts seem to agree that cheap nonunionized labor was the major inducement for this interregional shift. The labor force was composed of poor Piedmont rural whites increasingly forced out of agriculture, although blacks were used for the heaviest, most onerous, and lowest-paid tasks. Textile mill owners chose Piedmont locations in relatively small towns where they tended to dominate the wage labor force. Northern capital was lured by southern town citizens' committees who offered cash bonuses; in some cases northern merchants underwrote southern entrepreneurs. By 1902 the southern mills consumed more cotton than northern mills.[45]

The incidence of plant sitings in the South accelerated in the twentieth century. By 1930 the South exceeded the North in both numbers of plants and employment. Figure 9.21 shows the change in state and regional shares of cotton and synthetic spindles. The South's share surpassed the North's in 1924; by 1935 North Carolina and South Carolina each had capacity exceeding the leading New England state, Massachusetts. A shift in every branch of textiles was

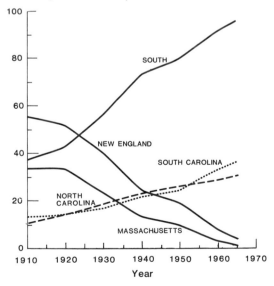

Figure 9.21
Regional and state shares of cotton-system spindles, 1910-1965. (Computed from Rowan, 1970:21)

apparent, with cotton production shifting from New England and hosiery production from the Middle Atlantic states. Woolens shifted more slowly. The New England climate favored woolen production. In addition, transportation costs of finished woolen goods were much lower than the raw material transport costs, so that factories nearer to sheepgrowers and import centers in New England enjoyed a cost advantage.[46] By World War II production in textiles had become more concentrated geographically than previously; fewer states accounted for the bulk of jobs.

The continued migration of textiles southward cannot be explained by the access to nearby cotton. By the twentieth century the best cotton was produced in the Southwest, where the climate was not humid enough to draw textile production. Second, cotton is frequently blended, and strains are purchased from many regions. Finally, cotton can be highly compressed and does not lose much weight in processing so that shipment of it is not a deterrent to profitable production. Wages continued to be the determining factor. In 1950 labor costs in Massachusetts constituted 34 percent of textile mill costs there but only 27 percent in the South, creating substantial differentials in profitability. In 1968 wages in southern knitting mills were only 70 percent of those in Massachusetts.[47]

Lack of unionization in the South has also been a significant pull factor. Unions tend to raise fringe benefits, to push for restrictive work rules, and can hamper production with strikes. Fringe benefits have been estimated to comprise half of all labor cost differentials between the two regions. A six-month strike in New Bedford in 1928 is believed to have crystallized textile mill owner decisions to leave.[48] In the South unions have always had difficulty organizing because of militant company opposition and the hostility of local business communities and politicians.

Racism has played a major role too. In 1890 and 1897 white workers in two Georgia mills walked out when employers hired blacks as operatives. Racism became institutionalized into the internal dual labor system in the mill. When Communist organizers promoted racial equality in their organizing efforts of the 1920s and 1930s, employers responded by equating communism with "nigger loving."[49]

Recent union victories may neutralize the role of racism and business opposition although too late to reverse the sector's abandonment of New England. In 1980 the Amalgamated Clothing and Textile Workers Union won a bitter seventeen-year fight with J. P. Stevens to organize ten of its plants with 3,800 workers. Their tactics included a boycott and stockholder pressure on board members. The ACTWU now represents 18 percent of all textile workers and, with workers in other sectors, has 485,000 members; its clout may increase with a proposed merger with the major apparel union.

Great differences among regions in social legislation and taxes have also encouraged the migration to the South. Southern states generally had no or very permissive restrictions on the work week and looser rules regarding women's hours and night work. Night shifts were favored by textile mills because running extra shifts saved on overhead, such as property taxes per unit output. Tax rates were deliberately lowered for new mills and exemptions sometimes given for initial operating years. Tax breaks were often paralleled with gifts of free mill sites. Recently one city council voted to bar a new factory from coming into the community because its plants have unionized workers in other locations.[50]

The location of cotton textile production worldwide has shifted irrevocably toward developing countries. While cheap labor is the dominating factor, Third World governments also provide the industry with subsidies. As imports have made increasing inroads on U.S. markets and mechanization has accelerated, employment has fallen dramatically in the United States. Losses have been concentrated in the northeastern states (table 9.6). The seven major northern producing states have lost more than 90 percent of their cotton textile jobs since World War II, continuing the trend begun in the late 1920s. The southern states have lost jobs as well, but at a slower pace—between 50 and 80 percent in each case. The net result is that the share of southern states has increased dramatically. North Carolina, South Carolina, Georgia, and Alabama have replaced the northern leaders as the top four states since World War II. As figure 9.22 shows, cotton textile production has reconcentrated spatially in the lowest labor cost locations, as hypothesized for late profit cycle stages.

Knitwear employment shifts, on the other hand, have lagged behind the cotton goods subsector. Because knits are more recent in origin, they have decentralized from their New York orientation (table 9.7). Knitwear employment actually increased in the Northeast until the early 1960s. Thereafter Virginia and North Carolina displaced New Jersey and Massachusetts among the top four states, and the number of jobs in New York and Pennsylvania began to decline absolutely. Knitwear appears to be following cotton

Table 9.6
State shares of cotton textile jobs

States	Jobs ('000)							Job change	Percentage change
	1947	1954	1958	1963	1967	1972	1977		
Maine	10.4	9.0	6.2	5.0	4.6	2.5	0.1	− 10.3	−99
New Hampshire	5.3	2.1	1.5	1.0	0.5	0.3	0.1	− 5.2	−98
Massachusetts	27.5	13.7	8.0	2.5	0.1	0.1	0.1	− 27.4	−99
Rhode Island	5.3	4.9	4.5	0.8	0.5	0.1	0.1	− 5.2	−98
New York	3.7	0.3	0.2	0.1	0.6	0.3	0.3	− 3.4	−92
New Jersey	3.2	2.3	1.1	0.8	0.9	0.5	0.3	− 2.9	−91
Pennsylvania	3.7	1.8	1.6	0.9	1.2	0.5	0.1	− 3.6	−97
North Carolina	71.0	69.3	53.1	49.4	45.5	32.5	35.4	− 35.6	−50
South Carolina	85.9	82.4	76.5	67.4	63.5	31.4	25.6	− 60.3	−70
Georgia	65.3	52.1	44.0	42.2	41.2	27.7	29.1	− 36.2	−55
Alabama	34.5	28.6	22.7	17.4	19.0	16.5	15.1	− 19.4	−56
Virginia	15.0	14.0	13.1	12.6	12.0	3.6	3.1	− 11.9	−79
Tennessee	6.4	4.7	3.1	2.5	2.5	1.8	1.7	− 4.7	−73
Texas	6.0	5.7	5.4	4.8	4.5	1.4	1.2	− 4.8	−80
United States	357.4	296.2	243.4	209.0	202.8	121.3	117.2	−240.2	−67

Source: *Census of Manufactures.*

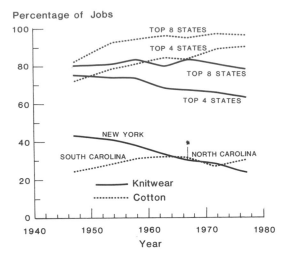

Percentage of Jobs

In 1967, North Carolina took over as lead cotton-producing state from South Carolina.

Figure 9.22
Geographical concentration in cotton textile and knitwear, 1947-1977

Table 9.7
State shares of knitwear jobs, 1947-1977

States	Jobs (000)							Job change	Percentage change
	1947	1954	1958	1963	1967	1972	1977		
Massachusetts	2.4	2.7	3.6	2.5	2.8	2.5	2.6	+ .2	+ 8
New York	14.9	18.8	23.2	22.7	22.5	20.6	17.5	+ 2.6	+ 17
New Jersey	2.8	4.1	5.0	4.9	5.3	3.6	4.2	+ 1.4	+ 50
Pennsylvania	5.9	8.8	12.9	14.1	13.7	13.6	12.6	+ 6.7	+ 114
Virginia	0.3	1.9	2.7	4.8	6.4	6.6	7.1	+ 6.8	+2,267
North Carolina	0.4	0.9	1.6	3.5	7.2	8.3	8.2	+ 7.8	+1,950
South Carolina	0.1	0.1	0.4	0.8	1.8	2.5	2.5	+ 2.4	+2,400
Florida	0.0	0.0	0.4	0.6	1.1	1.8	2.5	+ 2.5	+2,500
California	1.1	1.0	1.0	1.4	2.5	2.5	2.5	+ 1.4	+ 127
United States	34.8	46.4	60.7	68.6	73.8	74.4	73.0	+38.2	+ 110

Source: *Census of Manufactures.*

textiles south with a lag of about forty years. Decentralization is still in full force, a locational pattern consistent with stage III predictions.

Summary

The textile sectors display the hypothesized behavior of the profit cycle model. Each has passed methodically through the stages of the model, with accompanying firm, plant, and job growth and decline. Both are highly competitive, although some degree of market power began to emerge in the 1970s. As the older of the two, cotton textiles eliminated jobs at a faster rate, had higher concentration ratios, and had higher production to total work force rates than knitwear. Cotton textiles has also almost totally completed its relocation to the South, where lower wage rates and a better business climate draw it, whereas the more recent innovative history in the knitwear industry keeps it more closely tied to its New York-area origins, although it too is decentralizing.

9.5 Summary of the Producer Goods Sectors

Overall the producer goods sectors lend strong support to the profit cycle model. Each displays the hypothesized bell-shaped employment, output, and firm growth, although in the cases of aluminum and steel, the growth curve has been flattened and elongated by tight oligopolistic control. Each sector exhibits the predicted structural features, with top firm loss of market and job shares by sectors in innovative stages and large gains in market power during later stages. The exceptions to this rule occurred in steel and aluminum, where the top four firms lost market power to others in the top twenty during later stages. The producer goods sectors proved a perfect test of the occupational features of the model, as production workers formed a consistently lower and falling proportion of the work force of innovative sectors and a higher and increasing proportion in more mature stages.

The regional consequences of profit cycle behavior in these sectors proved to be consistent with the model's predictions. In the rapidly innovating sectors of computers and semiconductors, the top states increased their shares of employment and plants, although some of the secondary states lost relative shares. This can be explained by the beginnings of dispersion of electronics plants performing the more standardized functions, such as assembly, while the innovative research and prototype building is still carried out in core locations. In the more mature sectors—textiles, steel, and aluminum—dispersion from the original centers was strong and continual. Cotton textiles, the only one of these sectors approaching stage V, showed a tendency to reconcentrate in its historically newer sites, those with the lowest labor and public sector costs in the United States. Oligopoly in steel and aluminum had distinct roles in the regional deployment of productive capacity. Government actions—antitrust, wartime procurement, tariffs, research and development, labor laws—played a role in individual cases in shaping both the aggregate level of output and the regional array of facilities.

10   The Consumer Goods Sectors

In this chapter five consumer sectors—pharmaceuticals, women's apparel, autos, brewing, and shoes—are investigated. The sectors surveyed here produce a significant proportion of the basic necessities required by contemporary households. They range in recent experience from pharmaceuticals, with a job growth rate of 25 percent in the ten years from 1967 to 1977, to shoes, with a net job loss of 45 percent in the same period. One sector, autos, experienced a reversal in employment growth during the most recent decade. On the growth side of the profit cycle, both highly concentrated and highly competitive industries are represented in drugs and apparel, respectively. On the mature side brewing increasingly is oligopolized, while shoemaking remains highly competitive. Because of these differences, the reliance on advertising differs dramatically among the sectors, as do other aspects of business behavior. In general each sector offers strong empirical support for a profit cycle approach.

10.1 Pharmaceutical Industry

Pharmaceuticals are among the most interesting, controversial, and best studied of contemporary industries.[1] A $17 billion business by the mid-1970s, drugs now account for more than 20 percent of all health care costs. Chosen here as an example of a stage II consumer goods sector, pharmaceuticals are almost wholly a post-World War II phenomenon.[2] The industry is still highly profitable and growing rapidly. It is, however, extraordinarily concentrated, especially in subsectors. Thus it exhibits some characteristics generally found in a normal-plus oligopolistic stage grafted onto others associated with innovative sectors.

Profit Cycles, Output, and Jobs

Herbal remedies for illness and disease have been part of all known cultures. Yet in the United States, drugs did not become commodities until well into the nineteenth century. Initially preparations were imported from Europe, but the blockading of commerce during the Civil War, when drug needs were extraordinarily high, provided the impetus for the development of a domestic industry.

Two major rounds of innovation restructured the drug industry over the last century. First, the discovery of a chemical process for silvering or varnishing pills facilitated the large-scale manufacture of pills in place of hand rolling by the local druggist. Contemporaneously a few enterprising druggists expanded backward into manufacture of simple drug compounds. Yet the market remained limited; in 1920 only six drugs accounted for 60 percent of all prescriptions in the United States.

The second round of innovation began in Germany in the 1930s with the discovery of antibiotics. Between 1928 and 1949 the following miracle drugs were discovered and commercially marketed: prontosil, penicillin, streptomycin, and the broad-spectrum antibiotics. Wartime demands played a critical role; substantial government research and development funds were poured into the industry during World War II. From 1935 to 1966 patents grew enormously. By 1970 there were 200 sulfa drugs, 270 antibiotics, 130 antihistamines, and 100 tranquilizers on the market—some 10,000 prescription drugs altogether, in addition to 100,000 nonprescription drugs.[3] Ninety-five percent of today's drugs were unknown in 1950.

This second round of innovation dramatically boosted sales and profitability. Profits were indisputably and consistently high. Pharmaceuticals registered the highest profit rates of any other U.S. industry for most years from 1960 through 1972. In 1960 the drug industry realized a return of 15.5 percent on invested capital, in 1964, 16.3 percent, and in 1972, 19.7 percent. Comparable U.S. averages for manufacturing were 9.1 percent, 10.5 percent, and 10.7 percent, respectively.[4] Clearly the industry enjoyed superprofits.

A number of signs indicate that the rate of innovation is beginning to decline, however. From a high of 559 in 1949, significant new drug patents fell to a low of 83 in 1969. Except for antibiotics, where the mutation of certain bacteria to resist and narrow the spectrum across which a drug is effective has provided a continual demand for new forms, few new wonder drugs have been invented

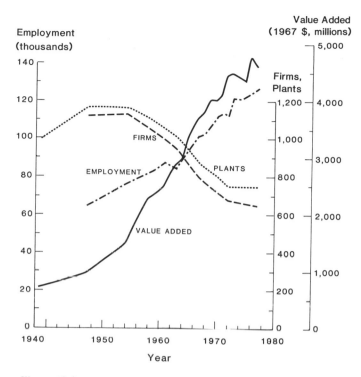

Figure 10.1
Pharmaceuticals industry growth, 1939-1977

recently. Most current major health problems—cancer and heart disease—are less responsive to chemical therapy than past ones. Meanwhile old patents are expiring. Thus continued high profits may be more a function of oligopoly in old drug lines than of innovation in new product markets. If so, the industry's superprofits era may be coming to an end.

Both output and employment have grown rapidly in this innovative era (figure 10.1). Value added for drugs has increased over five times in real terms since World War II. Output has increased continually because the manufacturers have been able to offer new medications and successfully penetrate the medical profession's practices with drug therapy. The average person filled 2.5 prescriptions annually in 1950 and 5.5 per year by 1972. The average doctor, it was estimated in the mid-1970s, prescribes $40,000 worth of prescriptions every year. While employment has grown less rapidly, it has climbed to more than 125,000 workers, almost double the number of 65,000 in 1947.

The work force in pharmaceuticals is relatively highly skewed toward nonproduction workers. Less than 50 percent of all workers were classified as production workers by the 1970s (figure 10.2), and this ratio has fallen continually. Compared to other U.S. manufacturing industries, the ratio is low and the differential is increasing, consistent with the profit cycle hypothesis for stage II. Several types of occupations account for the difference. First, since sales promotion is a huge part of competitive strategy, a sales force of some 20,000 is retained by the industry to inform and give free samples to doctors. Second, research outlays, which are also a central part of brand name ethical drug companies' strategy, are spent on skilled labor—chemists, biologists, lab technicians—who work in teams in drug laboratories. Technicians are also required for the extensive testing that accompanies manufacture. Third, a large clerical work force is employed in the promotional and regulatory end of the business. And finally, drugs are manufactured in relatively small plants and in small batches that require unusually high levels of supervisory and managerial personnel. Unionization rates are low, although the Oil, Chemical and Atomic Workers have made headway in recent years because of their commitment to worker health and safety issues.

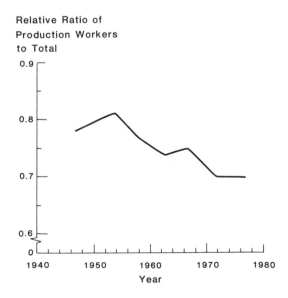

Figure 10.2
Occupational structure in pharmaceuticals, 1939-1977

Industry Structure and Conduct

The pharmaceutical industry appears to have a relatively competitive structure. There were still 650 firms in the late 1970s operating and about 750 plants (figure 10.1). The numbers have fallen rapidly since the 1940s, however, when more than 1,100 companies competed. This is not characteristic behavior for a stage II industry and suggests that effective oligopoly has coincided with this period of innovation. Great diversity characterizes the surviving firms. Firms vary dramatically in size. Only 31 ethical drug firms had more than $10 million in sales apiece in 1959 and were found to behave quite differently from 108 other small firms that produced their own specialty brand names and some 379 that produced generics only.[5] Some are multinational in nature, and others sell only domestically. Thirty companies (both European and American) control 50 percent of the market in developed countries and 70 percent to 90 percent of Third World sales. These large multinationals have pioneered overseas production at low-cost labor sites; 37 percent of their jobs are now located abroad.[6]

Some drug companies are subsidiaries or branches of large chemical corporations, such as Dow, American Cyanamid, or Johnson and Johnson. The larger drug companies have diversified into other commodities such as kitchenware, cosmetics, candy, and household chemicals, while others remain drug based. In 1969, of twenty pharmaceutical corporations with sales of more than $100 million, only eight had more than 50 percent of their sales in ethical drugs.[7]

In addition to differences in size and form, market power is severely concentrated in individual drug lines. One researcher found that 57.5 percent of all ethical drugs—both generic and brand names—were produced by only one firm, constituting complete monopolies.[8] In antibiotics, the most competitive of therapeutic drugs, eleven firms control 92 percent of output. Even generic drugs display high degrees of market dominance. Concentration results not from economies of scale in production, which is generally small batch in nature, or from economics in research and development, the medium-size laboratory being optimal, but from patent protection and extraordinary promotional behavior.[9]

The net result is that the pharmaceutical sector is highly concentrated. Fifteen firms control more than 66 percent of the domestic market sales. Concentration ratios (figure 10.3) fell through the early 1960s, as expected in an innovative sector, but increased thereafter. Ownership patterns (figure 10.4) confirm large corporate dominance. Multiplant corporations have steadily increased their share of establishments and control 93 percent of employment, a figure that has been steadily rising since 1950. This, too, is not characteristic of innovative stages of the profit cycle and reveals the overwhelming effect of market power in tandem with innovation.

The pharmaceutical industry is a rather unique instance of a sector in which active innovative performance is not inconsistent with excess profits and market power. The larger ethical drug companies do engage in a great deal of research designed to discover new drugs that will produce superprofits. Approximately 10 percent of all sales revenue in the industry is spent on research, although of this only 16 percent goes to basic research.[10] The larger drug companies have indeed been making permanent excess profits, a blend of superprofit and oligopoly profit. These arise in part from the seventeen-year patent protection afforded the industry for new innovations.

But normal-plus profits also stem from the extensive promotional campaigns that the companies engage in. Physicians rely heavily on drug company advertising and free samples. Drug companies spend approximately $5,000 per doctor per year to advertise products. Advertising absorbs even more money than research, approximately 12.5 percent of sales. Once its monopoly expires, a lead corporation generally maintains its market share because other firms have difficulty convincing doctors to switch to an equivalent product.

As a result of heavy promotion, patent protection, and physician behavior, little price competition exists. For instance, the firm with the highest price also has the largest market share in antibiotics. Drugstores pay drug companies a premium of approximately 52 percent to 62 percent above the lowest-priced antibiotics available, amounting in 1974 to $100 million in just this product line alone. One researcher estimated that the elimination of brand names and patent protection would have saved the consumer $617 million.[11]

Geography

Innovational imperatives have kept this sector agglomerated. Employment in the pharmaceutical industry is highly concentrated in major centers in the manufacturing belt (table 10.1). The two states of New York and New Jersey have consistently dominated the industry, together accounting for about one-third of all jobs in both 1947 and 1977. The share of the top state remained fairly constant over

Table 10.1
Employment shares in pharmaceutical jobs, 1947-1977

State	Jobs (000)							Job change	Percentage change
	1947	1954	1948	1963	1967	1972	1977		
Massachusetts	1.0	1.0	1.0	1.0	1.0	1.0	1.2	+ 0.2	+ 20
New York	12.9	17.9	18.6	17.1	19.0	15.1	16.5	+ 3.6	+ 28
New Jersey	7.7	9.8	10.6	14.4	19.1	25.2	23.4	+15.7	+203
Pennsylvania	4.4	6.5	8.0	9.5	10.7	11.9	13.6	+ 9.2	+209
Ohio	2.2	2.2	2.5	2.7	2.7	2.7	2.7	+ 0.5	+ 23
Illinois	7.0	7.9	8.2	8.0	10.0	11.3	14.5	+ 7.5	+107
Michigan	7.9	8.3	7.8	6.2	6.4	6.5	6.7	− 1.2	− 15
Indiana	8.8	10.1	10.6	10.5	12.1	13.4	13.1	+ 4.3	+ 49
Iowa	0.7	0.6	0.6	0.6	0.2	0.5	0.9	+ 0.2	+ 29
Missouri	3.3	2.8	2.5	2.7	2.6	2.5	2.9	− 0.4	− 12
Nebraska	0.4	0.3	0.4	0.5	0.8	0.7	0.6	+ 0.2	+ 50
Maryland	0.8	0.8	0.7	0.7	0.7	0.7	0.8	0	0
Tennessee	2.1	1.6	1.9	2.4	2.9	3.3	2.8	+ 0.7	+ 33
California	2.2	2.0	2.8	2.5	3.7	5.8	8.5	+ 6.3	+286
Texas	0.2	0.4	0.7	0.9	1.1	1.2	1.6	+ 1.2	+600
U.S.	65.4	76.6	82.0	85.1	102.6	112.0	126.4	+61.0	+ 93

Source: *Census of Manufactures.*

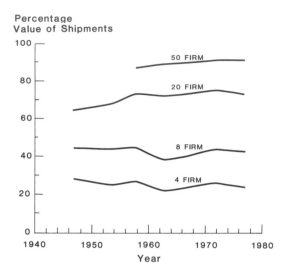

Figure 10.3
Concentration ratios in pharmaceuticals, 1947-1977

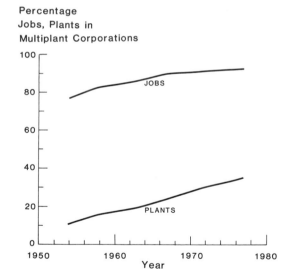

Figure 10.4
Ownership patterns in pharmaceuticals, 1954-1977

the period, and the shares of the largest four and eight states rose through 1963. The same eight states led in 1977 as in 1947. Notable job increases occurred in the less significant states of California and Texas, yet employment also grew dramatically in the more prominent states of New Jersey and Pennsylvania. Figure 10.5 shows the relative losses and gains of the most significant states.

Regional breakdowns (unavailable for all census years) are shown in table 10.2. The manufacturing belt states accounted for almost 87 percent of jobs in 1968, 75 percent of which were in the six states of New York, New Jersey, Illinois, Pennsylvania, Indiana, and Michigan. Within these states production is concentrated in metropolitan areas. In 1968 45 percent of all U.S. drug jobs were concentrated within a radius of forty miles from a point midway between New York City and Philadelphia. Five metropolitan areas—New York, Newark, Philadelphia, Chicago, and Los Angeles—hosted 55 percent of all jobs. If the SMSAs of Detroit, St. Louis, Cincinnati, and Indianapolis were added to these, they would account for 80 percent. Production was about evenly divided between suburban locations and cities in both the northeastern and Los Angeles areas, although cities claimed two-thirds of midwestern and southern jobs.[12]

The locational gravity of the industry has not prevented selective plant closings, however, as firms go out of business and products become obsolete. The OCAW (Oil, Chemical and Atomic Workers International Union) reports that many of their workers have been permanently laid off. In 1980 alone a Parke-Davis plant in Rochester, New York, closed, eliminating 1,300 jobs, and a Scherer capsule plant in Detroit, Michigan, closed, eliminating 155 jobs.[13]

This locational pattern confirms the hypothesis that an innovating industry will agglomerate around original centers of innovation. Drug companies need research personnel, advertising facilities, and access to the medical community, which they find in cities and in the manufacturing belt. Furthermore many drug companies buy and sell each other drugs as inputs into their own production process. A very slight tendency to migrate westward can be detected in the data, along with a movement of larger mass production operations toward suburban New Jersey. Given the skilled labor requirements of this industry, low-wage locations do not seem to exercise much pull on the industry in this stage; instead access to highly skilled labor dominates. But this centrality is not merely a function of innovational gravity. It is also a product of the need for marketing and public relations that marks oligopolistic practice. The magnetism of the

New York—Philadelphia—New Jersey core is thus a product of the fusion of innovative activity and oligopolistic market-regulating behavior.

Summary

The pharmaceutical industry is an outstanding case of a sector whose innovative period overlaps the emergence of oligopolistic control. Market power originates in strong patent protection. The larger drug companies have been able to parlay this edge into a postpatent position of monopoly power in many market segments, largely due to tremendous outlays on advertising. For present purposes the industry was classified as a stage II growth sector from 1947 to 1977, although on some variables it displays behavior more characteristic of stage IVa. In this thirty-year period the pharmaceuticals companies increased employment by 93 percent, and real value added climbed 365 percent; however, 42 percent of all companies and 13 percent of all plants disappeared. While the share of market controlled by the largest four declined modestly, the share of the largest twenty rose. Multiplant corporations substantially increased their shares of both plants and jobs. As was expected for an innovating sector, the share of production workers was below the U.S. manufacturing average and falling.

The regional distribution of pharmaceutical jobs confirms the stage II hypothesis. Four states in the manufacturing belt control 53 percent of jobs, 45 percent of these on the New York—Philadelphia axis. Furthermore the rate of concentration in the top four states increased over the thirty-year period, although the top state registered a modest loss in share. The regional pattern documents a strong centripetal attraction toward the core area, one that can be ascribed to both the agglomerative pull of innovation and the centralizing tendencies of oligopolistic activities.

10.2 Women's Clothing Industry

The ladies' garment industry, chosen here as a competitive stage III sector, is a classic example of a highly competitive sector.[14] Due to the absence of economies of scale, an extraordinary degree of labor intensity, and the unchanging nature of sewing machine technology, it has remained relatively less concentrated than most other mature U.S. industries. It has been even more sensitive to cheap and

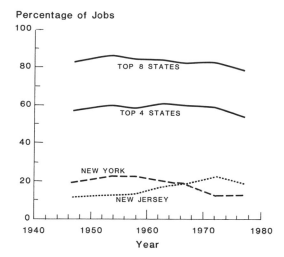

Figure 10.5
Geographical concentration in pharmaceuticals, 1947-1977

Table 10.2
Drug industry jobs by region, metropolitan area, 1968

Region/SMSA	Number of establishments	Number of employment	Percentage employment
Region			
Northeast		70,048	50.1
Midwest		51,071	36.5
South		11,393	8.2
Far West		6,878	4.9
Rocky Mountain		369	0.3
United States	471	139,759	100.0
SMSA			
New York City	37	20,804	14.9
Newark	21	20,286	14.5
Philadelphia	31	12,798	9.2
Chicago	26	18,906	13.5
Los Angeles	35	3,246	2.4
All five SMSAs	150	76,140	54.5

Source: Fletcher (1970:24, 25). Fletcher's data were collected for his specific project. He estimated that his sample covers 90 percent of the industry's employment.

unorganized labor than most other labor-oriented sectors. The industry became the target of militant organizing early in the twentieth century. At that time it was spatially centralized in New York City, where it formed a significant portion of the city's economic base. Since then it has migrated to more southerly locations in both California and the Southeast. Conflict around the social relations of production had thus been a determining factor in the industry's spatial reorganization.

Profit Cycles, Output, and Jobs

Through the nineteenth century, women's clothing, like that of other family members, was fashioned and produced by women in their homes for immediate family use, traditionally from handmade yarn, thread, and woven goods. With the mass production of textiles in the nineteenth century, purchased fabric supplanted homespun, but most clothing was still cut, shaped, and sewn at home, although elite classes could afford tailors. Sailors formed the first market for cheap, mass-produced clothing as early as the colonial period. Small commercial clothing firms met this demand in the Boston, New York, and New Bedford areas. But while cloth might be cut and clothing designed in these shops, most of the sewing was done by women at home.[15]

The Civil War precipitated the permanent transition of men's clothing from home to workshop. The sewing machine, invented in 1846, was innovated on a large scale during the war. Women worked in these shops since men were at war. The army's measurements of millions of men, used in ordering uniforms, provided the sizing statistics for the postwar industry. Women's ready-to-wear, as it was called, did not become a significant mass-produced item until the 1880s.[16] The innovative stage in women's clothing lasted from 1880 to 1910. A sustained competitive era then ensued. Both output and employment continued to grow at healthy rates as ready-to-wear penetrated the working-class and rural areas of the country.[17] By the postwar period growth rates of both value added and employment had leveled off, as did concentration ratios (figure 10.6).

In the postwar period competitive pressures on the industry appear to have reversed modest employment growth rates. Three factors account for this flattening out of employment. First, some economies of scale have been introduced, cutting labor costs. Examples are the large-scale blue jeans and work clothes plants like

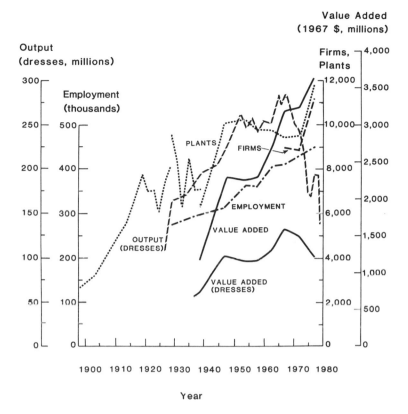

Figure 10.6
Women's clothing industry growth, 1900-1977. Data in this figure are for SIC 233, which subsumes SICs 2331, 2335, 2337, and 2339. Discontinuity make it impossible to reconstruct series before 1954 for four-digit SICs, except in the case of dresses, whose value added and output histories are included for comparison.

Farah's and Levi Strauss, which employ largely minority women in sunbelt areas from Texas through California. Levi Strauss operates more than 100 plants in the United States and abroad.[18] Second, some garment making has moved into Mexico, with only finishing touches added in the United States. Such items qualify as U.S. produced to permit companies to take advantage of lenient tariff regulations. This would register as a decline in employment per unit output (and probably as an increase in productivity). Direct and indirect imports constituted 25 percent of the U.S. market by the mid-1970s. Third, large numbers of small shops and putting-out operations have sprouted from Vermont to Los Angeles, employing immigrants without legal status and unemployed women at home. Because of the clandestine nature of some of these operations and underreporting, this also registers as job loss. To the extent that this phenomenon is significant, employment figures may be understated in census counts.

Employment conditions are poor in garment making. The industry is more labor intensive than any other major sector. The average rate of invested capital per worker is half that for textiles and less than one-fourth that for all manufacturing. Wages, as a result, are among the lowest in manufacturing. Average wages in the mid-1970s were still less than $3 per hour. Furthermore work is highly seasonal, and the average worker logs only forty weeks per year. Apparel is the largest industrial employer of women, and women comprise 80 percent of the garment-making work force. It is also a major employer of minority workers; more than half of New York City garment workers were nonwhite by the late 1960s.

For a brief period in the 1960s it appeared that the clothing industry might be successfully oligopolized. But in 1972 the trend toward concentration was sharply reversed as import penetration of garments cheaply assembled in the Third World eroded market control. U.S. corporations were forced to follow similar practices at home, fleeing organized labor in urbanized areas for unorganized, minority women in rural areas in the Southeast and recent urban migrants in Los Angeles. although profit rates are not available for these four-digit sectors, a survey of men's apparel plants in Georgia showed that profit margins ran only 2 to 4 percent in the early 1970s.[19] The women's clothing industry thus appears to mirror almost perfectly the profit cycle patterns hypothesized for a labor-oriented consumer good industry.

Industry Structure

Compared to most other mature industries, women's clothing is relatively unconcentrated. Concentration ratios vary across industry subsectors, as do their patterns of change over time. In general the top eight firms control no more than 20 percent of output (figure 10.7). This is not sufficient market power to prevent price competition but does permit extensive advertising by the larger corporations. Furthermore, if we take into account the prevalence of regional oligopoly in retail outlets, especially department stores with their large outlays on local media advertising, it is clear that some oligopolistic shaping

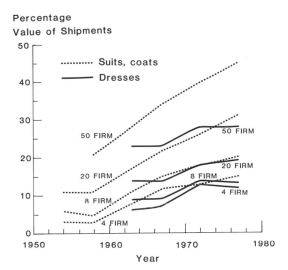

Figure 10.7
Concentration ratios in women's clothing, 1954-1977

of consumer tastes does take place.

The rise and truncation in concentration is also reflected in the data on establishment and firm growth rates (figure 10.6). During the lethargic growth period of the 1950s and continuing into the 1960s, many small marginal plants went out of business. But in the 1970s the number of both firms and establishments rose dramatically, documenting the heightened degree of competition forced on the industry by Third World imports. These new firms were almost all single-plant facilities, with small numbers of employees. In 1974 $50,000 was sufficient to set up a plant. About half of all plants employ fewer than twenty workers, with only 14 percent employing 100 or more. In a study of a related sector, men's apparel, researchers documented a 70 percent local ownership rate for Georgia plants, half of them Georgia natives starting with indigenous capital and half individuals and small privately held corporations that had relocated from the Northeast.[20]

The concentration trends characterizing profit cycle periods are supported by the data on ownership patterns (figure 10.7). The shares of employment accounted for by multiplant firms increased modestly in the 1950s and more rapidly in the 1960s. In 1972, as competition pinched in women's dresses, multiplant corporations lost their hold on employment share. In the suits and coats subsector, which is more insulated from international competition,

Despite the concentration, the majority of jobs in women's clothing remain within single-plant corporations.

However measured, the ratio of production workers is above the U.S. average and rising in the postwar period, consistent with stage hypotheses (figure 10.9). The ratio has declined in the industry as a whole from nearly 93 percent in 1943 to 86 percent in 1980, a modest fall in a still highly labor-intensive industry. Low levels of mechanization—even semiautomated processes are uncommon—result in the highest concentration of semiskilled jobs in manufacturing. Operatives make up 80 percent of employment compared to 45 percent for manufacturing as a whole.

Geography

The apparel industry serves a national market from relatively concentrated production sites. Yet the spatial distribution of jobs in women's clothing has dramatically decentralized over the last three profit cycle periods. Two different forms of decentralization dominate subsequent periods: intraregional decentralization through the early 1960s and interregional dispersion thereafter. In the newer locations intraregional dispersion has also taken place over the postwar period.

Until 1910 the garment industry was concentrated in New York City, which accounted for over 60 percent of its jobs. During the innovative rapid-growth period stretching from 1860 to 1910, home production was replaced by rapidly agglomerating production in Manhattan. The heart of early garment making was the Lower East Side, where Jewish small businesses dominated innovation in the industry. Both labor and entrepreneurial leadership were provided by Jewish immigrant tailors who taught their relatives the trade and set up small sweatshops where women did the sewing. Even as late as the mid-1960s, 100,000 garment workers labored in an eighteen-block area known as the Garment District, which had moved to the West Side of Manhattan.

As the competitive period set in, production began to decentralize to surrounding areas in both New York and neighboring states. Small batch production and rapid style changes held the industry within overnight trucking distance from the centers of design and marketing, which remained in New York City. The major centrifugal forces were lower wages and absence of unions in peripheral areas. In the initial periods of decentralization, the industry moved toward

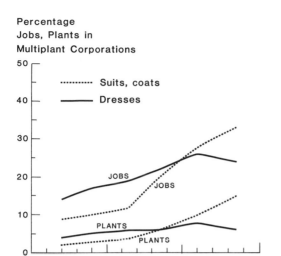

Figure 10.8
Ownership patterns in women's clothing, 1947-1977

Figure 10.9
Occupational structure in women's clothing, 1947-1977

In the initial periods of decentralization, the industry moved toward depressed anthracite mining areas of Pennsylvania and the textile towns of New England where a ready labor force of women waited.[21]

During the postwar period of heightened competition, the improvement of highway transportation and interregional pattern of dispersion dominated. Cheap air freight enabled the pull of lower wages to overcome the draw of accessibility to the center of fashion. Especially in standardized women's items such as pants, skirts, underwear, and nightwear, production rapidly decentralized to the cheapest labor areas. Hourly earnings for apparel workers were a stunning 43 percent higher in New York than in North Carolina in the mid-1970s. In addition 83 percent of northeastern workers were covered by pension plans compared to only 38 percent of southeastern workers, and the former logged 33 percent more vacation days than the latter. Right-to-work laws and strike activity also differentiated northern sites from the southern ones. The pull of California in particular is attributable to the large numbers of undocumented Latinos, many of whom work at home at piece rates in the Los Angeles area. The pressure to reduce labor costs was heightened by the even greater differentials between U.S. and Third World wage rates. In 1974 U.S. wages were $2.99 per hour in apparel; they averaged 57¢ in Hong Kong, 27¢ in Haiti, and 22¢ in South Korea, where workers could expect few additional benefits.[22]

In addition to lower labor costs and absence of unionization, southeastern sites offer apparel firms an additional advantage— proximity to the textile industry, which provides the major raw material input. Although the differentials in textile inputs costs are not nearly as great between North and South as they are in labor, raw materials constitute a higher percentage of input costs than does labor.[23] And although the northeastern plants have an advantage in closer proximity to markets, the transportation costs for finished clothing are considerably lower than for textile inputs due to loss of bulk in manufacturing. The input and transport cost structures, then, give the southeastern sites a small added advantage over the New York-area plants. But the limits of this line of reasoning are apparent in California's boom, which has taken place despite great distance from centers of clothmaking.[24]

The job cuts and shifts in the postwar period resulted in dramatic changes in shares of employment accounted for by states (tables 10.3 and 10.4). In both types of garment making, New York suffered a tremendous fall in job share. The decentralization of women's

Table 10.3
State shares of women's suits and coats jobs, 1947-1977

State	Jobs (000)							Job change	Percentage change
	1947	1954	1948	1963	1967	1972	1977		
Massachusetts	3.2	6.3	6.4	6.7	5.6	5.1	6.3	+ 3.1	+ 97
New York	46.9	46.0	39.2	39.4	32.3	25.1	21.0	− 24.9	− 54
New Jersey	8.6	12.6	11.6	14.2	13.7	12.3	12.4	+ 3.8	+ 44
Pennsylvania	2.4	3.7	3.7	4.6	6.2	3.4	5.3	+ 2.9	+120
Illinois	3.2	2.8	2.6	2.0	1.6	1.7	1.9	− 1.3	− 41
Missouri	2.3	3.3	3.1	2.7	3.1	2.4	2.2	− 0.1	− 4.3
Ohio	2.4	1.2	0.8	1.9	1.3	0.4	0.7	− 1.7	− 71
North Carolina	—	0.1	0.2	0.1	0.5	0.4	1.9	+ 1.8	+180
South Carolina	—	0.2	0.4	0.4	0.5	0.8	1.6	+ 1.5	+150
Florida	0.1	0.2	0.1	0.4	0.3	1.8	2.5	+ 2.4	+240
California	7.0	8.3	7.8	7.8	6.8	6.2	8.6	+ 1.6	+ 23
Texas	1.7	1.7	1.2	0.7	2.5	3.3	4.2	+ 2.5	+150
U.S.	82.6	96.0	84.1	83.3	83.8	75.9	84.9	+ 2.3	+ 2.8

Source: *Census of Manufactures.*

Table 10.4
State shares in women's dresses jobs, 1947-1977

State	Jobs (000)							Job change	Percentage change
	1947	1954	1948	1963	1967	1972	1977		
Massachusetts	8.8	12.5	11.9	11.5	12.3	10.8	6.7	− 2,100	− 24
New York	84.1	84.7	75.0	72.3	71.7	64.0	51.6	−33,500	− 42
New Jersey	11.0	11.6	12.3	12.5	11.8	10.9	8.4	− 2,600	− 23
Pennsylvania	18.7	24.6	25.8	33.9	35.4	35.0	24.5	+ 5,800	+ 31
Illinois	15.7	12.3	9.4	8.3	7.1	4.8	4.3	−11,400	− 73
Ohio	4.8	3.6	2.0	1.5	1.2	0.7	0.5	− 4,300	90
Missouri	9.3	8.0	5.5	5.4	4.5	3.5	1.9	− 7,300	− 80
North Carolina	0.2	0.5	1.1	3.8	4.1	4.3	4.5	+ 4,300	+ 215
South Carolina	1.0	4.3	5.4	6.9	8.6	7.6	4.9	+ 3,900	+ 390
Florida	0.3	1.8	1.8	2.9	4.5	9.6	8.2	+ 7,900	+2633
Texas	3.6	4.5	4.6	6.6	8.5	9.4	6.7	+ 3,100	+ 86
California	6.6	7.4	9.4	11.4	13.0	21.2	23.0	+16,400	+ 248
U.S.	182.4	197.8	184.7	200.0	209.6	211.6	168.6	−13,800	− 7.6

Source: *Census of Manufactures.*

garment making from its historic center in New York is distinctly
different through the stages of the profit cycle. In an earlier stage of
rationalization and competition, from 1947 to 1963, job shifts tended
toward regional centers in the manufacturing belt but outside New
York. Massachusetts, New Jersey, and Pennsylvania gained garment
making jobs in the period from 1947 to 1963, and the leading sunbelt states registered a modest hike in job share.

Beginning in the early 1960s loss of job share in the manufacturing
belt states accelerated, with regional employment centers outside of
New York declining even more rapidly than the SMSA. Concomitantly a rapid rise in employment was registered in the five major
sunbelt garment making states. Thus decentralization became
interregional in nature during a period of increasing concentration
but accelerated in the subsequent period of profit squeeze (figure
10.10). The shift cannot be accounted for by the general shrinkage
of employment in the sector as a whole. New York alone lost 39,100
jobs in these two subsectors from 1963 to 1977, while total U.S. job
loss was 34,800. Thus a substantial portion of job shift is accounted
for by new job creation in the sunbelt displacing jobs in the manufacturing belt.

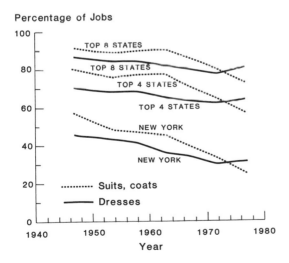

Figure 10.10
Geographical concentration in women's clothing, 1947-1977

Although the experience of the two subsectors is strikingly similar, two variations did occur. The shift to the sunbelt in dressmaking preceded the shift in coats and suits. This may reflect the innovation of a new product line—pants suits—which tied employment to the northeastern design center longer than was true for other garment sectors.

Second, the two subsectors demonstrated contrary tendencies toward dispersion within major regions. In 1947 five frostbelt and five sunbelt states together accounted for 85 percent of suits and coats employment and 82 percent of dressmaking; by 1977 the same states accounted for 77 percent and 85 percent, respectively. In other words suit and coat manufacture over the postwar period became less concentrated subregionally as states outside the major manufacturing centers gained almost a 10 percent share in employment. In dresses, on the other hand, employment became more subregionally concentrated in the major producing states.

Within the Southeast apparel manufacturing increasingly had gone to rural areas. Beginning in the 1930s garment plants shunned Atlanta for smaller town sites. In 1929 Atlanta had 36 percent of Georgia plants, by 1949 only 17 percent, and by 1969 only 10 percent. This preference was largely a response to increasing union activity in cities like Atlanta and to the prospects of controlling the entire community in small towns. Furthermore a labor force expelled from agriculture filled these low-paying job slots. The typical Georgia apparel plant was located in a town of 4,800, drew its workers from an extensive surrounding area, and was one of the three largest employers.[25]

The evidence on the women's clothing industry clearly indicates that employment became both intraregionally and interregionally more dispersed during the later profit cycle stages. The pace of decentralization quickened during the stages of limited market power and profit squeeze, despite the fact that total U.S. employment in this period fluctuated around an average of 84,000. In fact, in 1977 there were only slightly more workers in garment making in the United States than in 1958.[26] But while the median worker was still to be found in the frostbelt, large numbers of unionized garment making jobs had disappeared in the Northeast, displaced by cheaper sunbelt labor, largely black and Hispanic women. A clearer example of heightened sensitivity to labor organization and militancy by manufacturing capital faced with a profit squeeze could scarcely be found.

Summary

The women's apparel industry has passed through several stages in the mid-twentieth century, which reflect the structural and spatial transformations a highly labor-intensive, competitive sector undergoes in this era of internationalization. Despite an incipient oligopolistic stage, the stiff price competition from plants in developing countries has undermined market power of domestic corporations. In fact the employment record probably would be much worse today if it were not for the rapid expansion of jobs in low-cost locations like Los Angeles, where Third World women workers labor under sweatshop or home work conditions that permit their employers to remain profitable and competitive. Nevertheless, in one of the two subsectors studied here (women's dresses), employment declined by 27 percent in the mid-1970s, reflecting the impact of both imports and a shift to other types of women's clothing. The structure of the industry remains highly competitive, with the top four firms controlling only 9 percent and 15 percent of output in the two subsectors. In both subsectors the proportions of production workers were much higher than and increasing with respect to the U.S. average, supporting the profit cycle model suppositions.

Regionally the dispersal of women's garment making has followed the model's prescriptions. Concentration ratios for the leading one, four, and eight states fell during the competitive and subsequent period. Share losses were dramatic. The leading state, New York, lost 35 percent and 52 percent of its job share in the period. Only in the most recent profit-squeeze period in dressmaking did reconcentration appear; small gains in state concentration ratios occurred in the mid-1970s. The literature confirms that low labor costs, lack of unionization, and ties to the textile sector, which has similar spatial orientation, are dominant.

10.3 Auto Assembly and Parts Industries

The auto industry provides a clear case study of postwar oligopoly in the consumer goods sector.[27] Autos were a pivotal sector in U.S. economic history, ushering in a new era of profitability and capital accumulation in many related sectors. Autos stimulated the output of steel, glass, paint, upholstery fabrics, and rubber and, indirectly, the oil, advertising, and highway construction industries. Since autos permitted a massive restructuring of both interregional and urban space, a great round of accumulation in suburban development and sunbelt growth can be traced to this sector. By the postwar period some estimated that as many as one in six jobs was tied directly or indirectly to the automobile culture.[28]

Profit Cycle Stages

Henry Ford revolutionized production by installing the first modern automated assembly line in 1903. He then designed a simple basic black car, known as the Model T, which was to be low in price and targeted to a market of farmers and working people. Using interchangeable parts, highly differentiated work tasks, and a standardized design with no retooling for eleven years, Ford was able to cut the price of his car from $950 in 1909 to $295 in 1922. By 1922 Ford as a company was producing 2 million cars and controlled 55 percent of the market.[29] This innovative and expansionary period, ending in 1920, demonstrates the features of product innovation, process innovation, dramatic firm entry, rapid job creation, entrepreneurial daring, and volatile corporate growth (figure 10.11).

In the interwar period and up through the late 1960s, oligopolistic practices ensured normal-plus profits for the dominant corporations. No normal competitive period ensued because market power emerged directly out of the innovative period. Smaller firms failed in droves. Two-thirds of firms competing at the 1919 peak disappeared by 1933, and despite a brief hike during the war, their numbers have remained at below 1,000. Job growth became less dramatic as mechanization continually increased productivity. While oligopolistic restrictions on output growth are obscured by depression and war-related cycles, the long-term output expansion path does seem to be flattened and elongated from 1920 on. Furthermore the era of sales growth seems to have been prolonged by advertising expenditures of $100 million per year per major corporation to induce consumers to buy frequently.

By the early 1970s imports and the energy crisis began to destroy the industry's big car, nonprice competitive strategy, ushering in an era of less-than-normal profits. Since 1972 output of U.S. autos has fallen. Associated employment losses have been severe. Value added, on the other hand, has continued to rise, reflecting the change in quality in automobiles (more expensive materials), in addition to attempts at profit rate preservation by an industry still dominated by domestic oligopoly. While these events may reflect

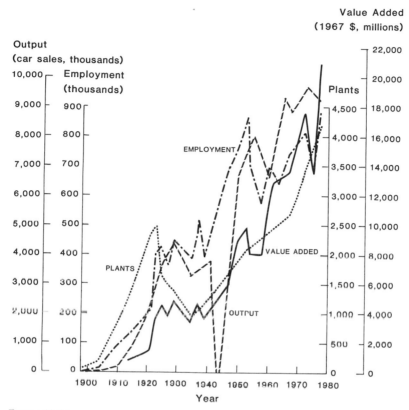

Figure 10.11
Auto industry growth, 1899-1980. Figures refer to assembly and parts production. Frequent redefinition makes it impossible to disaggregate into parts and assembly sectors over the longer run.

the ongoing economy-wide recession as well, there is good reason to believe that they may connote major competitive resurgence in the auto industry and the passage from stage IVa to IVb. In the late 1970s 300,000 auto jobs and 600,000 auto-related jobs disappeared with renewed competition, mechanization with robots, and movement of parts production abroad, such as engines made in Mexico.[30]

Industry Structure

During the innovative period the auto companies' energies turned from product innovation toward methods designed to grab and hold market share. General Motors (GM) soon grabbed the lead from Ford, which had a strategy of growing internally by reinvested profits, by swallowing up its competitors.[31] Competition eliminated the majority of smaller producers, whose scale of production was not as efficient as the larger companies or who succumbed to buy-outs. Those that remained independent tended to produce small parts and survived with the blessing and patronage of the larger companies. By 1930 three corporations controlled 90 percent of the finished auto production; by 1941 only twelve companies produced cars at all.

During this era of growing concentration the largest firms remained profitable by employing techniques such as advertising and frequent style changes to lure buyers. In addition they built extensive dealership networks, which proved essential in attracting and holding a market share. The independent wholesaler was eliminated. The oligopoly secured its market power through these methods plus basing point pricing practices. After 1940 no new entrant managed to build an auto corporation anew. Kaiser, which entered after the war, found that it was impossible to create a sufficient dealer network and merged with Willys Jeep.

The domestic auto industry has become more concentrated since World War II, measured by both control of value of shipments and value added. The four largest auto corporations controlled less than 60 percent of all auto and parts production in 1947 but more than 80 percent in 1977 (figure 10.12).[32] Yet since 1970 concentration of domestic output has remained almost unchanged. This pattern suggests that the oligopolistic possibilities in autos and parts were largely exploited by the end of the 1950s. After that the giant auto firms increasingly diversified into other lines. Concentration has been lowered over the last fifteen years by successful penetration by European and Japanese manufacturers; however, even with these entrants, the sector remains oligopolized.[33]

The evidence on ownership form further supports this two stage interpretation of postwar auto sector experience (figure 10.13). Little change in plant and job share firms took place during the normal-plus profit era. After 1967, however, single-plant corporate firms increased their share of plants significantly, although most of this change represented the conversion of noncorporate operations to the corporate form. A small erosion of establishments accounted for by multiplant firms occurred in the latter period.

The relative importance of production workers declined in the postwar era from its previous high of 85 percent in 1940 to 77 percent in 1972 (figure 10.14). But the ratio has risen steadily above the U.S. average, consistent with hypothesized profit cycle behavior. The oligopolistic era ushered in a greater demand for engineering,

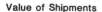

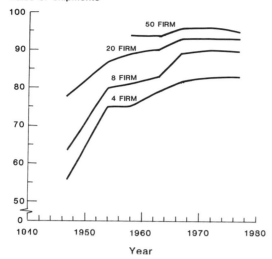

Figure 10.12
Concentration ratios in autos, 1947-1977

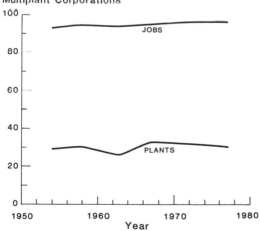

Figure 10.13
Ownership patterns in autos, 1954-1977

Relative Ratio of
Production Workers
to Total

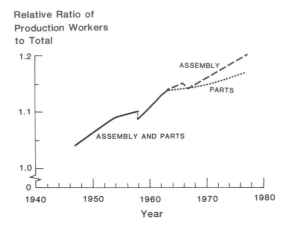

Figure 10.14
Occupational structure in autos, 1947-1977

marketing, and management personnel to manipulate the industry's oligopolistic and hidden persuasion strategies. The redesign efforts of the industry's oligopolists, their push to automate production, and their huge assault on the public sector for industry relief appear to have shifted occupational requirements in favor of professional-technical management and workers and away from production workers.

Postwar Geography

The automobile grew out of the carriage industry. Entrepreneurs in the 1880s and 1890s in all regions from Boston through Chicago experimented with ways of making the buggy horseless. By 1893 the Duryea brothers in Springfield, Massachusetts, had successfully produced a motorized car, and in the same year, the German Benz reached the United States. The experimental stage dates from 1893, when the first motorized cars appeared, to 1899, when mass-produced cars first recorded a profit. From 1899 to 1920 a period of tremendous innovation set in, as the number of parts and assembly plants reached more than 2,800, the number of manufacturers of complete cars reached 181, and employment grew to 400,000 (figure 10.11). From the earliest days regions specialized in distinct auto technologies: steam in Massachusetts, electric in Connecticut, gasoline in Detroit. The last, which triumphed, was linked to the development of gasoline-powered marine engines for lake-going freighters.[34]

The Detroit area had a number of advantages. It had fostered the carriage industry with its luxuriant stands of nearby hardwoods and by the persistent demand for better transportation in this prosperous flat farm region where public transportation was poor and distances traveled significant. In turn the carriage business had engendered a parts sector making malleable iron, steel, brass parts, springs, rubber tires, paints and varnishes, and machine tools. Small-scale entrepreneurship in both carriage and bicycle manufacture lent a competitive dynamic to the adaptation of the auto. Durant, the creator of GM, was a Flint, Michigan, carriage manufacturer, and Ford, born on a farm near Detroit, was a bicycle maker. Detroit straddled both rail and river transportation links and was notorious in the 1890s as an open-shop, nonunion town. By 1903 73 percent of all autos were made in Michigan.

The oligopolistic era was so quickly grafted on the industry that it did not begin to disperse much from its center of innovation and agglomeration. Both the marketing and distribution functions tended to anchor jobs in the Detroit area. In addition, in 1936 the automakers through their trade group, the Automotive Manufacturing Association, adopted a basing point price quotation system similar to that for steel. It raised the quoted price of an assembled car substantially above what it would have been without the system and is reported to have amounted to 42 percent of all GM's profits in 1938, or $33 million.[35] This monopoly premium fell disproportionately on consumers in locations remote from Detroit, so that the market-depressing effect slowed the decentralization of auto assembly.

Thus anchored in the Detroit area, competitors could keep close watch on each other and draw on a pool of engineering and executive talent, as well as the skilled labor force that had developed. Assembly began to be decentralized as early as 1910, when Ford built a branch plant in Kansas City. But management, design, prototype construction, and parts production remained quite heavily concentrated in Michigan. The auto industry sported an hourglass shape, in the image of one scholar. A plurality of 25,000 components manufacturers sold to a handful of carmakers that made engines, transmissions, and frames and assembled this in a Detroit-based subassembly process, then sent these units to semidispersed assembly plants for ultimate distribution to 45,000 dealers. The assembly plants were the first to be spun off from Detroit because twelve knocked-down (unassembled) cars could be shipped on one freight car compared to only four fully assembled autos. If a regional market could support sales of 100,000 cars, it became a candidate for an assembly plant.[36]

The dramatic unionization of the Detroit plants in the 1930s, best remembered by the Flint sitdown strike, also contributed to decentralization in this period. The auto corporations bridled at their dependency on a large urban pool of skilled workers. Now more vulnerable to strikes and work stoppages and confronted with an unusually strong and competent union leadership, they sought cheaper, more tractable labor in far-flung locations. Thus the profit-swollen oligopoly was sensitive to the challenge from organized labor and used new siting patterns to respond.[37]

The postwar geography of the auto industry is characterized by further dispersal of assembly, with parts manufacture slowly following that downstream activity out of Detroit.[38] The impetus to disperse came from three factors: the push of government policy, the push of an organized labor force, and the pull of new markets. In 1951 President Truman inaugurated the National Industrial Dispersion Program, which instituted accelerated tax write-offs and defense contracts to decentralize U.S. manufacturing. GM, for instance, sited a plant at Arlington, Texas, to meet government defense contracts during the Korean war. Second, desire to escape a toughened work force was strong. As one scholar put it, "The deviation in the industry from traditional patterns of nucleation is due in large measure to the desire to mitigate as much as possible the volatility and antagonism found historically in the Detroit region."[39] Suburbanization and the growth of sunbelt metropolitan areas provided a final incentive.

As a result new assembly plants built after the war were overwhelmingly sited in regional centers: Los Angeles (GM, Ford, and Chrysler), Atlanta (GM, Ford), Louisville (Ford), San Jose (Ford), New Jersey (Ford), Wilmington, Delaware (GM), and Framingham, Massachusetts (GM). Not only were these plants located far from Detroit, but they tended to gravitate toward suburban locations in large metropolitan areas. By the late 1960s, plant clusters appeared in the Bay Area (two), Los Angeles (four), the Dallas area (two), Atlanta (three), St. Louis (three), Kansas City (three), New York-Baltimore (eight), and Chicago-Milwaukee (three) in a pattern reminiscent of Hotelling's prescription.[40] As assembly spread out, parts manufacture, particularly the stamping of car bodies, began to migrate toward these new regional centers.

The broad outlines of job dispersal can be seen in table 10.5. The record shows that employment has dispersed from its previous agglomerative core in Michigan. That state employed 57 percent of all auto workers in 1947 but only 38 percent in 1977. Michigan lost 68,000 auto jobs in this period, despite the tremendous gain by the sector as a whole. Ohio was one of the biggest employment gainers in this period, but even the growth of that state could not counterbalance the Michigan loss. The share of the manufacturing belt states declined significantly in importance during the postwar period. New York, New Jersey, Illinois, Wisconsin, Indiana, and Missouri, all of which had jobs in the tens of thousands in the immediate postwar period, were unable to share proportionately in employment growth in the country as a whole. While Michigan's employment losses slowed in the 1960s and 1970s, other manufacturing belt states lost at even more rapid rates than previously. Sunbelt states accounted for most of the job share gains.[41]

Dispersion is shown even more clearly in the data on plant location.[42] The plant share of Michigan, the industry's historic center, has declined dramatically since 1954 (figure 10.15). The establishment figures (table 10.6) show that Michigan's losses led the manufacturing belt as a whole into a persistently declining share of auto plants. The share of plants accounted for by states outside the manufacturing belt has increased dramatically, from nearly 29 percent in 1954 to over 47 percent in 1977.

The spatial evidence modestly contradicts the model specifications that anticipate a higher rate of decentralization during the IVb stage. In this case, the counteracting urge toward a major product innovation—the lightweight, energy-efficient auto—has allayed spatial centrifugal forces. More designers and engineers are needed to counteract the combined onslaught of energy price hikes and import competition, but it is likely that this reversal will be short-lived. The rash of plant closings since the late 1970s could result in a greater employment share loss for Michigan.[43]

Summary

The auto industry case study supports a profit cycle interpretation of structural and spatial change. From a highly innovative and competitive sector at the turn of the century, an effective oligopoly emerged

Table 10.5
State shares of auto assembly and parts jobs, 1947-1977

State	Jobs (000)							Job change	Percentage change
	1947	1954	1948	1963	1967	1972	1977		
Massachusetts	3.07	5.00	2.51	2.93			(1.5)		
New York	38.91	44.24	32.81	(38.39)	(29.5)				
New Jersey	12.86	13.55	13.49	12.16	(3.0)	(3.1)	(2.1)		
Pennsylvania	20.55	13.87	15.99	13.60		(7.3)	(8.8)		
Ohio	61.45	72.48	74.36	105.22	97.2	112.8	114.9	+53.5	+87.0
Indiana	52.69	50.65	41.72	56.96		(48.3)	(49.2)		
Illinois	14.86	16.47	20.59	(12.1)					
Michigan	371.80	341.91	229.20	261.15	289.6	294.7	303.9	− 67.9	− 18.3
Wisconsin	21.42	19.12	24.19	35.08					
Missouri	14.03	14.58	15.53	21.62	(6.2)	(6.1)			
Tennessee	3.47	1.99	2.35	3.40		(10.2)	(12.9)		
Texas	1.61	4.59	3.95	5.99	(2.0)	(3.1)	(3.7)		
California	12.12	21.01	19.71	23.19	29.3 (6.4)	(10.5)	(14.6)		
U.S.	653.17	649.27	546.04	649.93	686.1	739.1	794.3		

Source: *Census of Manufactures.*
Note: Figures in parentheses are for SIC 3714 parts only.

Percentage of Plants

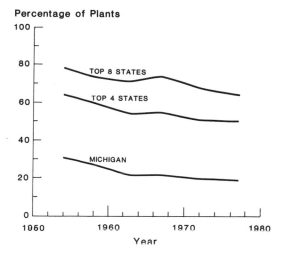

Figure 10.15
Geographical concentration in autos, 1954-1977

Table 10.6
State shares of auto parts and assembly plants

State	Number of Plants[a]						Plant change	Percentage change
	1954	1948	1963	1967	1972	1977		
Massachusetts	9	12	15	13	16	13	+ 4	+ 44
New York	41	33	44	46	48	38	− 3	− 7
New Jersey	13	14	19	23	30	22	+ 9	+ 7
Pennsylvania	18	24	30	36	31	33	+ 15	+ 18
Ohio	86	96	121	106	117	116	+ 30	+ 35
Indiana			67	67	75	82	+ 15[b]	+ 22[b]
Texas				27	38	39	+ 12[c]	+ 44[c]
Michigan	201	177	200	202	206	208	+ 7	+ 3
Illinois	62	57	57	57	66	61	− 1	− 2
Wisconsin	21	23	22	20	24	28	+ 7	+ 33
Missouri	12	15	22	29	35	24	+ 22	+138
California	66	58	102	116	135	147	+ 81	+123
U.S.	649	651	909	915	1052	1116	+469	+ 72

Source: *Census of Manufactures.*

a. Plants with more than twenty employees.

b. 1963-1977 only.

c. 1967-1977 only.

that has lasted to the present and whose profits were to become squeezed only by the competitive pressure from imports. Oligopoly extended the growth period by restricting capacity additions to preserve profits and by using advertising and planned obsolescence to encourage frequent new car buying. Jobs in automaking increased until the early 1970s, although only slowly after the war, while value added climbed dramatically. In auto parts, much more competitive than assembly, new firms entered in large numbers in the postwar period. But even with parts included, industry-wide concentration was severe and increasing over the period, as the top four and top twenty firms controlled 83 percent and 93 percent of shipments, respectively. In the postwar period multiplant corporations also increased their shares of both plants and jobs, so that 96 percent of all autoworkers were employed by such large corporations by the 1970s. Consistent with mature stage behavior, the production work force comprised a higher than average and increasing share of employment.

The auto industry shows a classic agglomeration-decentralization pattern, from its Detroit-area homeland to regional centers throughout the country. Agglomeration was sustained after the innovative period had ended by the oligopolistic needs of the sector: an emphasis on marketing and frequent style changes, a spatially biased basing point system, and the locational buildup of suppliers around Detroit. So concentrated is this sector in Detroit (and so unparalleled by any other local sector) that the city has been dubbed the Motor City, and its name is synonymous in the business press with the auto industry even today.

Only after an enlarged national market developed and a home-based militancy erupted in the area's labor force did the industry disperse its assembly plants, encouraged by federal government policy. Gradually parts manufacture began to decentralize as well, sometimes outside the nation's borders. Headquarters activities remain in Detroit, however. The sudden restructuring forced on the industry by the usurpation of a large market share by imports, intensified by the 1970s energy crisis, resulted in numerous plant closings and efforts to roll back wages and benefits. The net spatial change from this profit-squeeze period cannot yet be documented, but it is quite likely that robotization and a dramatically downsized auto will further decentralize the U.S. industry. Ironically the only corporations currently attracted by Detroit's labor and supply sector resources are precisely those international corporations (such as Toyota) whose arrival has cast the sector into chaos.

10.4 Brewing Industry

The brewing industry is a good case study of a consumer goods sector in transition from competitive to oligopolistic stature. Brewing is
more protected than most other sectors from the growing integration
of the world economy since its product is extremely heavy per unit
price and thus not easy to import. Despite recent in-roads by Mexi-
can beers and other imports (many of which are now manufactured
domestically under franchise by the largest U.S. brewing corporations), the industry's leaders have successfully oligopolized the
domestic market in the 1970s. Brewing has thus passed through two
distinct profit cycle stages in the 20th century: a long competitive
stage up through the late 1950s, followed by rapid oligopolization.
Each placed its mark on spatial restructuring.

Profit Cycle Stages, Output, and Jobs

Brewing was once a home industry, brought to the United States by
early English and Dutch immigrants. It was one of many activities
of the diversified family farm, although frequently those who made
beer produced for others besides their immediate household. During
the nineteenth century the brewing of beer became standardized,
mechanized, and urbanized in small breweries that served local
markets, a result of the German immigrants' introduction of lager
beer in the 1840s. With beer consumption still largely confined to
Northern European immigrants in the grain belt (New York through
Minnesota), each local or regional brewery produced a style of beer
distinctive to its available makings and local tastes. Factory production of beer increased throughout the nineteenth century, prompting
a sustained growth in the ranks of brewery workers, until the end of
the first decade of the twentieth century (figure 10.16).

The maturation of competition in brewing was signaled by the
turning point in proliferation of commercial breweries in 1904. A
competitive stage commenced in which demand was met by mechanization and expansion of existing plants. The temperance crusades,
wartime austerity, and prohibition (1920-1933) severely retarded the
growth dynamic until repeal in 1934.

The fortunes of brewing faltered in the postwar era as hard liquor,
wine, and soft drinks promotional campaigns cut into the beer

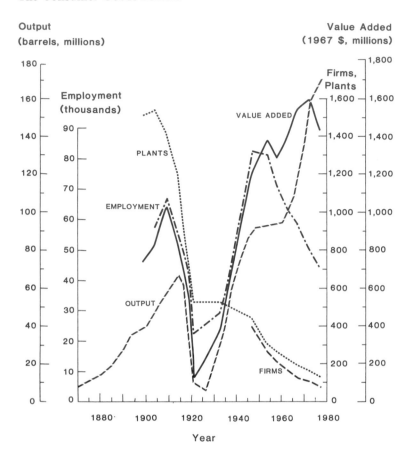

Figure 10.16
Brewing industry growth, 1870-1977. Value added series before prohibition includes
internal revenue taxes. Prohibition lasted from 1920-1933.

market. From 1940 through 1960 output grew at rates less than 0.5
percent per year, in part due to the relative decline in the youth content of U.S. society. Per capita consumption hit low points in 1958
and 1961. Employment fell dramatically, and only the larger, more
efficient plants survived.

A few enterprising corporations began to fight back by engaging in
advertising campaigns at a regional and then national scale and by
packaging their output for grocery stores as a way of shedding the
"tavern" stigma. The industry directed its sales pitch at both women
and white working-class males by creating new premium and (later
light) beers and by sponsorship of spectator sports. Packaged beer
favored large-scale production, which in turn engendered greater

market power by leading brewing firms. They succeeded in reviving beer drinking by expanding the pool of beer consumers beyond traditional beer-drinking ethnic males, beyond the regional borders within which they form a significant portion of the population, and beyond the neighborhood bar into the home.

Sustained heavy advertising budgets were possible only as the investment and accompaniment to successful oligopolization, since the advertising outlays would have to be passed along in the price to the consumer. The initiation of this stage of normal-plus profits can be dated at 1958, a year in which concentration ratios began to climb precipitously and in which value added for the industry again began to rise. Profit data suggest that rival beverage advertising created a brewing profit squeeze up through 1958 but that oligopoly permitted margins to rise thereafter.[44]

In the twenty-year period of successful beer industry oligopoly that has ensued, beer drinking has continued to boom with only a slight downturn in the early 1980s. This resurgence in output is clear evidence of the ability of oligopoly and advertising to prolong a product's life cycle in a consumer goods sector. Not all breweries have shared in the benefits. Predatory price cutting, prohibitive advertising outlays, and growing economies of scale cut into small single-plant companies' profitability.[45] Many have closed down. Furthermore the reversal in profitability and output growth rates has not translated into a reversal of job loss. Since 1947 almost one in two brewing jobs has disappeared, and half of these losses have occurred since the industry's revitalization.

Industry Structure

Consistent with the profit cycle model, the brewing industry has persistently suffered plant losses since the turn of the century. Where there were once more than 1,500 local breweries, now fewer than 150 remain. While the greatest number of closings took place prior to and during prohibition, the scrapping of plants in the postwar period has also been significant. Approximately two out of every three plants surviving World War II are now closed.

Advertising, which enlarged the aggregate market, played a central role in the restructuring of brewery concentration. In the 1940s and early 1950s a few large brewers broadened their market horizons to a national level by developing premium beers. The top five increased their market share by 10 percent in this manner, while the second largest five increased their share by only 4 percent. Several of these firms were based in Wisconsin, although one—Anheuser Busch—was headquartered in St. Louis. In 1953 a Milwaukee-based seventy-six-day labor strike cut deeply into the nationals market, and when workers won a substantial wage hike, brewers raised their beer prices to maintain profit margins. Both the stoppage and higher prices gave a group of smaller regional breweries (Falstaff, Carling, Hamm, and Schaefer) a chance to fight their sales erosion by entering the advertising fray. From 1952 to 1958 these medium-sized firms increased their market share by 5 percent compared to 2 percent for the nationals. Once recovered from the strike, the latter—Anheuser-Busch, Schlitz, and Pabst—aggressively entered regional markets, bought and built breweries at distant locations, developed their own low-priced brands, and sustained large advertising bills. The smaller breweries had no choice but to engage in the advertising battle or close down, accelerating attrition in brewing ranks.

Thus the rates of concentration within the industry have persistently risen throughout both twentieth-century stages and appear to have accelerated with the era of successful national oligopolization. The eight largest corporations controlled only a bit over 15 percent of national output in the late 1930s but control over 80 percent currently (figure 10.17). Twenty corporations control virtually all contemporary brewing, whereas in 1947 they controlled less than 45 percent. And as the oligopoly emerged, share growth by the largest four and eight corporations accelerated in the period after 1958.[46] Changes in ownership form over the postwar period also confirm that oligopolization is intensifying. Since 1954 single-plant firms have fallen from 72 percent to under 40 percent of all establishments, while multiplant corporate enterprises have risen from less than 35 percent to about 60 percent of all plants (figure 10.18). Employment patterns suggest that multiplant corporations are almost completely hegemonic at the present time. From about 65 percent of jobs in 1954, they now control 96 percent of brewing employment.

Undetectable from the census data is the degree to which brewing corporations have been attractive to and thus bought up by related conglomerates in the 1970s. The first big entry was Phillip Morris's buyout of Miller's in 1971. Phillip Morris immediately commenced a heightened advertising campaign around its products, especially its newly introduced Miller Lite, that forced other corporations to follow or yield up shares of the market. Phillip Morris brought tremendous

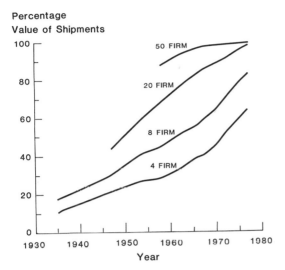

Figure 10.17
Concentration ratios in brewing, 1935-1977

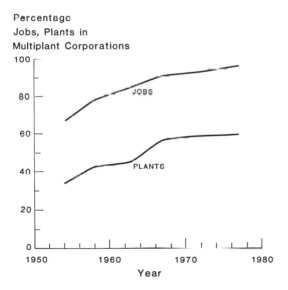

Figure 10.18
Ownership patterns in brewing, 1954-1977

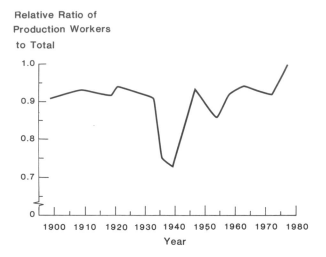

Figure 10.19
Occupational structure in brewing, 1900-1977. Series was discontinued on 1939-1947.

resources in both cash and marketing experience to the industry, aiming in the long term to oligopolize and dominate. Strapped for cash to mimic the conglomerate, other brewing corporations became candidates for conglomerate acquisition as well. The new product innovations, trumpeted with slick advertising ideas such as the slimming, even athletic attributes of light beers, have resulted in a product that is cheaper to make (it uses less expensive hops) but sells at a higher price. The normal-plus profits that accrue to the big beer corporations are split between advertising budgets and higher stockholder returns and retained earnings.[47]

The proportion of production workers to total in brewing has fallen substantially over time (figure 10.19). In 1900 85 percent of workers were engaged in production; the current average is nearer 65 percent. When blue-collar representation is compared to the U.S. pattern, the brewing industry shows a recent tendency, in its latter stage, toward an increase, although proportions remain slightly below the national norm. The rate of change thus conforms to expectations.

Geography

Traditionally every medium-sized town in the grain belt had its own brewery, sometimes several. Beer was marketed in kegs, to be consumed in public taverns, and in returnable bottles. The relatively heavy weight of beer to its value kept the market localized. This prior structure was not necessarily as competitive as the national figures on concentration would suggest. Each region had a relatively small number of firms serving its market area. Regionwide marketing did emerge as early as the 1880s, with Milwaukee leading the way. Milwaukee brewers had a superior natural ice supply, cheap cooperage prices, and entrepreneurial response to the challenge of a limited local market area.[48] But until the postwar period, markets remained regional. Even the product was regionally differentiated. California breweries manufactured "steam beer" which did not require refrigeration as did lager beer.

California brewers were well enough organized in the 1930s and 1940s to prevent lower shipping rates that would have permitted midwestern brewers to penetrate their markets and won discriminatory wholesalers' fees that favored California beers. Fogarty presents strong evidence that the strategy of postwar nationals to build plants in California was motivated largely by their need to overcome this regional monopoly on its own turf, especially since the West Coast population boom provided greater market potential than did their home regions. The improvement in interstate highways in the postwar period was also a significant factor in the interpenetration of local markets by regional plants of national firms.[49]

With the postwar revival of the brewing industry, the major brewers faced immediate and vigorous competition from each other. Dramatic interregional changes grew out of their efforts to enlarge average plant size, close 182 plants, and reduce employment per unit output. The grain belt states bore the brunt of the plant cuts (table 10.7). The single exception was Wisconsin, where brewers with major headquarters have substituted several new experimental plants for smaller, older operations. Meanwhile both southern and western regions gained plant shares. Two forms of behavior produced this interregional shift. First, the bigger corporations sited their new, ultramodern plants in southern or western regions, frequently in states or communities that had no previous experience with brewing, and where workers would not be unionized. Second, plant and job cutbacks took place largely in the older regions where the labor force was militantly organized and the plants relatively inefficient.

Absolute plant losses are recorded in table 10.7, which shows that no state enjoyed net gains in plant, with the exception of Colorado. Plant closings were greatest in those states with the initial largest

Table 10.7
State shares of breweries, 1947-1977

State	Number of Plants							Plant change	Percentage change
	1947	1954	1948	1963	1967	1972	1977		
East									
Massachusetts	14	8	7	6	4	4	3	− 11	− 79
New York	46	26	26	16	15	14	12	− 34	− 74
New Jersey	12	10	10	9	7	8	8	− 4	− 33
Maryland	8	6	7	8	7	6	5	− 3	− 38
Pennsylvania	61	34	30	29	23	20	14	− 47	− 77
Midwest									
Ohio	37	20	14	10	8	7	4	− 33	− 89
Illinois	39	22	17	15	10	8	6	− 33	− 85
Michigan	24	14	11	8	6	8	4	− 20	− 83
Indiana	12	7	4	5	5	4	2	− 10	− 83
Wisconsin	55	44	38	28	20	14	10	− 45	− 82
Minnesota	17	14	13	12	9	7	5	− 12	− 71
Missouri	12	10	7	6	6	4	3	− 9	− 75
South									
Louisiana	6	4	4	3	3	4	4	− 2	− 33
Texas	7	6	7	8	9	8	7	0	0
West									
Washington	12	8	8	5	6	6	6	− 6	− 50
California	16	17	16	15	13	13	11	− 5	− 47
Colorado	3	4	4	3	3	2	1	− 2	− 67
United States	440	301	258	222	185	167	131	− 309	− 70

Source: *Census of Manufactures*
Note: For this sector, the figures for all establishments rather than those with greater than twenty employees were used to permit comparisons back to 1947. By 1977, most beer plants employed more than twenty workers.

concentrations: New York (20), Pennsylvania (31), Wisconsin (17), Illinois (22), and Ohio (23). A general dispersion in brewing location is apparent in the figures for state concentrations, which show that during this postwar competitive period, the proportion of plants accounted for by the previous leading brewing states decreased.

The growing domination of large brewing corporations and the entry of conglomerates into the field appear to have accelerated this pattern of dispersal and net interregional shifting since 1958. Wisconsin's share of plants was cut nearly in half, while the entire midwestern region's share fell substantially. Plant share in the southern and western regions continued to increase. Although no state increased its number of breweries, the southern and western states lost relatively fewer plants than did their northeasterly counterparts. Dispersion of plants toward newer sites in states with previously insignificant brewing production is reflected in the continued decline in concentration ratios for the top one, four, and eight states (figure 10.20). This behavior confirms the model's suppositions about spatial outcomes when an industry oligopolizes late in its maturation.

What cannot be read easily from this state-level aggregation of the data is the intraregional concentration of employment that has accompanied the average rise in plant scale. Disproportionate numbers of small local breweries have closed in medium-sized cities

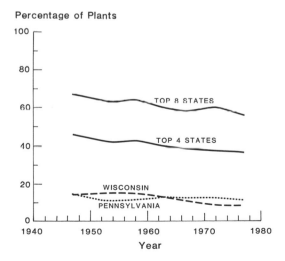

Figure 10.20
Geographical concentration in brewing, 1947-1977

(for example, Fitger's in Duluth), victims of the heightened penetration of their markets by the big national breweries. Many of the new high-volume plants serving regional markets are located in or near major metropolitan areas, often in Hotelling-like juxtaposition with competitors. Thus the largest employment displacement problems have occurred in the medium-sized towns of the grain belt, not necessarily in the larger multiplant brewing cities.

Job dispersal has accompanied shifts in plant incidence. The lead state of Wisconsin has suffered less drastic employment reductions than states like New York and Pennsylvania; this center of agglomeration still leads the United States with 18 percent of all jobs. New York lost 10,200 brewing jobs from 1954 to 1977, Pennsylvania lost 4,000, and Wisconsin a modest 1,400. Wisconsin breweries are on average larger than the more eastern breweries and are also linked to national headquarters of several firms. Sufficient modernization has occurred in this beer-drinking heartland to permit Wisconsin to increase slightly its share of employment while suffering a fall in the number of establishments. Employment dispersed less rapidly than plants, therefore, over this era. However, the largest employing states—New York, New Jersey, Pennsylvania, Wisconsin, and California—collectively lost employment share from 49 percent in 1954 to about 43 percent in 1977. Meanwhile Texas, Colorado (through one brewer, Coors), and Oregon showed dramatic increases in employment over the period.

As transportation costs have decreased with the interstate highway system, regional markets can more easily be served by breweries in more tractable communities. Union demands for higher wages and union opposition to plant closings have encouraged the larger brewers to build new plants outside the grain belt. Schlitz, for instance, told distributors that it would supply its midwestern markets from Memphis rather than Milwaukee in the event of a threatened strike, perhaps permanently. New superbreweries in places like Winston-Salem and Memphis incur lower labor costs and higher profits. In addition to lower labor requirements—for example, two workers per shift where once there were twenty-four—the ability to supply markets from alternative locations is used to tame labor at the bargaining table. In 1981 striking brewers making Iron City beer agreed 254 to 32 to accept a contract that just two days earlier they had rejected 207 to 111 because the firm, Pittsburgh Brewing Co., had ordered action to begin closing the company's brewery. The company reversed the closing order within an hour of the second vote.[50]

Brewing remains an industry with strong regional identification. In a number of cases communities have responded to announced closings by forming coalitions proposing to take over the plant or issuing calls for incentives to permit the small local brewing company to survive. Brewers at Iron City are trying to encourage beer drinkers to buy local out of loyalty. But to date such responses have not stemmed the tide of movement toward the South, West, and other locations.

Summary

The brewing sector has passed through the intermediate stages of the profit cycle and is now a successful oligopoly. Once a very labor-intensive and highly localized activity, producing a product consumed collectively in taverns and bars, the brewing industry has become relatively mechanized and nationally integrated and produces a highly advertised set of brands marketed through and drunk in front of a television set. In the immediate postwar period, brewing became highly competitive. Attempts to increase market shares of a moribund market through advertising proved too costly for many small breweries to survive; 41 percent of plants and 10 percent of all jobs were eliminated in the short period from 1947 to 1958. By 1958 advertising had reversed the public abandonment of beer for other forms of alcohol and had begun to pay off for a small elite of nationally oriented firms. Concentration rates climbed, and by the 1970s four firms controlled 64 percent of the market and the top twenty, 98 percent.

Geographically the industry has dispersed with its maturation. Originally concentrated in the grain belt for cultural reasons but dispersed in medium-sized towns throughout, the sector developed a new node in the Milwaukee area when the introduction of premium beer permitted several firms to become national in scope. A severe labor strike in 1953 aided non-Milwaukee competition, and in response the national brewers began to decentralize plants through buy-outs and new construction. New breweries cropped up in metropolitan-area clusters and more recently in southern small to medium-sized towns, where labor problems are minimal. Small breweries in the older centers, particularly in states like New York and Pennsylvania, closed their doors while their citizens bought beer trucked in from Virginia. Oligopolistic practices did reinforce

Milwaukee's centrality, at least in job share, since many of the larger corporations are headquartered there. However, other oligopolistic practices, such as the enlargement of the aggregate beer market through consumer taste formation and conglomerate financial restructuring, have resulted in a degree of decentralization that would probably not otherwise have occurred.

10.5 Shoe Industry

Shoemaking is a case of a troubled, mature consumer goods sector. Shoemaking was an old and respected profession in colonial times. As it became commercialized, it remained an almost totally labor-oriented industry, although its requirements shifted over time from skilled to semiskilled labor. Clear stages of the profit cycle can be demarcated, and most of the hypotheses characterizing stages of the cycle, including geographic ones, are borne out by the data. A competitive sector throughout, U.S. shoemaking entered stage V decline in the late 1960s, largely because of the preemption of the market by synthetic materials and cheap imports.[51]

Profit Cycle Stages, Output, and Jobs

The commodification of footwear in the United States encompassed three forms prior to factory manufacture. In the more remote settlements and in poorer households, family members made their own shoes. In villages of modest size, artisan shoemakers fashioned shoes that were individually fit to the wearer's foot. In the largest towns, like Boston, where a sizable demand for boots came from the fishing and sailing industries, a putting-out system evolved, with women and children of seafaring men organized into standard-sized shoe production. The entrepreneur, often a merchant, would distribute hides to home workers, who would cut and stitch it.[52] Thus shoemaking became a low-wage occupation in its capitalist origins, although the prior craft had been a much more prestigious occupation.

The innovative expansionary period in shoemaking dates from the Civil War, when a great demand for men's boots and shoes had to be met with a depleted labor force. The industry was rapidly mechanized by the introduction of the McKay sewing machine, which solved the labor shortage. Tremendous experimentation in shoemaking machinery dominated the thirty-year period from 1870

to 1900; some 100 shoe machinery firms competed in Lynn, Massachusetts, the center of agglomeration. Shoemaking was forced to
conform to the imperatives of its supplier industry. Within twenty
years most shoemakers and small firms mechanized their operations,
which cut labor costs by 80 percent to 90 percent. The industry
became male dominated in this period, as labor savings and increased
productivity raised wages but cut employment.

The mechanization of the industry introduced vigorous cost competition even while output and value added continued to climb
(figure 10.21). Employment grew to a high of 250,000 in 1923,
although job gains lagged output because productivity increased 8
percent between 1900 and 1919 and another 16 percent between
1919 and 1927.[53] Employment fell almost 20 percent in this latter

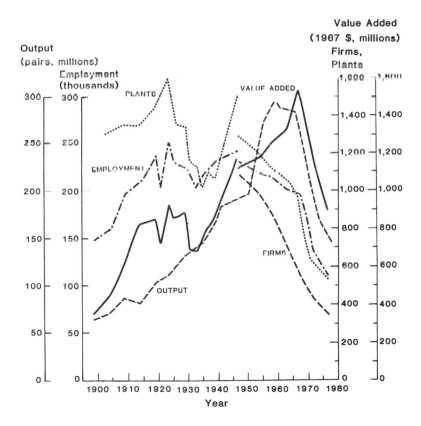

Figure 10.21
Shoe industry growth, 1899-1977. (Source: Hoover, 1937:130)

period, or by more than 47,000 workers. Establishments peaked in 1923 at 1,600, when productivity gains and tough competition began to erode their ranks rapidly, falling to 1,150 in 1931 and 1,020 by 1935.

Between World War II and 1967, the U.S. shoe industry entered a period of intensified competition, heightened by cheap imports, which forced many plants below the level of minimum acceptable profits. Some 340 plants disappeared during this less-than-normal profit period. Jobs fell by 17.5 percent, or 42,000 workers. Although domestic output continued to rise, up a net 42 percent, and value added rose consistently, price competition proved too severe for many firms. Imports, a mere 2 percent of the market in 1946, had captured 25 percent, by 1968. In an industry where wage costs comprise 35 percent of output, the cheaper wage rates of Southern Europe and Asian countries had proved too difficult for many small U.S. firms to meet.[54]

The decade beginning in 1967 was disastrous for the U.S. shoe industry. It is perhaps not alarmist to consider it one of negative profit and abandonment. Even though demand did not abate, imports captured more than 60 percent of the domestic market. The inability of almost one in every two plants to reach even a minimal profit level was revealed in a plant shutdown rate of 43 percent (figure 10.21). Some 410 firms disappeared during the decade as output plummeted even faster than previously to just half of what it had been in 1965. Employment losses mirrored plant closings. Some 43 percent of all workers were displaced, for a total of 86,000 in ten years. These patterns of output, jobs, and firm growth confirm the hypothesized sequences of the profit cycle model.

Industry Structure

The innovative stage in shoemaking occurred so long ago that it is difficult to detect any degree of concentration from a superprofits experience. It is likely that in local and regional markets, the first shoemakers to mechanize did prosper at the expense of their fellow craftsmen. Beginning in the 1880s the shoe industry began to settle into a prolonged era of fierce competition. Ironically fragmentation and preservation of small firms in shoemaking was largely a by-product of concentration in the shoe machinery sector, which by 1899 had become the monopoly of one corporation, United Shoe Manufacturing Company. United Shoe adopted several practices that helped keep the shoe industry competitive. First, it refused to sell its machines, preferring to lease them. It then charged the same rent per unit output regardless of how intensively the firm used the machine. This permitted small firms with irregular production schedules to compete with larger firms. Second, the company charged the same lease and maintenance rates regardless of the location of the user, so that Boston-area firms (where the United Shoe machinery factory was located) had no advantage over midwestern ones.[55] Despite the extraordinary casualties among firms, the industry remained unconcentrated into the 1930s, with the largest firm, International Shoe, controlling less than 15 percent of the market.

In the profit-squeeze period following World War II, the continued loss of small firms did not make the industry much more concentrated (figure 10.22). In fact shares of output of the largest four and eight firms declined slightly, although those of the largest twenty and fifty increased; however, marketing advantages had begun to concentrate employment in multiplant firms. As figure 10.23 shows, multiplant firms increased their share of plants from 25 percent to over 50 percent in the period and their share of employment from 50 percent to more than 80 percent. The larger firms, such as International Shoe (based in St. Louis) and Kinney's, had better growth rates due to franchise retail outlets and aggressive marketing in this postwar period.[56] The greatest relative increase in production workers to total took place during this era (figure 10.24), confirming the rationalizing preoccupations hypothesized for profit-squeezed firms.

Structurally, this latest period of stress has only modestly increased concentration among the top eight and 50 firms and actually decreased the largest four's share slightly (see figure 10.22). But the share of plants accounted for by multiplant corporations decreased slightly. This confirms a stage V tendency for more profit-rational firms to close, switching their assets into other commodities and regions, more quickly than small firms whose owners may be tied to the community. Harrison's (1983) study of net job loss from plant closings by type of firm in New England confirms this tendency. He found that shoe conglomerate investment and plant closing behavior from 1969 to 1976 resulted in the net destruction of 28 percent of their jobs, compared to rates of 13.4 percent for corporate owners and 24.7 percent for independent owners. In other words both the smallest and largest ownership forms recorded more rapid closings and job destruction than did the traditional shoe corporations.[57] The trend toward higher production to total work force continued during

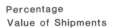

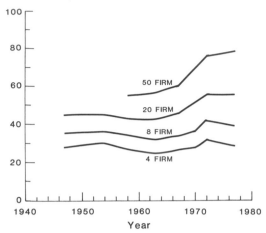

Figure 10.22
Concentration ratios in shoes, 1947-1977

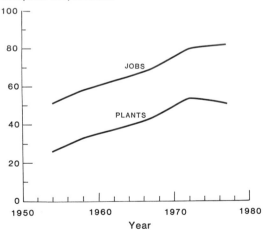

Figure 10.23
Ownership patterns in shoes, 1954-1977

this decade although less rapidly (figure 10.24).

Geography

In its precommodity form, shoemaking was highly decentralized. The first long-distance trade in stock shoes appeared around 1815, when local leather supplies began to be depleted. Leather tanneries sprang up in concentrated clusters around seaports, particularly Boston. Here the supply of hides, a by-product of meat packing, could be purchased from ships stopping in at Latin American ports. The first regionally oriented shoe firms originated near these tanneries, as at Lynn, where they also served a growing demand from Boston. Low-wage female labor helped New England footwear firms compete in the emerging midwestern market, where the high cost of scarce labor on the agricultural frontier handicapped the growth of an indigenous industry.

The initial geographical effect of mechanization of the industry was to agglomerate production further in the New England states. The states of Massachusetts, New Hampshire, and Maine increased their shares of shoe output from 51 percent in 1849, to 57 percent in 1859, to 65 percent in 1869, and 66 percent in 1879 (figure 10.25). Rapid changes in innovative processes seem to have reinforced the importance of New England through the era. Through the nineteenth century, these three states were the only ones to specialize in shoemaking far beyond their shares of U.S. population.[58] Not until the 1880s did this overwhelming concentration begin to lessen, coincident with the initiation of a thoroughly competitive stage and due in large part to machinery leasing practices.

Both the end of innovational ferment and the coming of organized labor led to decentralization of the industry away from its concentration in New England cities. The former factor enabled shoe manufacturing to follow markets and leather supplies westward, without fear of becoming cut off from market-unsettling production changes. Between 1879 and 1900 the states of New York, Ohio, Pennsylvania, Illinois, and Wisconsin gained in share of shoes produced (figure 10.25), building on an indigenous industry set up largely by German immigrants. In the more western states, these shoes were generally a lower grade, principally men's boots for use in agriculture and lumbering, made from cattle hides. As women's shoes took on important style features, production remained in specialized New England firms or gravitated toward the New York

Relative Ratio of
Production Workers
to Total

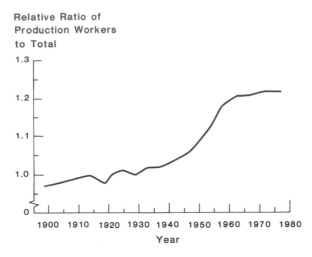

Figure 10.24
Occupational structure in shoes, 1939-1977

fashion center. Mechanization and standardization of machines abetted this trend by rendering specialized skills in shoemaking tools and custom machinery unnecessary. By 1900 the industry's ratio of production to total workers was already in excess of the national norm (figure 10.24).

While the deskilling that accompanied mechanization in this industry provided a centrifugal force, so did unionization in the older centers of shoemaking. Beginning in the 1860s the male Knights of St. Crispin began organizing New England shoe factories. By the 1870s they were engaged in strikes over pay and working conditions. Entire towns were organized at once, and the communities tended to support the workers. By the 1930s more than 60,000 workers were unionized, or between 30 and 50 percent of the work force depending on the source. Workers by the 1920s were including clauses in contracts that prevented employers from conducting job analyses designed to increase productivity. The draw of cheap labor began as early as 1900, accelerating after the 1920s.[59]

Competition, standardization, and labor union challenges produced two distinct spatial tendencies in this era. First, a shift from east to west severely cut into New England's dominance; by the 1930s that region was losing jobs in absolute numbers. New England's share of total output fell from 63 percent in 1898 to 35 percent in 1933. Consistent with the profit cycle predictions for stage III dispersion, the most important state, Massachusetts, lost the greatest percentage

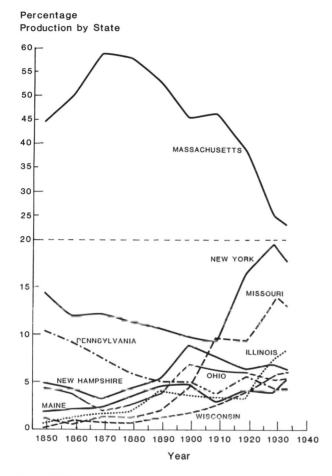

Figure 10.25
State shares of shoe output, 1849-1933

share, down from 53 percent to 23 percent in the same period. The share of Missouri, Illinois, Wisconsin, and Ohio, meanwhile, rose from 11 percent to 33 percent.

Labor cost and militance seem to have been primary propellants along a second axis of movement—from older regional centers to outlying areas within the same and neighboring states. Maine increased its share of shoe production after 1900, while New Hampshire and Massachusetts declined precipitously. From 1879 to 1933 the following major shoe-producing cities lost their share of their states' production dramatically: New York from 50 percent to 39 percent; St. Louis from 83 percent to 23 percent; Chicago from 78 percent to 25 percent; Philadelphia from 93 percent to 21 percent; and Cincinnati from 97 percent to 8 percent. In each case the major movements were to peripheral areas where depressed agricultural or other conditions kept wages low. For example, in Pennsylvania, production moved to depressed anthracite regions. St. Louis's production moved to low-wage areas in Kentucky, Arkansas, and Tennessee, while only headquarters, general assembly, and warehousing functions remained in the city. These patterns accelerated in the next two decades, with wholesale abandonment in parts of New England. New England lost 16,000 jobs in shoemaking from 1929 to 1947; Massachusetts lost more than seventy-nine firms in the 1930s alone. These job shifts constituted an important share—as much as 5 percent to 10 percent—of total U.S. manufacturing shifts of this period.[60]

In both types of shift aggressive recruiting often wooed shoe jobs away from older, more costly centers. Boosterist organizations offered lower taxes, free rent, free transportation of machinery (for plant relocations), and even cash bonuses. The town of Seabrook, New Hampshire, posted a $5,000 bond against labor troubles payable if organizers should interfere with the Bloomfield Shoe Manufacturing Company, recruited and moved from Lynn in 1934. Wisconsin shoe firms got some local governments to agree to pay transportation costs for a firm to leave town if it should be the target of labor troubles. Unorganized labor was the greatest relocation inducement, according to Hoover. In some cases firms left towns like Lynn for cities like Boston, where immigrant labor was less organized and without community support, confirming Gordon's (1978) thesis. More often, however, plants migrated to satellite communities in the periphery.[61]

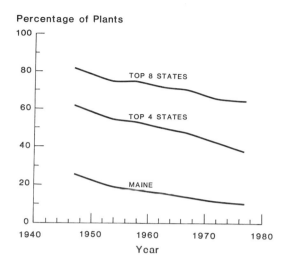

Figure 10.26
Geographical concentration in shoes, 1947-1977

Locational readjustments have been dramatic in the most recent periods as well (figure 10.26). Immediate postwar losses were heaviest in the Great Lakes area, which lost 11,000 workers by 1954. Subsequently Missouri also lost job share, down 16 percent as employment declined from 34,300 to almost 18,000. The largest four states—Massachusetts, New York, Pennsylvania, and Missouri—lost the biggest plant share. Meanwhile the southern states, especially Tennessee, Arkansas, and Texas, increased their job share from 10 percent to 21 percent. Ironically New England also gained in employment due to the movement of shoemaking into peripheral Maine, which registered gains of 13 new plants from 1947 to 1967, up 13 percent (table 10.8). The intraregional shift within New England can be accounted for wholly by the desire to secure labor at a lower cost.[62]

Under the recent period of negative profitability, the industry has continued to shift interregionally. The four most important states again suffered plant closings at a faster rate than others, their share of plants dropping from 47 percent to 37 percent in ten years, while job share dropped from 40 percent to 31 percent. The South accelerated its gains in plant share, from 8 percent to 13 percent. And the South was not only gaining relatively. In the midst of disaster, plants were still being set up in the South. In these ten years when almost one in two plants closed nationally, North Carolina

Table 10.8
State shares of shoemaking plants, 1947-1977

State	Number of Plants							Plant change	Percentage change
	1947	1954	1958	1963	1967	1972	1977		
Maine	67	73	73	74	80	80	63	− 4	− 6
New Hampshire	63	55	59	60	62	50	44	− 19	− 30
Massachusetts	338	226	202	167	134	95	81	− 257	− 76
New York	249	207	182	152	124	91	66	− 183	− 73
Pennsylvania	108	125	127	127	118	91	70	− 38	− 35
Illinois	52	52	42	35	28	22	14	− 38	− 73
Ohio	31	27	23	20	19	15	9	− 22	− 71
Wisconsin	53	59	53	41	47	45	32	− 21	− 40
Missouri	109	96	89	76	69	58	57	− 52	− 48
Virginia	9	9	9	10	10	11	9	0	0
North Carolina	1	2	3	8	6	10	10	+ 9	+900
Tennessee	21	30	36	37	37	37	37	+ 16	+ 76
Kansas	8	5	6	7	9	15	20	+ 12	+150
Arkansas	7	9	10	17	20	24	27	+ 20	+286
Texas	13	49	36	28	23	30	24	+ 11	+ 85
California	64	55	53	55	42	34	35	− 7	− 11
United States	1288	1196	1115	1040	951	826	733	− 555	− 43

Source: *Census of Manufactures*.
Note: SIC 3143, 3144, 3149. From 1947 to 1963, these subsectors were subsumed under SIC 314.

hosted four new plants, Kansas eleven, Arkansas seven, Texas one, and California fifteen (table 10.8). The southern region increased its job share from 13 percent in 1967 to 21 percent in 1977. The shift south must be interpreted as purely a shift to lower-wage, nonunionized sites. If it were a market-oriented phenomenon, the West would also have gained; yet the western states, despite their ample supplies of leather, have not increased their share of shoe production at all. Recent gains in California are attributable to cheap Latino labor in the southern portion of the state.

This recent period shows how temporary the initial movements to outlying locations in the manufacturing belt have been. Spatial shifts became purely interregional in this decade, and suburban-rural locations in the frostbelt lost jobs as well. Maine lost seventeen plants in the period, more than it had gained in the twenty years previously, and it lost almost 10,000 jobs, or more than it had added since the war. Although Maine surpassed Massachusetts in the 1970s as the country's largest shoe production center in terms of employment, its decline has been precipitous since the late 1960s. There is no reason to believe that the same pressures will not close down southern plants in the decades to come.

Summary

The shoe industry presents a classic profile of a sector's passage through the profit cycle. It exhibits a bell-shaped employment growth curve, whose down slope registers the success of both substitute materials and vigorous import competition. Firm population peaked prior to jobs, which in turn peaked before output measures. Plant closings have accelerated in the postwar period, as jobs declined by 52 percent and three out of four plants closed. It has been and remains a highly competitive sector, although the number of firms competing has fallen dramatically. Oligopolization at an early juncture seems to have been prevented by the unique monopolistic practices of its companion shoe machinery sector. Production workers have become an increasingly large proportion of the work force, compared to the U.S. average.

The mass-produced shoe has a classic geographical pattern as well. At its outset, the sector clustered around Boston, where an initial seagoing market of sailors and a ready labor force of women and children combined to supplant the individual formfit shoemaker. It was here, too, in nearby Lynn, that the first tanneries were built, the first large-scale entrepreneurs competed to produce a shoe-stitching machine, and the first union organizing began. As innovation subsided and labor militancy grew, shoe companies dispersed across the United States, especially toward midwestern conurbations. They were aided in this by the practices of the United Shoe Machinery monopoly, which serviced its leased equipment for the same price regardless of location. As competition heightened in the twentieth century, production again shifted toward rural, cheap-labor locations in both the North and the South, as Maine hosted firms fleeing from Boston, and Kentucky and Tennessee welcomed plants moving from St. Louis. The U. S. shoe market is increasingly supplied from abroad and increasingly from Third World production sites rather than Southern Europe. Thus the growth and dispersal of production is continuing on a world scale but has precipitated a stage V crisis in shoemaking domestically.

10.6 Summary of the Consumer Goods Sectors

Each of the sectors studied in this chapter displays an employment expansion path that conforms to the profit cycle model, although several have peaked only recently and perhaps not permanently. In each postinnovative case, output and employment growth patterns diverged, confirming that the latter was a better indicator of sectoral status and behavior than output. All exhibited the expected structural characteristics: firm entry and exit, concentration, and occupational composition. Only in the case of pharmaceuticals, where superprofits from the innovation of some patent-protected drugs overlap with monopoly profits from market power in other drug lines, did a sector display features from stage II superimposed on stage IVa.

All of the sectors show geographical agglomeration and dispersion tendencies corresponding to profit cycle stage status. All five clustered around an innovative location in their early stages of commercialization: pharmaceuticals in the New York-Philadelphia corridor, autos in Detroit, brewing in Milwaukee, apparel in the New York metropolitan area, and shoes near Boston. In the two mature sectors in which oligopoly never appeared—apparel and shoes— dispersal occurred soon after innovation subsided, aided in the case of shoes by certain practices of a monopolistic supplier, United Shoe Machinery. These two sectors were and are increasingly drawn to low-wage sites in the sunbelt.

In the other three sectors the emergence of strong market power and the leadership of a few corporations reinforced the role of the agglomerative center in expansionary periods, in some cases because of output restriction and spatially biased pricing systems, as in autos, and in all cases because the management of markets (advertising, distribution, product differentiation, interfirm cooperation, political lobbying) favored a centralized location with disproportionate numbers of professional and technical and managerial workers. In the case of pharmaceuticals, continued product innovation also contributed to centripetal tendencies, while in autos the design changes forced by the successful foreign innovation of down-sized cars has recently reinforced activity in Detroit. When oligopolies have experienced profit squeezes, as in autos and brewing, they have been quick to disperse, although in both cases market extension through advertising practices has also fed into decentralization.

The desire to evade organized labor was a major dispersing force in all cases but pharmaceuticals. But even in drugs, routine production runs are being moved to Third World countries where they are a much-heralded part of international development strategies. Apparel, autos, and shoes face stiff import competition, which hastens their search for cheap and docile labor and, in the case of autos, for international sites for production and reimportation. In autos unions have begun resisting spatial movement as a corporate strategy, demanding that workers in core regions like Detroit not bear the entire brunt of plant closings. In apparel the international labor force has come to the United States rather than vice-versa; in this sector recent dramatic employment gains are almost entirely ascribable to Latino and Asian women working in areas like Los Angeles in sweatshops or at home.

11   The Resource-Oriented Sectors

The resource-oriented sectors comprise those industries whose location is closely tied to one or more critical natural inputs whose availability is unevenly distributed across the earth. Five sectors are studied in depth in this chapter: fish processing, wineries, soybean oil mills, cigarettes, and sawmills.[1] All demonstrated significant profit cycle behavior. One industry, wine, demonstrated a clear pattern of recycling through a second innovative stage. Another, fish processing, was revealed on investigation to consist of three distinctive commodity types: fresh packaged, canned, and frozen fish; the last two subsectors were thus investigated separately since they were found to be in quite distinct stages of their profit cycles. Industry structure tended to be more competitive in this group than in the producer goods sectors, but large firms exist in nearly all of them and seem increasingly interested in dominating their respective markets.

Although geographical mobility was highly irregular, these industries exhibited clear propensities to move, for reasons encompassing both oligopolistic strategy and cost-cutting incentives. Most show agglomeration at early stages, followed by dispersion, with a tendency among the mature ones toward reconcentration in the later stages. Only wineries and tobacco lack straightforward spatial tendencies associated with the profit cycle. Although tobacco manufacturers moved north during the sector's most competitive stage and returned south as oligopoly structures emerged, they remain highly concentrated in a few locations. Wineries have tended to disperse fastest during innovative or growth eras, defying profit cycle logic.

The case studies permit the study of aspects of the industries not readily apparent from the data. For instance, the early emergence of a pure monopoly in the tobacco industry profoundly affected its future growth patterns. Similarly growing concentration in both sawmills and wineries appears to be reshaping these sectors.

Technological change was significant in altering the location of the fishing industry. The transformation of forestry into scientifically managed farming is anchoring the lumber industry in the South in a manner that was never possible before.

11.1   Wine Industry

The wine industry traditionally has been very significant to subregions in northern California and the Great Lakes.[2] It is also the sole example of an industry in the set that seems to have recycled clearly through profit cycle stages, experiencing three periods of distinct growth. The politics and culture of temperance explain this unusual pattern, interrupting the sector's normal expansion path. Winemaking is an industry with a dual corporate structure (and product), with large vintners producing (and popularizing) for a mass market and small vintners producing for a more exclusive market. This duality lends a distinctive character to recent expansionary performances.

The resource base in the wine industry is climate, since grapes require a predictably sunny and dry spell during maturation. As in Europe, regions specialize in wine types, corresponding to the four-season continental grapes and the two-season Mediterranean varieties. The comparable North American divide is the Rocky Mountains; regions east of the Rockies share the continental climate, while the West Coast parallels the Mediterranean. Within regions different localities grow varieties especially suited to the soil, rain, and temperature conditions. The regional distribution of wineries has been historically quite stable, and yet important shifts, openings, and closings have accompanied sequential periods of profitability.

Profit Cycles, Production, and Employment

Winemaking and its consumption as a beverage are ancient human activities. European colonists tried repeatedly to grow the continental vine, *Vitis vinifera,* on the new continent, but their efforts east of the Mississippi were defeated by a series of rots and diseases. Colonial wine drinkers had to settle for a strong-tasting variety produced from native American vines.

The poor prospects of the U.S. wine industry were dramatically altered by a catastrophe in Europe. In the mid-nineteenth century, a previously undetected New World root louse, *Phylloxenia,* traveled on some American vine roots to Europe, where it destroyed the

European grape. It became clear that this indigenous louse was responsible for the death of virtually all imported European roots. American winemakers were forced to innovate by grafting European vines onto American roots. Two additional benefits of the European disaster stimulated a U.S. industry. It created a strong export demand for the hardy midwestern native root stocks, onto which European varieties were then grafted, and it set off a stream of experienced European immigrant winemakers who brought their expertise to the American vineyards.[3]

Winemaking was slow to evolve. It took years to determine the superior vines for local soils and additional years to perfect the bottling and aging process. Yet growth, even from the earliest years, approximated a boom-bust cycle. During the mid-century boom, wineries popped up with great rapidity. In northern California, where winemaking followed the gold rush, the number of vines planted rose from 1.5 million in 1856 to 10.5 million in 1862. The state had thirty-two wineries by 1860. By the 1870s gluts were not uncommon. Furthermore periodic bouts of disease in isolated regions altered the overall supply, as in the 1880s when the root louse invaded California vines. By the 1890s, price instability from gluts and grape famines and vigorous competition had provoked the wineries to organize trade associations. The California Wine Association, for instance, initiated by the seven most prominent companies, was formed in 1894 and by 1918 controlled 84 percent of the state's wine output.

This relatively competitive, normal profit era was abruptly truncated by the passage of prohibition in 1919. Wine output fell from 43 million gallons in 1913 to 5 million between 1918 and 1932. Only ten wineries in California survived, most making sacramental wine. Vineyards were ripped out, some to be planted to the raisin grape. Some growers managed to market their fine wine grapes to the home wine industry, which expanded dramatically during the period. (Per capita consumption of wine actually went up about 60 percent during prohibition.) Wineries were dismantled, some converted to novel uses such as mushroom farming in cold, damp cellars.

Immediately after the repeal of prohibition, small wineries appeared in all former wine-producing areas. The start-up was crippled by lack of good varieties of grapes, the scarcity of trained winemakers, dried out and leaky containers, and no stocks of aged wine. From the outset dessert wines dominated the market since they could be manufactured easily from the sweet, tough-skinned

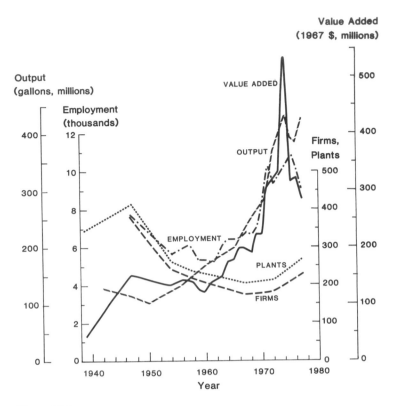

Figure 11.1
Wine industry growth, 1939-1977

grapes planted during the Great Depression. Enormous quantities of cheap, sweet wines were produced. Periodic gluts depressed wine prices, discouraging wine growers from planting higher-quality, higher-priced grapes. The 751 wineries that had started up again in 1934 dwindled to 374 by 1949. Government appropriation of vineyard output for wartime raisin procurement hastened the closure of the weaker firms. In addition the mechanization of harvesting after the war and severe downward pressure on prices resulted in a sustained postwar slump where value added languished and employment fell dramatically, even though gallons produced steadily rose (figure 11.1).[4]

A third profit cycle was set off in the mid-1960s, caused by several factors. First, better wine grapes began to be produced by maturing vines. Second, a series of protective taxes on wine and restrictions on winery location that had been set up after prohibition were eliminated or liberalized in the late 1960s and early 1970s. Third, a concerted marketing strategy by large firms, exemplified best by Gallo, which produce the lower-grade table wines, substantially shifted American tastes from hard liquor toward wine. As standardized mass-produced wines grew more popular, a market for higher-quality wines also developed, prompting the entry of a number of small, specialty wineries. The dramatic reversals in employment losses and firm attrition rates are clear from figure 11.1. This reinvigoration may have reached a peak by the mid-1970s, since after that date value added fell precipitously and employment flattened out as well.

Industry Structure

The wine sector exhibits an industry structure that conforms closely to the profit cycle model. Some degree of collusion existed in regional markets prior to prohibition, as the California Wine Association case demonstrates. After prohibition several factors conspired to ensure the dominance of large firms, at least in the mass market segment. First, growers shifted to table and raisin grape wines, which favored large-scale production. Large wineries have accounted for about two-thirds of output since 1933. Second, vintners began to integrate vertically. By 1951 at least 75 percent grew some of their own grapes, amounting to 35 percent of grape tonnage, and many of the larger wineries produced their own bottles. Third, mechanical harvesting sharpened the edge that large wineries held over the smaller ones. The number of giant wineries, those producing more than 9 million gallons per year, increased from nine in 1941 to thirty-six in 1977. Three out of four wineries existing in 1934 had closed by 1965; half of all surviving the war had disappeared by 1967 (figure 11.1).[5]

Not only did small firms fail compared to large ones, but expansions and mergers dramatically boosted the incidence of multiplant corporations (figure 11.2). Since the 1950s noncorporate family vineyards have declined as a percentage of both establishments and employment. Multiplant corporations have increased their share of jobs from 32 percent in 1954 to over 75 percent in 1977. Thus multiplant corporations with national marketing and advertising have captured the lion's share of the market. Nevertheless there has also been a revival of the small winery in the most recent boom.

Percentage
Jobs, Plants in
Multiplant Corporations

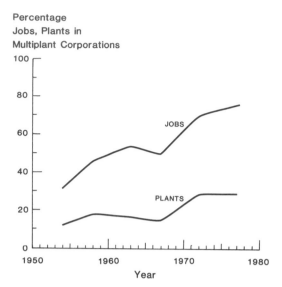

Figure 11.2
Ownership patterns in wines, 1954-1977

Concentration of market power in the wine sector has methodically increased in the postwar period (figure 11.3). The share of value added accounted for by the four largest corporations grew steadily, to over 52 percent by 1972. Even with renewed competition, the twenty top corporations maintained their control of 85 percent of the market. The wine industry is thus becoming an oligopoly.

Greater concentration in fewer corporate hands has resulted in vigorous trade organizations, which have successfully curried state support. In California, for instance, the state Wine Advisory Board has levied taxes on wine sales to finance public relations, advertising, and research. The Giannini Foundation at the University of California researched the control of vine diseases, perfection of distillation processes, engineering of temperatures for fermentation, and development of finer varieties.[6]

In the wine industry the job share of production workers has been unusually low compared to the country as a whole—only 77 percent of the U.S. average for manufacturing in 1977 (figure 11.4). The relatively low ratio is a result of both substantial quality control and a large number of individual proprietors in the business. What is more striking is the tendency for the ratio to rise during the stage III period from 1947 to 1958 and to reverse dramatically with the return of the sector to a stage II growth period. The decline since the 1960s

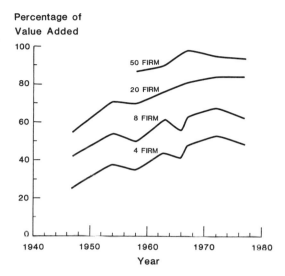

Figure 11.3
Concentration ratios in wines, 1947-1977

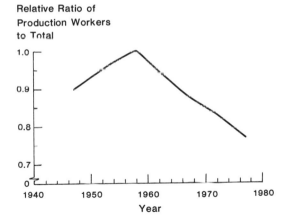

Figure 11.4
Occupational structure in wines, 1947-1977

growth era began is a function of both large marketing outlays (and the personnel required to oversee them) and the increase in small vineyards with a preponderance of nonproduction personnel. The reversal fits the profit cycle model.

Geography

Wineries are spatially much more tied to their resource base than most other sectors because they require such extraordinary horticultural conditions. Fruit orchards for the distilled members of this group are found in California, Washington, and the Great Lakes belt of Michigan, Illinois, Ohio, and upstate New York; good conditions for table wine grapes are restricted almost entirely to the Lake Erie region, California, and Washington.

Wine is the quintessential regionally differentiated industry. European varieties are known by the district where they originate. The U.S. wine industry has exhibited waves of decentralizing impulses followed by reconcentration. Nineteenth-century efforts to cultivate good wine grapes were recorded in Georgia, Tennessee, Virginia, Michigan, and Missouri. By the 1860s this eastern wine industry had gravitated toward the Lake Erie region due to disease and failure elsewhere and to the high level of innovative and experimental activity in that area. Within the Lake Erie region entire communities sprang up to service the wineries' needs for cooperage, casks, and vats. In the West winery expansion centered around the northern California region, and by 1870 California wine output exceeded that in the East. A spirited rivalry between the two major wine regions was sparked by the completion of the transcontinental railroad, which permitted the finer-tasting, European-parented western wines to undercut the heavier, pungent eastern wines. While the latter were easier to clarify and to store and were closer to the major wine market of the nation, they contained massive amounts of sugar to improve their palatability. After twenty years of relative agglomeration, notable efforts to disperse production again appeared in the 1880s, as eastern vintners experimented in Texas, Alabama, Kansas, and Pennsylvania.[7]

Prohibition decimated wine establishments and interrupted what might otherwise have been a slow but continual diffusion of the industry outward from its major centers, climate and soil permitting. New York grapes were converted into grape juice, which softened the disruption in that location, while California growers shifted to a thick-skinned, large, and high-yield grape for transcontinental shipment to the home wine market. Within California this resulted in the expansion of the San Joaquin Valley vineyards at the expense of north coast vines.

The location of wineries has not reflected the profit cycle predictions of agglomeration during innovation and dispersal thereafter. Just the opposite phenomenon prevailed, with dispersal typical of growth eras and concentration in subsequent stages. The major states increased their shares during the long 1947-1967 retrenchment, when 213 wineries closed (figure 11.5 and table 11.1). California and New York suffered the largest number of winery closings, although Illinois lost a higher percentage of its plants than did California. Fluctuations occurred in the interim. In the late 1960s boom, California registered a modest loss in its share of the nation's wineries as new states, including Washington, entered the table wines market. The share loss also could be accounted for by mergers and consolidations in larger-scale operations in California. In the subsequent period of high prices and cost cutting, California seems to be regaining its lost share. The new small wineries starting up in the 1970s clearly cluster around this major winemaking center, consistent with the agglomeration hypothesis. Thus the continued innovation in the quality wines market accounts for a persistence of agglomeration even when the sector as a whole is retrenching due to the predominance of standardized mass market wines.

The disclosure rules make it difficult to chart regional employment, but figures for California and New York, shown in table 11.2 and figure 11.5, also reveal that expected wine employment tendencies were not realized. Despite numerous winery closings, employment in the industry rose during the postwar period, with the largest absolute gains in California (3,500 workers since 1954). New York's winery jobs in 1977 were identical to those in 1947—a zero overall growth rate. The persistent rise in California's job share seems to be a result of both the concentration and success of the largest wineries there and the numerous start-ups of small specialty wineries. While rationalization in the larger wineries undoubtedly has cut jobs per unit output, employment has nevertheless risen in California (as opposed to the rest of the country) because of the sheer increase in volume and the appearance of the smaller wineries. Overwhelmingly the fact that stands out in the case of wine is the permanence of its job concentration in the California and Lake Erie regions, despite a roller-coaster expansion path.

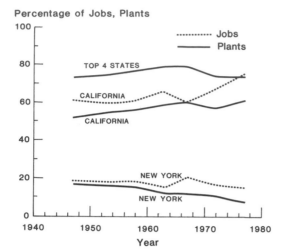

Percentage of Jobs, Plants

Figure 11.5
Geographical concentration in wines, 1947-1977

Table 11.1
State winery shares, 1947-1977

	Number of Wineries							Winery change	Percentage change
	1947	1954	1958	1963	1967	1972	1977		
New Jersey	11	10	11	12	11	9	8	− 3	−27
New York	70	43	37	27	25	23	24	− 46	−66
Illinois	6	1	4	5	3	3	2	− 4	−66
California	218	143	133	131	123	122	165	− 53	−24
United States	418	262	239	222	205	213	269	−146	−36

Source: *Census of Manufactures.*

In sum, winemaking appears to be spatially insensitive to the profit cycle because it is so highly resource tied. Climate is (at least to date) a very unreplicable aspect of land, and no conceivable amount of capital expenditure can make greenhouse grape growing competitive with Napa Valley or Finger Lakes vineyards. While some degree of agglomeration occurs during growth eras, new regions also show greater propensity to enter the competition during such periods. Clearly no marked tendency to decentralize characterizes the periods of slow growth and retrenchment.

Summary

Winemaking in the United States has an extraordinary history due to the interruption of prohibition, a massive political proscription on the legal production of the commodity. Since winemaking requires a substantial investment period, particularly in vineyards but also in fermentation, this fourteen-year hiatus largely destroyed the natural and physical capital in the sector. A substantial informal wine sector evolved, but its demands for grapes and labor had entirely different qualities and spatial implications than the preexisting industry. After repeal the wine industry was slow to recover its former preeminence, sidetracked for a time into the production of cheap, sweet dessert wines. Nevertheless, by the mid-1960s a truly innovative stage commenced, with dramatic reversals in job, value added, and firm growth. This innovative revival and its profit gains attracted new entrants whose numbers decreased the sector's trend toward concentration. During the innovative decade, the ratio of production workers to all workers fell more rapidly than in the bracketing periods, reflecting the marketing and managerial ferment of revival.

Table 11.2
State job shares in wine making, 1947-1977

	Jobs (000)							Job change	Percentage change
	1947	1954	1958	1963	1967	1972	1977		
New York	1.4	1.0	1.1	1.0	1.4	1.6	1.4	0	0
California	4.7	3.4	3.6	4.0	4.1	6.3	6.9	+2.2	+47
United States	7.7	5.7	5.9	6.1	6.8	9.4	9.2	+1.5	+19

Source: *Census of Manufactures.*

Spatially the wine industry has been and remains concentrated in the Lake Erie and California regions. During the most recent boom, winemaking has spread to regions like the Pacific Northwest, as small, experimental wineries try to cash in on the lucrative fine wines market. If anything, the industry has shown a greater tendency to agglomerate in its established centers during periods of retrenchment rather than innovation. Thus the search for better wine varieties in new locations seems to override the agglomerative impulse to share personnel, process experiments, and marketing economies during rapid growth stages.

11.2 Soybean Oil Industry

The soybean industry cultivates and processes the most outstanding example of a miracle crop in recent history. Long produced as a food and feed staple in Asia, soybeans were introduced to the United States in the 1920s. Within fifty years soybeans have become our leading agricultural export, second only to corn. The fifty-year soybean growth rate of an average 25 million additional bushels per year may never be duplicated by soybeans or any other crop in the future. Soybeans are a renewable resource-oriented sector because the arable land devoted to soybean cultivation may be transferred into other crops such as corn, grains, sunflower seeds, and cotton, and is not used up in the process.[8]

Structural and locational change in the soybean industry is proxied here by data on the soybean oil milling sector, SIC 2075 (previously SIC 2092 and 2883). This is an appropriate choice since farmers first planted soybeans on a large scale in response to the emerging commercial market for oil. Through World War II, soybean oil still accounted for over 50 percent of soybean use, although more recently the demand for soybean meal in livestock operations has topped oil demand.[9] Furthermore both oil and meal are produced jointly in the same mills, so that location of oil mills is by definition coterminous with the processing of all soybean products. The location of mills will not perfectly reflect the location of soybean cultivation, but the movements of milling capacity do reflect the spatial extension of cultivation across the country. Some mills included in the data process solely soybeans, while others, generally smaller and more southern, process cottonseed oil as well as soybean oil.

Profit Cycles, Production, and Employment

Soybean growers never enjoyed a prolonged period of superprofit associated with risking acreage on this new commodity. Farmers may have cashed in during early years, but the tremendous competition within agriculture, where many thousands of relatively small firms compete, transfers to the middlemen any excess profits from an imbalance between supply and demand. Soybean oil mills, on the other hand, were in a better position to reap abnormal profits from soybean product innovation. They could directly exploit the difference between production cost and what the market would yield, a function of the price of available substitutes such as butter, margarine, and other vegetable oils. Oligopolistic supplier firms were also in a position to reap some of the soybean farmers' initial profits; John Deere's 1929 farm machinery catalog was entitled *Soybeans for Profit*.[10] Soybean oil processing is a sector that jumped from an innovative stage directly to an oligopolistic one. Oligopoly market management smoothed out the expansion path, although the sector as a whole experienced severe short-term swings, particularly in the 1970s. Profit cycle stages, output, employment, and firm growth are displayed in figure 11.6.

Soybean output rose from a modest 4 million bushels in 1922 to 1.2 billion in 1976. Consistent with the preoccupations of a dynamic innovative sector, employment in soybean oil mills grew dramatically through the 1940s. But after 1947 superior consumer substitutes that were scarce during the war once again competed, and military needs subsided. Total real value added slumped as prices fell and did not reach wartime peaks again until the early 1960s. Employment growth was curtailed during this period, consistent with maturity and oligopoly strategy. In part the languishing of job growth behind output reflects the switch, beginning in the early 1950s, to a chemical solvent extraction process that favored larger, more mechanized plants. Sustained growth in soybean oil peaked in the late 1960s, with intensified competition from other oil seeds (cottonseed, peanuts, sunflowers, and safflower). The market for soy products has been supported largely through a concerted effort on the part of producers and the government to boost exports to Europe and Asia, which now consume more than half of all U.S. sales of soybeans, meal, and oil.

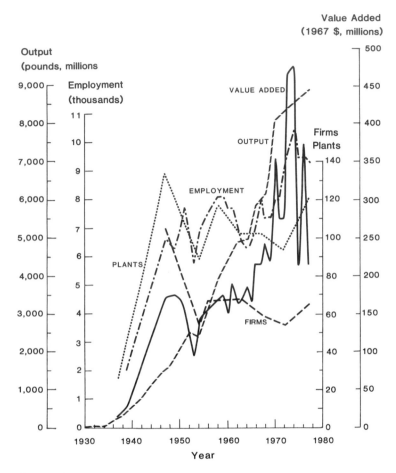

Figure 11.6
Soybean oil industry growth, 1930-1977

Industry Structure

The great additions of soybean oil capacity took place, as expected, in the period of innovation (figure 11.6). From 1939, when the figures begin, to 1947, the number of plants climbed from 36 to 133, an all-time high. With the postwar readjustment, a net of 45 plants disappeared, or 1 in 3. An industry expert characterizes the period from 1947 to 1970 as one in which 200 small, inefficient, multiproduct plants rationalized into a 130-plant complex of largely single-product operations.[11]

Processors first organized and colluded in the 1930s, largely in response to raw soybean supply problems. At that time, they adopted the so-called Peoria plan, a form of guaranteed delivered price that stabilized the market. At the same time they began lobbying for import tariffs for their nascent sector and won substantial protection in the Smoot-Hawley round.[12] Concentration was already fairly well established by 1947 when four corporations controlled almost 45 percent of oil shipments (figure 11.7). Concentration gradually became more pronounced, with rationalization greatest during periods of slow growth or adverse market circumstances. For instance, the gain in share of the four largest from 40 percent to 55 percent of oil shipments occurred entirely between 1958 to 1967, the worst years of the postwar period and the poorest in terms of employment performance. By 1977 the twenty largest companies produced almost 95 percent of soybean oil output.

The predominance of multiplant corporations in the business was already assured by the early 1950s. The multiplant firms controlled nearly 65 percent of plants and more than 80 percent of employment by 1954 (figure 11.8). Job concentration ratios have remained relatively stable since. Multiplant firms have gained in share of plants, although this gain was eroded somewhat in the mid-1970s. Single-plant firms remain relatively unimportant as employers, accounting for less than 10 percent of all jobs.

A key oligopolistic strategy in soy oils has been the recruitment of government aid. The Marshall Plan absorbed 60 percent of all soybean oil output between 1948 and 1952, and from 1954 on, the major U.S. foreign aid programs underwrote more than 50 percent of soybean product exports, permanently establishing the export ties that were to sustain the sector thereafter. Price supports for raw soybeans kept prices to processors above what the market would have brought in one out of every two years between 1957 and 1968, which

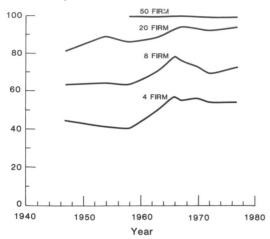

Figure 11.7
Concentration ratios in soybean oil, 1947-1977

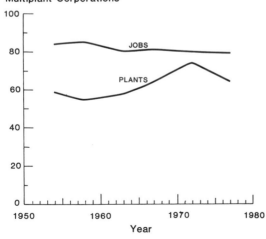

Figure 11.8
Ownership patterns in soybean oil, 1954-1977

prompted the processors to call for a free market in agricultural commodities. Significant research activities funded by the U.S. Department of Agriculture and state universities yielded superior hybrids and improved processing techniques. In addition cotton and corn policy indirectly affected decisions by farmers to plant soybeans, while the Korean war engineered a tremendous increase in export demand when Japan shifted its soybean purchases to the U.S. from China.[13]

The data on production workers as a percentage of total work force show a lower-than-average ratio throughout the innovative stage and a clear tendency for the proportion to rise over both the innovative and the competitive stages (figure 11.9). During the mid-1960s to mid-1970s employment slump, the ratio declined relatively, suggesting that production workers bore the brunt of cutbacks. By the early 1970s the ratio was consistently above the national manufacturing average. These results confirm the occupational hypothesis.

Spatial Distribution

Soybean mills were first concentrated in the cornbelt—the states of Ohio, Indiana, Illinois, and Iowa—because it was here that tremendous yield increases in corn had released rich farmlands for soybean acreage. Sporadic attempts to start up profitable soybean oil mills date from 1911 in Seattle and 1915 in North Carolina, but both failed. The center of innovation and agglomeration in processing

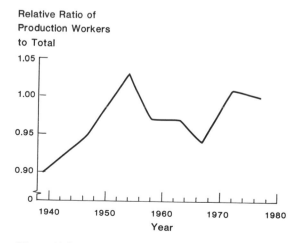

Figure 11.9
Occupational structure in soybean oil, 1939-1977

became Decatur, Illinois, where in 1922 a corn processor named Staley set up the first commercially successful mill. The four cornbelt states accounted for more than 61 percent of all plants in 1947, the end of the rapid-growth era (table 11.3). As competition heightened, transportation economies became increasingly important to processors locating new plants. Soybeans are cheaper to transport than their meal and oil successors, so that plants tend to be closer to markets than to farms. But since the transportation costs for meal are higher than for oil, mills are located nearest to major livestock centers. In the Midwest soybean growers and livestock farms are located in close proximity so that mills remain near soybean supply areas. The rate of decentralization may well have been retarded by the joint effects of output control, the Peoria plan, and the transportation rate structure of railroads, at least up to the mid-1950s.[14]

Eventually the oligopolists themselves engineered a net shift away from the Iowa core. In the postwar period the cornbelt leaders lost plants at a rate three times as great as the nation as a whole, for three reasons. First, the very large-scale, highly efficient chemical solvent processing plant was pioneered in this region, supplanting the smaller, older plant. Second, as cotton production techniques

Table 11.3
State shares in soybean oil mill plants, 1947-1977

	Number of Plants							Plant change	Percentage change
	1947	1954	1958	1963	1967	1972	1977		
Ohio	13	10	8	7	5	6	5	8	62
Indiana	10	4	4	3	5	5	7	3	30
Illinois	27	21	20	21	15	12	16	11	41
Iowa	32	20	19	18	18	16	19	13	41
Minnesota	3	6	5	5	5	5	7	+ 4	+133
Kansas	5	4	3	4	4	4	4	1	20
Missouri	3	5	5	4	3	3	3	0	0
North Carolina	5	1	3	2	3	3	3	2	40
Kentucky	4	3	3	3	2	2	2	2	50
Tennessee	3	3	7	5	8	4	5	+ 2	+ 67
Texas	4	0	1	2	1	0	0	4	100
Arkansas	2	2	5	4	5	4	5	+ 3	+133
California	1	3	12	6	7	6	7	+ 6	+600
United States	133	88	117	102	102	94	121	12	9

Source: *Census of Manufactures.*

improved radically after the war, planters converted southern cotton acreage to soybeans. By the 1970s the three southern states of Mississippi, Louisiana, and Arkansas accounted for almost 20 percent of soybeans grown. In parallel fashion many small cottonseed oil plants began to press soybean oil. Third, states like California and Minnesota reaped the rewards of research on adapting soybeans to their climates.[15] Four late starter states (Minnesota, Tennessee, Arkansas, and California) increased their share of postwar production at the expense of cornbelt states (table 11.3).

The net result of these rationalizing and centrifugal forces was a clear dispersion of productive capacity. A group of late starters— states with a collective total of less than 6 percent of plants in 1947—accounted for almost 17 percent by 1977. These states— Minnesota, Tennessee, Arkansas, and California—are fairly evenly distributed across the agricultural regions of the country. The shifting tendency seems to have passed over other nearby and earlier starter states such as North Carolina, Kansas, Kentucky, and Texas. Indeed a general dispersion of plants toward states without any previous substantial production is also indicated by the fact that the top eight states declined in share over the period, from more than 75 percent to about 59 percent (figure 11.10).

The dispersal of plant shares overstates the extent to which employment has decentralized. The largest, most efficient plants are still concentrated in the cornbelt, and Illinois and Iowa remain the states with highest incidence of mills (table 11.3). Employment data, which are very slim due to disclosure requirements, show that in 1977 Illinois still had the largest work force, followed by Iowa. Yet since mechanization has increased productivity, the jobs per gallon of oil output are fewer in this core region. In the South, where mills may be as small as 30 to 40 tons per day (compared to 1,700 tons in Iowa), soybean oil processing creates more jobs per gallon, though these jobs pay predictably lower wages.[16]

Summary

The soybean sector, the premier miracle crop of the twentieth century, has been oligopolized since before World War II and has grown consistently if fitfully throughout its history. It has displayed cycle-consistent behavior in the postwar period, increasing employment at about 2 percent per year (a rate far below output growth) but increasing concentration and consolidating jobs in fewer and larger

Percentage of Plants

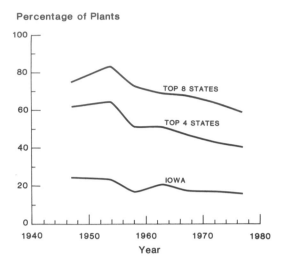

Figure 11.10
Geographical concentration in soybean oil, 1947-1977

plants. Only the conversion of southern cottonseed oil plants to soybean oil production for at least portions of the year has mitigated the trend toward concentration of employment in multiplant firms. The proportion of production workers is about average for the United States but is rising, consistent with stage IVa predictions.

Spatially the processing of soybeans has methodically diffused outward from its innovative center in Iowa and Illinois. Mills generally have been built (or converted from other oil commodities) as the locations of soybean supply and agricultural markets, largely livestock, have moved across the country. Particularly significant in this respect are the adaptation of soybean varieties to California cropland and the supplanting of cotton acreage with soybeans in the South. Soybean production clearly clustered in its midwestern heartland at the outset and subsequently has dispersed. Oligopolistic practices may have retarded dispersal from the 1930s through the mid-1950s, while innovation and management still irradiate from the older core region. While this is consistent with the predictions of the profit cycle model, the widespread suitability of soils to soybean cultivation and the ubiquity of livestock husbandry has played no small role in this dispersal. Lower labor costs also figure in, permitting smaller multiproduct southern mills to remain competitive with the large cornbelt mills.

11.3 Fish Processing Industry

The fishing industry encompasses both fishing activity and fish processing. The former is still pursued almost entirely by small entrepreneurs in coastal areas. Fish processing has taken three distinct forms: fresh, canned, and frozen fish.[17] Each segment has had distinct geographical patterns, which generally support the profit cycle hypotheses.

Profit Cycles, Output, and Jobs

Fishing has long been an important U.S. commercial activity. By 1660 Boston and Gloucester were shipping a substantial volume of codfish to European nations. Fish exports were an important contribution to colonial mercantile profits and to the development of the transportation and financial sector. Characteristic of an expanding sector, employment grew more rapidly than output (figure 11.11), up through 1900.[18] Over the last century the evolution of protein and oil substitutes has imposed natural limits on the expansion of commercial fishing. After 1900 fish became less attractive than other protein alternatives such as beef, poultry, and pork in the American diet. By 1949 civilian per capita consumption of fish was only 6.5 pounds compared to 146 pounds of meat.

Heightened competition forced greater productivity on the industry (larger trawlers, new techniques). As a result employment began to plateau around the turn of the century, even though output grew dramatically until World War II (figure 11.11). Furthermore employment was much more sensitive to cyclical fluctuations, as the 1930s experience shows.

Since the 1950s the fishing industry as a whole has experienced below-normal profitability. This substitution is counteracted by growing demand for fish meal as a feed for farm animals, so that a product shift from consumer to producer commodity is also involved. Since World War II profits in fishing have been decidely below other U.S. sectors, including the umbrella category of agriculture and forestry, as well as manufacturing. In addition to the continued popularity of meat, severe compaction from imports has cut into returns. Currently imports account for more than 60 percent of U.S. fish consumption.[19]

The profit cycles of the three basic forms of consumer fish products can be sequentially inferred from the data. Until World War I,

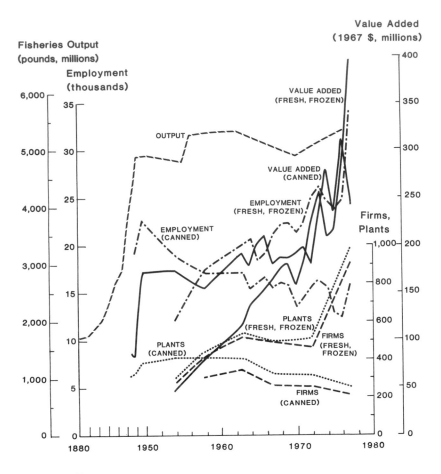

Figure 11.11
Fish processing industry growth, 1890-1977

most fish was either marketed fresh in cities near the fishing grounds or cured and sold farther inland. By the war's end canning of fish, as of other food products, began to replace fresh fish and greatly expanded the consumer market. Canned fish became ascendant by the later 1930s.

Canned fish was eclipsed by the advent of frozen fish. The freezing of fish commenced in the 1910s, when the U.S. Bureau of Fisheries transplanted French technology to New England shores, giving a Mr. Birdseye his start in the frozen food business. But it was not until the perfection of filleting in the early 1920s that transcontinental shipment became profitable and product differentiation possible.[20] Sales of frozen fish dramatically rose during the same period when canned fish sales declined persistently. Frozen fish received a further boost from the introduction of fish sticks and fish sandwiches in fast-food operations in the 1970s. This source of increased demand has reversed the tendency in the 1960s for fishing to decline as an industry. The profit cycle stages are depicted for each segment in figure 11.11. Employment in fish curing and canning peaked in 1947 and has fallen by 30 percent since that time. Jobs in frozen fish, on the other hand, have risen dramatically.

Industry Structure

The fishing industry is dominated by small firms, even on the processing end. Plant openings and closings (figure 11.11) closely parallel job growth and decline. The basic size of plant has not changed much. In canned fish plants with more than twenty employees closed down at a faster rate than smaller ones. The growing predominance of small firms holds true for the fast-growing frozen segment as well, where the larger firms fell from 46 percent to 41 percent of total plants in the same period. That there appear to be no significant economies of scale in production may stem from the small size of catch at any one site rather than the technical capabilities of fish processing.

Even in this highly fragmented industry, concentration is growing. The majority of plants in both industry segments are owned by single-plant firms. Multiplant firms, however, are far more important as employers. In canned fish almost 85 percent of jobs are in multiplant corporations, even though these account for only 38 percent of establishments (figure 11.12). This concentration has increased rapidly since the 1950s, during stage IVa, indicating that

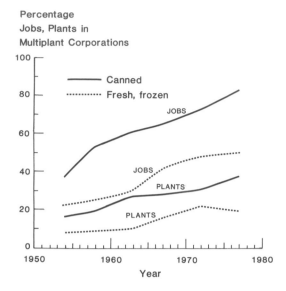

Figure 11.12
Ownership patterns in fish processing, 1954-1977

while small plants have superior survival rates, small firms do not since they lack the marketing advantage of multiplant firms. Similarly, for frozen fish the expansive growth phase has encouraged dominance by multiplant firms, whose job share grew from less than 25 percent in 1954 to 50 percent in 1980.

Growing market power is clearest in the more dynamic frozen fish sector. Concentration of control over output has declined for canned fish but increased for frozen fish (figure 11.13). Canning remains by far the more competitive sector, where the largest four firms control less than 15 percent of output, while in frozen fish they control over 50 percent. Marketing imperatives explain the persistent increase in frozen fish concentration, which is not characteristic of an innovative sector. The stage IVa decline in market power in canned fish is consistent with the hypothesis that small marginal producers may continue to ply their trade even in the face of a profit squeeze because they cannot easily shift their assets or skills to any other commodity production.

Government policy has been a central feature in the structure and fortunes of the fishing industry. Not only has it restrained the propensity to overfish by establishing catch limitations, but it has also long been engaged in promoting the fishing industry through direct subsidies. The federal Fishing Fleet Improvement Act of 1964 was aimed at reversing fleet casualties by subsidizing up to 50 percent of the construction cost for new vessels.[21]

This relatively mature industry employs disproportionate numbers of production workers (figure 11.14). While this would be expected for canned fish, it is somewhat surprising for frozen fish. The cause lies in the continued high proportion of fish handling, which requires manual labor; while machines can fillet, fish must be trimmed by hand, battered and breaded, and hand packed. But the ratio was significantly lower for the frozen category until 1963, consistent with predictions for an innovating subsector.

Geography

Fish processing has been remarkably mobile. Historically over 90 percent of fishing industry activity has been coastal, with the rest associated with the Great Lakes. While the proximity of processing facilities to fishing grounds has not changed, the type of processing has. Four different regions have dominated the industry sequentially: New England, the Middle Atlantic, the Gulf states, and the Pacific (figure 11.15).

The Northeast (New England, Middle Atlantic, and Great Lakes) accounted for over 70 percent of all fish caught in 1870, when most fish was sold fresh in urban markets. In part local custom and taste explain the prominence of this region. New Englanders have always consumed much more fish, on average, than their more western neighbors. In the late 1960's New Englanders ate 30 pounds of fresh fish per capita compared to 11 pounds per capita of both fresh and frozen fish nationwide. The demand by Catholics for fish on meatless Fridays and during Lent inflated fishing revenues by almost 20 percent.[22]

The first geographical shift moved down the coast. The northeastern region still accounted for slightly more than half of output in 1910, when the era of fresh fish began to give way to canned fish. New England's dramatic decline, which began in the late nineteenth century, was due in large part to depletion. The center of the East Coast fishing industry moved successively south, from New England and New York to the Chesapeake (Virginia and Maryland) from 1870 to 1890 and then farther south to the Gulf.[23]

The second shift went from east to west. Canned fish boosted the Far West and the Gulf states—Louisiana, California, Florida, and Texas in particular—into prominence (figure 11.15). Canning

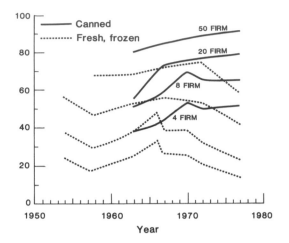

Figure 11.13
Concentration ratios in fish processing, 1954-1977

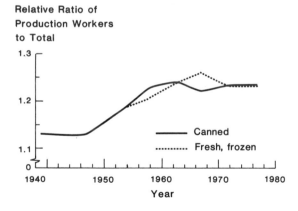

Figure 11.14
Occupational structure in fish processing, 1939-1977

Percentage Share by Region

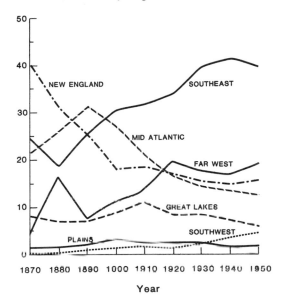

Figure 11.15
Fisheries employment by region, 1870-1950. Adapted from Perloff, et al. (1960:135, 239) The share of the Mountain region never exceeded 190.

techniques had been pioneered in both California and Florida and were easily adapted to fish. Both salmon and tuna fed the canneries of the West. In the Gulf menhaden was harvested for animal feed and oil. The fresh fish states of Maryland, Virginia, Illinois, and New Jersey suffered the biggest losses in this era. In the nineteenth century loss of a region's share of national employment did not necessarily mean displacement, since employment was still growing rapidly. But beginning in 1900 the Middle Atlantic region began to suffer net losses in fishing jobs, and whole villages were depressed. After 1910 this region was joined by communities in New England and the Great Lakes.[24]

The transportability of canned fish integrated what were previously regional markets into one national market. The Gulf and western states proved to be the most profitable producers in this national competition. By 1950 canned fish had propelled the southeast, southwest (mainly Louisiana), and western states to a control of 64 percent of the national output (figure 11.15). As might be expected with a relatively mature sector, labor problems and wage costs have been a major inducement for plants to close in older centers. White (1954), for instance, cites a series of strikes in the 1940s that kept the fishing fleet in the Boston area shut down for thirteen months over thirteen years. Imports have undercut the frozen fish market domestically because workers in nations like Canada and Iceland earn much lower wages than in New England and tend to be nonunionized. Fascinating issues of worker-entrepreneur-dealer conflict have punctuated recent history. On the West Coast and in Alaska, native American fishing rights form the basis of sometimes violent regional clashes, and in some urban areas, fishermen have fought the development of marinas that replace fishing wharf space.[25]

Since 1950 the canned fish industry has been retrenching. As the profit cycle model predicts, the industry has tended to decentralize yet more (table 11.4 and figure 11.16). The strongest producing state, Alaska, has steadily lost plant share except for a brief spurt in the mid-1960s. California has been the largest consistent loser, dropping from over 12 percent of plants in 1947 to less than 7 per-

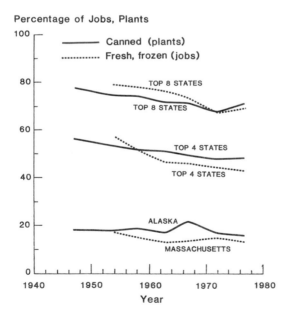

Figure 11.16
Geographical concentration in fish processing, 1947-1977. Plant share for Alaska in 1947 was estimated to be the same as in 1954.

cent in 1977. Only Virginia, Oregon, Washington, and Louisiana experienced a net increase in plant share in the period.[26]

Contrary to the decentralizing trend in canned fish, the growth of frozen fish has clearly led to an agglomeration of production around the Gulf and western states (table 11.5). The states where frozen fish was innovated registered the largest percentage job gains: Florida, Oregon, California, Washington, and Alaska. By 1967 Florida had become the single largest producer, growing from 4 percent of the segment to 15 percent in 1972. The rise in Gulf Coast sales is due in part to the discovery of new shrimp beds, as well as the growing popularity of seafood once freezing techniques solved spoilage problems.

Summary

The fish processing sector, closely allied to the activity of fishing

Table 11.4
State shares of canned and cured seafood plants, 1947-1954

State	Number of Plants							Plant change	Percentage change
	1947	1954	1958	1963	1967	1972	1977		
Massachusetts	11	12	10	11	10	10	8	− 3	−27
Maine	61	45	44	40	29	27	23	− 38	−62
New York	32	30	28	27	22	14	17	− 15	−47
New Jersey	6	6	13	14	13	13	9	+ 3	+50
Pennsylvania	3	4	3	1	⩽ 2	⩽ 3	3	0	0
Illinois	11	7	8	11	4	3	5	− 6	−55
North Carolina	8	9	5	6	8	10	8	0	0
Maryland	11	14	15	12	13	15	8	− 3	−27
Virginia	11	14	13	16	10	16	13	+ 2	+18
Mississippi	15	14	9	11	9	9	5	− 10	−67
Louisiana	35	32	34	30	23	24	23	− 12	−34
Washington	56	56	57	67	42	44	37	− 19	−34
Oregon	20	12	10	12	10	11	11	− 9	−45
California	60	40	35	24	19	17	16	− 44	−73
Alaska	84	73	76	70	67	53	40	− 44	−52
Hawaii	5	4	2	5	6	5	5	0	0
United States	470	406	411	405	320	310	255	−213	−46

Source: *Census of Manufactures.*

itself, has passed through several profit cycles associated with dramatically different commodity forms: fresh packaged, canned, and frozen fish. The contrast between the last two affords an ideal opportunity to test the profit cycle model. Both highly competitive and dominated by small firms, frozen fish has been an innovative sector for most of the postwar period, while canned fish has been a declining sector, because of the substitution of the former for the latter. Frozen fish posted all the expected job, output, and firm growth gains, while fish canning eliminated one job in five and almost one of every three firms. The top four firms in frozen fish control only 14 percent of their market, compared to 52 percent in the canning sector, although both sectors posted similar gains in the percentage of plants and workers accounted for by multiplant corporations. Perhaps because of their close substitutability—a cannery plant can be converted to a freezing plant—the ratio of production workers to total was almost identical in both, which means that frozen fish has an abnormally high rate for an innovating sector.

Table 11.5
State shares of fresh and frozen packaged fish jobs, 1954-1977

	Jobs (000)						Jobs change	Percentage change
	1954	1958	1963	1967	1972	1977		
Massachusetts	2.1	2.7	2.6	2.4	2.5	3.8	+ 1.7	+ 81
Maryland	1.6	1.8	1.9	1.7	1.1	2.2	+ 0.6	+ 38
Virginia	2.0	2.6	2.2	2.1	2.3	3.3	+ 1.3	+ 65
Georgia	1.3	2.0	2.2	2.3	1.6	2.2	+ 0.9	+ 69
Florida	0.5	1.7	2.3	2.7	3.8	4.6	+ 4.1	+ 820
Louisiana	0.9	0.5	0.9	0.6	1.0	1.5	+ 0.6	+ 67
Texas	0.7	1.6	1.9	2.5	2.3	1.3	+ 0.6	+ 86
Washington	0.6	0.9	1.1	1.0	1.4	2.1	+ 1.5	+ 250
Oregon	0.4	0.4	0.6	0.6	1.0	1.5	+ 1.1	+ 275
California	0.2	0.5	1.0	1.0	1.5	2.5	+ 2.3	+1,150
Alaska	0.1	0.2	0.3	0.8	1.2	3.0	+ 3.0	+1,000
United States	12.3	17.7	20.1	21.4	24.7	34.3	+22.1	+ 181

Source: *Census of Manufactures.*

Fish processing of both types has tended to disperse throughout the postwar period. In the case of frozen fish significant agglomeration has taken place on the Gulf and western coasts, but this fact is partly obscured by the inclusion of fresh fish, largely an East Coast phenomenon, in the figures. Dispersal is a function in both cases of complex interrelationships among international competition, fishing ground depletion, the development and marketing of new species such as shrimp, the differential wage and unionization rates of the regions, and the policies of state and federal governments.

11.4 Tobacco and Cigarette Industries

Of all the industries studied here, tobacco ranks among the most mature. Although it passed its historical apex many years ago, the industry has kept alive through tight oligopolistic control of price competition, import protection, government subsidies, and extravagant advertising campaigns that shape consumer tastes and carve out market share for individual corporations. The monopolistic practices of the industry seem to have retarded growth in the early periods by restricting output to raise prices and stretching out expansion over a relatively longer period than might otherwise have been the case. The industry's staying power was also enhanced by its successful campaign to induce consumers first to switch to cigarettes from cigars and other tobacco products and then to keep smoking despite proved health hazards. Its center of gravity has shifted from Manhattan cigar shops to North Carolina cigarette factories.[27]

Profit Cycles, Production, and Employment

The tobacco industry was a small-scale hand manufacturing operation originally. By 1840 it had become a distinct commodity production item, employing about 8,000 to 9,000 workers in small factories, 40 percent in Virginia near the older centers of tobacco production. A distinct growth and innovation stage began about 1840. By the 1880s a competitive era had set in, and trade wars broke out. Due to an extraordinary effort in trust building, by the turn of the century, the entire industry, except for cigars, was dominated by one large combine. This early and sudden appearance of monopoly has marked the history of the industry ever since.

The trust was engineered by J. B. Duke, who perceived the possibilities in the small cigarette sector. Unlike cigars, a highly skilled and labor-intensive field where a workman could go into business with a few tools and a small amount of capital, cigarette production saw machinery developed that cut labor requirements to one-tenth and introduced scale economies. By the 1880s the tiny industry already had 90 percent of its output controlled by five companies in four major locations: New York City; Rochester, New York; Durham, North Carolina; and Richmond, Virginia. A series of trade wars ensued, and by 1880 Duke had forced all the companies to combine as the American Tobacco Company, controlling 90 percent of the market. He consolidated its power by monopsonizing the tobacco machinery business, by further buy-outs, by selective price cutting (especially targeted against small firms in North Carolina and Virginia), and by gaining control of jobbers, extending it into snuff and cigars. Throughout its lifetime the trust restricted output and enjoyed profit rates estimated at 25 percent.[28]

Antitrust action in 1911 broke up the monopoly but, in order not to hurt stockholders, the federal courts created and sanctioned a three-way oligopoly. Fourteen companies were carved out of the trust, but in each market segment three or four dominated. In cigarettes three companies—American Tobacco, Liggett and Meyers, and Lorillard—continued to account for 80 percent of U.S. output, and among these, each dominated a specific type (luxury, cheap Turkish, blends). These firms, though subsequently challenged for industry leadership by three new entrants, still belong to the six-firm oligopoly that comprises the industry today.

An all-time employment high was reached in 1914 at over 150,000 workers, after which competitive pressures and cigar mechanization, partly in response to unionization, began to drive the remaining small cigar firms out of business in droves (figure 11.17). Despite hefty oligopoly profits, job levels declined precipitously. From 1919 to 1939 almost half of all tobacco industry jobs were eliminated. Between 1939 and 1954 the tobacco sector suffered the greatest percentage losses in employment of any other two-digit manufacturing industry; another 20 percent of its jobs disappeared.[29] During this stage cigarettes first started to catch on as a mass-consumed form of tobacco, and sustained and dramatic growth in cigarette output dates from the post-World War I era.

Within the tobacco industry, the cigarette sector began to outsell cigars in the 1920s. Cigarettes were easier to mass produce than cigars, so prices were cheaper on the market. Previously considered a refined, even affected form of smoking, cigarettes became a

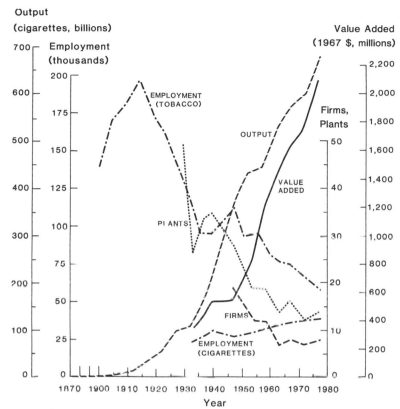

Figure 11.17
Cigarettes industry growth, 1870-1977

working-class consumption item. After the war gains in cigarette jobs began to offset declines in cigar making, although they have never been sufficient to counteract net job losses in the industry.

Ultimately a sustained profit squeeze has plagued the industry despite its market power. Since the 1970s cigarette sales have posted near-zero growth rates. An intense consumer-education campaign around health issues has succeeded in stemming the spread of smoking. No growth is expected to continue into the 1980s; industry experts predict growth rates between −0.3 percent and +0.7 percent.[30]

Industry Structure

The tobacco sector historically was transformed from a thriving small business sector to one with only six serious corporate competitors

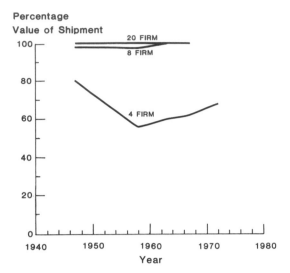

Figure 11.18
Concentration ratios in cigarettes, 1947-1977

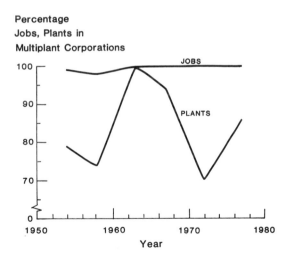

Figure 11.19
Ownership patterns in cigarettes, 1954-1977

and very large plants. As figure 11.17 shows, the decline in numbers of firms since 1904 has been catastrophic: from 16,000 to 6. Despite the increase in cigarette sales and employment, production was methodically concentrated in fewer and fewer plants until the early 1960s, when numbers stabilized at around 14.

The casualties among smaller firms were the consequence of the oligopoly created by the 1911 settlement. Since then only three new companies have made it into the ranks of the top corporations. These three—R. J. Reynolds, Philip Morris, and Brown and Williamson—proved more innovative and stronger than their predecessors. Virtually all output has been controlled by these largest six firms continually since World War II, and four firms consistently have produced more than 79 percent of all U.S. cigarettes (figure 11.18 and table 11.6). While a few single-plant corporations did survive, 99 percent of employment was concentrated within the multiplant corporations dominating the industry (figure 11.19). Price leadership was continually exercised by R. J. Reynolds, and profits, although less than under the monopolization, remained historically high for these companies among U.S. manufacturers as a whole.[31]

Since the market has not and is not expected to expand and oligopolistic discipline keeps any one firm from price cutting, competition takes the form of lavish advertising outlays. In 1980 the industry spent $800 million on brand competition; R. J. Reynolds alone spent $280 million in 1981. Competition centers on securing market

Table 11.6
Cigarette corporations' market shares, 1980

Corporation	Market share (percentage)	Sales (billions of cigarettes)
Reynolds	32.76	200.4
Philip Morris	30.78	188.3
Brown and Williamson	13.74	84.0
American	10.72	65.6
Lorillard	9.80	60.0
Liggett	2.20	13.7
Total	100.00	611.8

Source: *Business Week,* December 15, 1980.

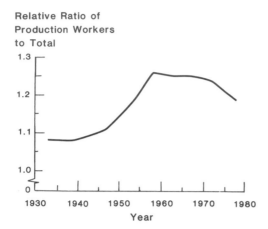

Figure 11.20
Occupational structure in cigarettes, 1933-1977

shares in successive new product lines. Since the 1970s there have
been two major rounds of new low-tar cigarettes, designed to counteract adverse publicity regarding health problems. In the 1970s
fifty-five low-tar cigarettes were introduced, of which only ten brands
survived. Currently the industry is in the throes of an intense competition over the introduction of new ultra-low-tar brands, which are
expected to rise from 8 percent of the market in 1980 to 22 percent
by 1985. Innovations tend to be marginal improvements of the product, such as new filters and more porous paper.[32]

The occupational structure of the industry confirms its stage IVa
status (figure 11.20). The ratio of production workers has been
higher than the manufacturing average throughout the postwar
period. By 1958 it was 26 percent higher than the norm. Subsequently, and corresponding to the stabilization of the cigarette oligopoly, the ratio has declined both relatively and absolutely due to
large increases in marketing and professional occupations related to
the sales effort.

Geography

The tobacco industry has become more concentrated in its late stages
of the profit cycle, as massive shop and plant closings eliminated
regions where cigar manufacture once thrived. Good data exist on
the historical location of the industry, better in fact than for the most
recent period, when geographic and firm concentration have invoked

Percentage Share by Region

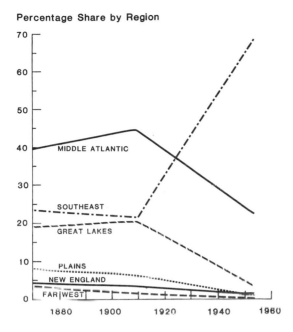

Figure 11.21
Regional shares of tobacco employment, 1870-1954. (Source: Perloff, et al., 1960:129) The Southwest and Mountain regions never registered more than 190 in any given year.

disclosure rules. The original states of tobacco manufacture—New York, New Jersey, and Pennsylvania—grew in employment share up through 1910, due mainly to labor-intensive cigar production's demand for skilled labor. The monopoly's cigarette plants, on the other hand, were spread between North and South. All other regions, with the exception of the Great Lakes group, lost share as locally oriented firms lost out to nationally made and marketed products.

In the oligopolistic period sharp reversals in this pattern occurred. The previous regional gainers lost share dramatically for the next fifty years. The locational dispersion occurring during this period propelled the southeastern region into prominence (figure 11.21). Lower wages, absence of unionization, and accessibility to tobacco seem to have been the major drawing factors accompanying the shift from cigars to cigarettes. Tobacco was an unusual case of an industry that became more, rather than less, resource oriented as its

skilled and ample labor requirements were lightened by mechanization. From 1929 to 1954 tobacco was among the most mobile of all
U.S. industries and is an outstanding example of reconcentration of
employment. While four states controlled 56.4 percent of tobacco
jobs in 1929, the same four accounted for 68.4 percent in 1954.[33]

Job losses were severe for some regions during the oligopolistic
period. From 1929 to 1954 the Middle Atlantic states lost more than
7,000 jobs (26 percent), the East-North Central region lost an equal
number (more than 67 percent), and New England lost over 1,000
jobs (57 percent). The big gainers were the East-South Central
region, with 5,000 new tobacco industry jobs, an increase of 56 percent, and the South Atlantic, which gained 33,000 jobs, up 33 percent. Kentucky was the largest and most consistent gainer
throughout the interwar period.[34]

Spatial reconcentration has occurred as the industry has faced hard
times (figure 11.22). North Carolina has been the only state to host
new plants, and its share climbed from 18 percent in 1947 to 43 percent in 1977. North Carolina's share of jobs has, however, remained
relatively stable, fluctuating between 51 percent and 46 percent over
the period. The biggest job gainer in the postwar period was Kentucky, whose employment grew from 3,800 in 1947 to a high of
9,500 in 1972 before dropping to 8,300 in 1977 (table 11.7). But
even this predominance has not proved stable; since 1963 states outside the big three have increased their share of plants from zero to
14 percent, although it is impossible to tell whether employment
shifts have followed.

Summary

Experiencing its first profit cycle stages in the nineteenth century,
tobacco is an industry that was encumbered by severe monopoly
power early on. This domination facilitated a successful campaign to
shape consumer tastes around the cigarette form of inhalation rather
than cigar smoking. Concomitantly labor needs shifted from highly
skilled and unionized cigarmakers to a highly mechanized, nonunionized, and relatively unskilled sector. Hundreds of thousands of jobs,
largely in cigarmaking, were destroyed prior to World War II. While
most tobacco subsectors were being decimated, the cigarette industry
behaved like a classic normal-plus profit sector, increasing output at a
rate below demand growth and closing plants and firms at the rate of
more than one in two.

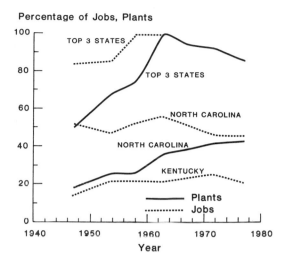

Figure 11.22
Geographical concentration in cigarettes, 1947-1977

Table 11.7
State shares of cigarette plants and jobs, 1947-1977

	Number of Plant							Plant change	Percentage change
	1947	1954	1958	1963	1967	1972	1977		
Plants									
Virginia	5	5	5	5	6	3	3	− 2	− 40
North Carolina	5	4	5	5	5	5	6	+ 1	+ 20
Kentucky	4	4	4	4	4	3	3	− 1	− 25
Rest of United States	14	6	5	0	1	1	2	−12	− 86
Jobs									
Virginia	7.7	8.3	8.7	8.7	>2.5	>2.5	>2.5	n.a.	n.a.
North Carolina	14.1	14.2	17.7	19.5	18.5	17.6	17.9	+ 3.8	+ 27.0
Kentucky	3.8	6.2	7.2	7.3	8.3	9.5	8.3	+ 4.5	+ 118.4
Other United States	2.1	1.3	.2	.1	n.a.	n.a.	n.a.	n.a.	n.a.
United States	27.7	30.0	33.8	35.6	36.6	38.1	39.0	+11.7	+ 45.9

Source: *Census of Manufactures.*

The tobacco industry in the United States initially agglomerated in the Virginia area, then centered on skilled cigar wrapping in the New York area, and then migrated back to the tobacco belt in the mid-twentieth century. This shift represents a complex response to lower labor costs, a better business climate, and the proximity to tobacco cultivation. Without the carefully engineered societal shift from cigars to cigarettes, however, the industry probably would have pursued a very different spatial path.

11.5 Lumber Milling Industry

The lumber industry presents a striking example of a resource-based industry with substantial interregional movement.[35] These movements are partly ascribable to the long-term profit cycle through which the industry has passed. In lumber profit cycle behavior is complicated by remarkable differences between regions in industry structure, caused in turn by disparate landownership patterns and differences in labor force composition. The industry has also responded to resource depletion and to abrupt changes in relative regional profitability due to product or process innovations that have accompanied the later stages of the profit cycle.

Profit Cycles, Jobs, and Output

Lumbering was an integral element in colonial production, as wood was used for housing, roads, heating, ships, and wagons. For the most part it was carried on by small operators, often farmers, for commercial sale locally or for home use. Lumbering became a relatively larger-scale operation, with wage workers housed in lumber camps, after the 1830s, when lumber became the basic material in the grand spurt of national development, city and farm building, and road construction. The industry's dramatic expansion leveled off near the end of the century as accessible stands of timber were depleted and new substances competed with wood, particularly in the building industry. Stone, brick, and reinforced concrete challenged wood as more durable, cheaper, easier to work with, and less prone to disastrous fire. High stumpage costs (a form of rent to landowners) and low labor productivity in logging and milling further hampered lumber's performance in this interindustry competition. The use of wood as a fuel, which had accounted for as much as half of all consumption in the 19th century, peaked in 1890. Per capita consumption of all lumber peaked in 1904, and absolute quantity output reached an all-time high in 1909.[36]

A highly competitive stage ensued in which rationalization and re-structuring were severe. Over the next quarter-century, annual output declined 10 percent, and job loss amounted to 23 percent, down 165,000 workers from an all-time high of 715,000 (figure 11.23). During this stage more than half of all mills closed down; by 1928 there were about 19,000 mills in place of more than 42,000 in 1909. Following the depression, when many lumber workers were employed by the Civilian Conservation Corps to reforest the nation, the fortunes of the lumber industry were not restored by World War II, unlike many other U.S. sectors.[37] Output continued to register zero growth rates, and employment fell more rapidly than before the depression. While many mills had reappeared briefly after a 1937 low, their numbers again declined precipitously, particularly from the mid-1950s on.

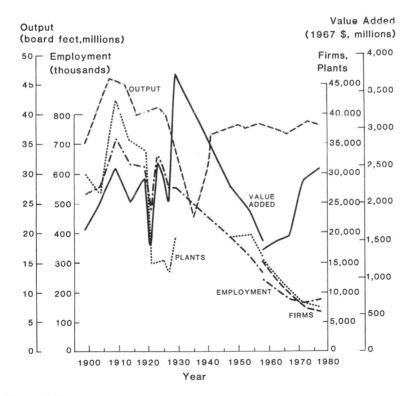

Figure 11.23
Lumber mill industry growth, 1900-1977. Industry definition changed in both 1929 and 1963.

In a reversal somewhat exceptional for a U.S. industry, the lumber industry seems to be entering an oligopolistic stage after a prolonged less-than-normal profit stage. The shift can be dated to 1972, although its origins appear in the late 1960s, and seems to be tied to the energy crisis.[38] After 1972 jobs rose by 5 percent over five years. Value added began rising dramatically in 1967 (figure 11.23), even though output performance was lethargic; however, the expansion has been highly regionally specific.

Industry Structure

From its origins and intensifying around the turn of the century, the lumber industry has been characterized by fierce competition. More than one out of every two mills closed down after 1909. The larger companies attempted to organize trade associations and to manipulate regional competition, but the labor-intensive nature of the production process, the careful crafting of decisions in the sawmill, and the fractionated patterns of landownership tended to keep economies of scale in the sector low.[39]

During the mid-century period, the industry remained dominated by small firms making marginal profits. The persistence of a below-normal-profits stage was confirmed by a leading forestry expert in 1969:

The lumber industry, which is a sick industry and, indeed, has been in ill health for a great many years, has relied rather heavily upon subsidy from its labor in the form of low wage rates. Amongst the little mills which are exceedingly prominent in this industry, family labor is common and the firm resembles, in many ways, the sub-sistence farm family. In those segments of the industry which use employed labor, there has been some tendency to gravitate toward rural areas which are depressed or which, for some other reason, offer a supply of cheap labor.[40]

Throughout this period, as figure 11.24 shows, the proportion of production workers to total employees not only was high compared to the U.S. norm but continually rose. This was in part a result of the disappearance of many small operators counted in the managerial category as their mills succumbed to intense competition.

In the past two decades, large national corporations appear to be oligopolizing the industry. The emergence of oligopoly is clear from the data on concentration; the fifty largest firms increased their share of output from 30 percent to over 50 percent in the ten years follow-

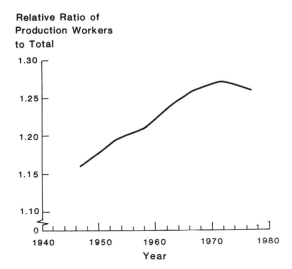

Figure 11.24
Occupational structure in lumber mills, 1947-1977

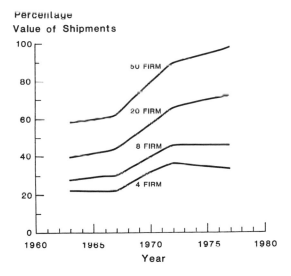

Figure 11.25
Concentration ratios in lumber milling, 1963-1977

ing 1967 (figure 11.25). Similarly the decline of the noncorporate mill accelerated in the 1970s, as corporate ownership surpassed noncorporate for the first time in 1977. By 1977 more than 55 percent of lumber mill jobs were concentrated in multiplant firms (figure 11.26). Concentration was even greater within regional markets. In California, for instance, four firms controlled the bulk of milling and processing and owned more than 50 percent of all private timber lands. Concentration seems to have been led by growing lumber company control over land, following a 1970s buying spree in which large corporations speculatively invested in forest lands in both the West and the South. By 1980 Weyerhauser owned 2.8 million acres in the South and 3.1 million in the Northwest, while Georgia-Pacific owned 2.7 million in the South and 1 million in the Northwest.[41]

A final correlate of oligopolistic status is the reversal in the most recent period of the trend toward relatively high proportions of production workers (figure 11.24). New process innovations account for this shift. The sawyer, a venerated mill figure for his ability to gauge the quality, shape, and size of a log for sawing, began to be replaced by numerical control techniques where computers read the log. New techniques for peeling smaller logs made previously marginal second-growth stands profitable. Genetic engineers have developed a square tree that grows fast and will provide the maximum board feet per acre. Product innovations, too, have favored cheaper woods, particularly plywood, pressboard, and hardboard, as substitutes for traditional lumber.[42] Both government and private corporate owners moved toward sustained-yield forest management policies. Forests can now be more accurately called tree farms, at least in some regions. The proportions of production workers do, however, remain relatively high compared to other manufacturing sectors.

Geography

Until 1840 the lumber industry was concentrated in the Northeast where the bulk of the population was housed and employed. But as the 1840s saw the opening up of the prairies and plains to homesteading farmers and the cities industrialized to provide manufactured goods for the country, the tremendous demand for lumber was met by rapacious commercial timber operations that accompanied railroad expansion into the Great Lakes region. By 1869 the Midwest was the largest regional producer of lumber, accounting for nearly half of national output.

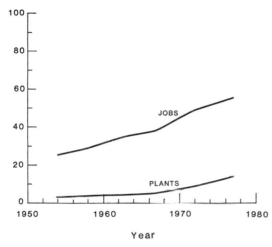

Figure 11.26
Ownership patterns in lumber milling, 1954-1977

Throughout these initial stages the lumber industry was persistently mobile, following virgin timber stands across the country (figure 11.27). Each region—Northeast, Midwest, South—sequentially experienced a dramatic increase in output, followed by a period of embattled dominance and then a precipitous decline in share of national production. With the techniques then employed, which consisted of clear-cutting and absence of any reforestation or conservation measures, depletion of the resource base was the most important locational factor, followed by the availability of rail transportation. Great Lakes exploitation preceded that of southern stands due to the destruction of southern railroads in the Civil War and the East-West orientation of transcontinental railroads. By the 1880s midwestern timber harvesting had peaked, leaving behind it the persistent unemployment of the cutover region. Southern production reached its peak in 1909 when it accounted for nearly 54 percent of total national lumber output.[43]

The dramatic ascendancy of production in the Far West was just emerging at the close of this era, having begun with the Northern Pacific Railroad's arrival in Washington in 1882. Harvesting of the magnificent California redwoods and Pacific Coast douglas fir had been stalled by the immense size of the trees and prohibitive trans-

Percentage
Share by Region

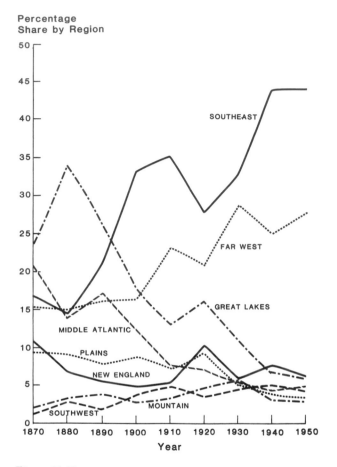

Figure 11.27
Regional shares of lumber production, 1870-1963 (Source: Perloff, et al. 1960:135, 239)

portation costs, given the tremendous distance to market and the rough mountainous terrain. The development of steam shipping and steam technology (power loaders and skidders) for use in the woods, as well as techniques for funneling railroad tracks directly into the woods, also enabled penetration of the western forests. Mills continually followed the forests, since milling takes 85 percent of the weight off the product. Some 92 percent of all sawmills were, and are today, located within seventy miles of their supply.[44]

During this period the West increased its share of output at the expense of every other region. Improved techniques had further enhanced western lumber profitability, and publicly owned western forest land was available in large, concentrated stands at relatively cheap rates. But vast differences began to differentiate western from southern timbering. Chiefly these revolved around landownership patterns and the availability of labor.

In the South landownership was divided into relatively small, individually owned parcels and worked by a southern rural black labor force. Even in 1960 73 percent of all commercially viable southern forest land was controlled by nonindustrial private owners. Small parcels discouraged the use of mechanized techniques. Furthermore lumber on this land could be harvested cheaply using black labor, which as late as the 1960s accounted for 42 percent of the southern lumber industry work force. Low wages, as in southern agriculture, were enforced by the unavailability of alternative jobs for blacks, who were assigned the heaviest, most hazardous, and largely unskilled jobs in forests and mills. Throughout this period the southern milling industry remained highly labor intensive, organized in small companies or by individual farmers, whose portable mills were nicknamed "peckerwood mills." Low wages and small parcels stunted the drive toward mechanization and higher productivity. In the West, on the other hand, wages were high and the industry highly mechanized. Unionization rates predictably differed as well, being much higher in the western timber regions than in the South.[45]

During the postwar era the depletion of the southern forest finally negated the southern low-wage differential, and the southern share of output fell rapidly. The South lost 19,000 sawmills between 1947 and 1967, with only 5,000 left at the latter date.[46] The Far West, aided by still newer techniques such as hydraulic peeling and larger machinery for mastering rugged terrain, increased its share from 41 percent in 1929 to almost 60 percent in 1958, although the sector's location within the region had steadily shifted south from an initial start in Washington.

Changes in job shares complement plant share changes. The share of employment of the nine most important southern states declined from a high of nearly 50 percent in 1947 (when they accounted for a share of output close to 40 percent) to 34 percent in 1977. Meanwhile the four states of Oregon, Washington, California, and Idaho increased their share of jobs through 1972 from 27 percent to 42 percent. While these shifts were substantial and were accompanied by absolute employment losses of greater than 15 percent for many southern states (table 11.8), the tying of lumber production to

Table 11.8
State shares in lumber mill jobs

	Number of jobs							Job change	Percentage change
	1947	1954	1958	1963	1967	1972	1977		
Maine	4.9	4.3	2.5	2.1	1.8	2.3	2.9	− 2.0	− 41
Pennsylvania	6.6	6.2	4.6	4.1	4.1	3.2	3.6	− 3.0	− 46
Wisconsin	4.1	3.4	2.5	2.0	1.5	1.5	2.4	− 1.7	− 42
Michigan	6.0	4.1	2.5	2.5	2.5	2.0	2.4	− 3.6	− 60
Tennessee	9.1	11.8	6.8	5.6	4.2	3.1	3.6	− 5.5	− 60
Virginia	17.9	15.4	11.9	9.0	6.8	5.2	5.8	− 12.1	− 68
South Carolina	10.5	10.5	8.0	5.5	5.2	5.0	4.8	− 5.7	− 54
North Carolina	22.2	19.7	16.5	12.1	8.4	7.7	8.5	− 13.7	− 62
Texas	21.5	10.9	9.1	7.3	6.9	6.7	4.3	− 17.2	− 80
Georgia	25.8	19.4	12.6	8.9	7.0	6.6	8.0	− 17.8	− 69
Louisiana	21.7	12.4	9.4	7.8	6.5	5.2	5.0	− 16.7	− 77
Arkansas	14.4	14.5	11.1	10.2	8.2	7.4	7.4	− 7.0	− 49
Alabama	31.4	19.4	14.4	10.8	9.7	7.6	8.3	− 23.1	− 74
Mississippi	20.7	12.2	9.1	7.4	6.3	5.6	6.7	− 14.0	− 67
Idaho	7.2	8.6	7.5	7.2	6.7	6.7	7.5	+ 0.3	+ 4
Washington	26.8	21.9	18.3	17.4	16.0	15.9	15.8	− 11.0	− 42
Oregon	41.3	44.3	31.7	26.4	24.6	26.8	25.1	− 16.2	− 39
California	25.4	30.8	26.1	23.5	19.6	19.9	19.4	− 6.0	− 24
United States	380.5	321.2	245.7	207.4	180.5	166.6	175.2	−205.3	− 54

Source: *Census of Manufactures*.

the forests that supply them resulted in a slight increase in the concentration of employment in the largest states (figure 11.28), a result inconsistent with the general prediction's of the profit cycle model.[47]

The recent emergence of oligopoly seems to have hastened the removal of the industry back toward its low-wage, low-cost locations. New harvesting techniques, plus a corporate commitment to cost cutting, have shifted the industry back to the South, particularly the coastal plains states, Virginia through Georgia (figure 11.28). As the western states lost about 10 percent of their share of national output in the mid-1970s, the coastal states began to increase their share. The southern gain can be attributed to a combination of factors. The climate is amenable to rapid reforestation; rainfall is even, and temperatures permit a long growing season. Logging can be carried out all year long, and the topography is relatively gentle. Southern pine forests had had a chance to regenerate since the 1930s; CCC-planted forests had come of age in the 1970s. The technical innovations favored the second- and third-generation southern forests. Perhaps even more important, southern labor earns only half the wage of western woodworkers. The average southern worker in lumbering received just over half the pay of his or her western counterpart. Such wage differentials in a still heavily labor-intensive industry gave a big push to companies to move back to the South. Georgia-Pacific

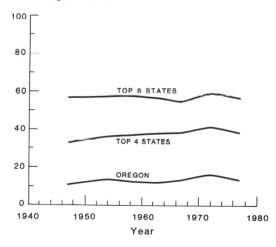

Figure 11.28
Geographical concentration in lumber milling, 1947-1977

moved its headquarters to Atlanta from Portland, Oregon.[48]

Meanwhile severe displacement hit the western lumber industry in the 1970s. The highly mechanized logging operations became prohibitively expensive in some areas as equipment costs climbed. Rail transportation rate increases placed eastern markets out of profitable reach, and in some cases western marketing was undercut by a closer, revived southern industry. New sustained-yield policies and the large Redwood National Park formed in 1968 and extended in 1978 withdrew some National Forest lands from production. Demand from the western market lagged as skyrocketing interest rates depressed housing construction. Some of the slack was taken up by Japanese imports—West Coast lumber provided 20 percent of the wood for new Japanese housing—but most of this was exported as raw logs so that sawmills remained idle.[49]

The result was the deepest depression in the western logging industry in fifty years and one that U.S. Forest Service research concluded was permanent, predicting job losses of 45 percent in western Oregon and Washington in the next twenty years. In just six months from November 1980, 7,000 of 76,000 Oregon timber industry jobs were eliminated, and Washington had lost 7 percent of its 52,000 such jobs since 1979. In the California redwoods region in 1981, only 9,464 of 23,900 workers still held full-time jobs, and 60 percent of all lumber workers were either unemployed or working only part time. Similarly only 39 of 116 coastal California sawmills were operating full time, with another 38 at reduced time.[50] Entire regions dependent primarily on the lumber industry, like Eureka, California, were experiencing one big plant closing.

Summary

The lumber industry has been a mainstay of the U.S. economy since colonial times and has been among the most mobile of sectors. Until 1905 the sector expanded dramatically; after that substitute building materials and depletion of accessible first-growth timber stands resulted in the initiation of a competitive, slower growth period. Sawmill jobs have disappeared at the rate of almost 2 percent per year since 1947, as more than 60 percent of both plants and firms closed. While still relatively competitive (the top twenty firms control only 36 percent of the market), concentration has been increasing rapidly, and oligopolization in some market segments may be commencing. As expected for a mature and profit-squeezed sector, the ratio of production to total workers is high and growing compared to the U.S. norm.

Serious regional rivalries exist in the lumber business. Although sawmills follow the availability of trees, widely disparate wage levels and unionization rates are believed to encourage migration toward southern forests. This move is reinforced by the successful development of southern tree farming, using hybrids that will grow straight and rapidly to facilitate frequent and efficient harvesting. At least one of the largest corporations has moved its headquarters from the Pacific Northwest to the South. While the larger southern sawmills flourish, communities in Oregon, California, and Washington have been devastated by plant closings that constitute large portions of their economic base.

Summary of the Resource Sectors

The resource-based sectors studied here comprise a remarkable set of distinctive experiences. All offer strong support for the profit cycle model's predictions of employment, output, firm, and establishment growth, as well as occupational structure. In each case a significant role was played by government and, in all but fish processing, by the presence of or tendency toward oligopoly. In the innovative stages these industries tended to spawn more plants and more rigorous competition, with the sole exception of frozen fish processing, whose experience may be obscured by its compilation with fresh fish. In the mature stages all showed a tendency toward plant closings and firm failure as concentration intensified.

Regionally the resource sectors conform to the profit cycle model only in the broadest historical sweep. When taken from their origins to present, all but wineries show substantial interregional movement. Tobacco and lumber are both reconcentrating in their most mature stages, while soybean and fish processing continue to decentralize. Only wineries clearly refute the spatial counterparts to the model's sequential stages. Because the draw of new vineyards overrides the magnet of agglomeration at the core during expansionary periods, the sector contradicts the model's predictions. Although the geographic tendencies of these sectors do not precisely follow changes in source and rate of profit, they do confirm tremendous mobility, generally away from initial centers of innovation.

12   Case Study Summary and Implications

The case studies presented in this book confirm that it is both possible and fruitful to use the profit cycle model in charting sectoral dynamics. It proved relatively easy to select a set of distinct yet highly disaggregated sectors for empirical investigation of the model. All but one of these sectors displayed the predicted sequential stages. In general the case studies confirm the superiority of job growth and decline as the delineator of stages. They also confirm the predicted timing of peaks in net new firm formation, job expansion, and output growth. Similarly, at least for the postwar period when a single data series can be marshaled as evidence, the case studies support the hypotheses regarding relative concentration and ownership tendencies and the changing ratio of production to total workers.

The tendency for plants and jobs to bunch up at a limited number of sites in initial stages and to disperse thereafter was generally borne out by the studies. Two difficulties, however, make the findings less compelling on this account. First, the disclosure restrictions on publication of place-based production data in the Census of Manufacturers dictated the spatial scale; even at this state level, job data were often suppressed. Second, many of the resource-oriented sectors turned out to be too spatially sensitive to one or more resource inputs to detect methodical decentralizing tendencies. These sectors were indeed highly mobile but were more likely to display life-long trails in search of new resources rather than a pattern of agglomeration followed by dispersion. The case studies yield a substantial number of cases that confirm the striking role of oligopoly in reshaping development paths and in biasing regional distribution of plant and jobs.

Two types of comparisons—temporal and cross-sectional—can be made in summarizing the case study results. First, the conclusions were based on longitudinal studies, which evaluate the model's fit over time within individual sectors. They confirm that sectors do pass through distinct eras of profitability and that a spatial pattern of agglomeration succeeded by dispersion holds in a number of cases. To the extent that profit data were available, they have been included. These results offer strong support for the model because they address the essential dimension of the project: changes in industry behavior over time.

Yet readers may feel uncomfortable with the assemblage of evidence in these studies, which was drawn from diverse industry materials and secondary sources. The treatment of industries individually makes it difficult to compare stage-specific behavior across the sample. Therefore in this chapter I draw corroborating evidence from comparisons across the set by comparing the performance of sectors in each stage for the postwar years for which Census of Manufacturers data are available. Taken together the eighteen four-digit sectors yielded twenty-four cases of identifiable stages in the postwar period.

12.1 Longitudinal Results

The studies indicate that employment is indeed a better measure of sectoral evolutionary progress than output. While the forces underlying the bell-shaped employment curves are complex rather than monocausal, the employment variable tends to exhibit a methodical historical rise and fall in all sectors studied here (except those still in initial stages). This employment pattern appears to prevail in the long run regardless of output pattern; that is, it is possible, even probable, as the model suggests, for output to continue to rise but employment to decline steadily. Increasing demand therefore does not necessarily engender more jobs. The profit squeeze may settle in on sectors that are still experiencing growth in output, an event better gauged by monitoring employment rather than sales or value-added figures. Burns (1934) erred, therefore, in proposing a product life cycle that assumed that the rise and fall of market demand for a commodity would capture the essence of industry dynamics rather than the more complicated interaction among use values, technology, oligopoly, and marketing strategies.

In all but one sector, the hypothesized sequential stages were easily identified. That exception was wineries, whose volatile history suffered because of prohibition. Wineries appear to have had three distinct expansionary periods, the last two associated with two waves of postprohibition adjustment. Four sectors—computer mainframes, pharmaceuticals, aluminum, and soybean mills—seem to have skipped over a textbook competitive stage entirely, and three others—autos, steel, and tobacco—endured such brief competitive stages that they hardly registered. In at least two cases, textiles and lumber, an oligopolistic era of normal-plus profits seems to be emerging after a period of prolonged profit squeeze. The signs of emerging oligopoly in many recent sectors, including innovative ones like semiconductors and troubled mature ones like textiles, suggest that questioning the suitability of the competitive model and developing one that highlights innovation and oligopoly power is useful.

The studies show the tendency for sectors embodying new technologies or materials to supplant others with historical regularity. Cigarettes displaced cigars; automobiles and trucks outmoded locomotives and streetcars; synthetics conquered cottons; minimills undercut integrated steel; soybean oils substituted for cottonseed and animal oils; frozen fish replaced canned. Within sectors too, new technologies create waves of change; the three generations of semiconductors are a good example. The case studies pointed out instances of intersectoral linkages that tie one sector's fortunes to another; a recent example is the depression in steel linked to the restructuring of the auto industry.

In most cases the four-digit breakdowns provided important detail that would not have been available with a larger-grained data base. In apparel, fish processing, textiles, and autos, subsectors had dramatically different growth and diffusion patterns. Auto assembly, for instance, is deployed spatially in much different patterns than are auto parts plants. In fact four-digit sectors proved too highly aggregated to detect important differences in internal products and processes in sectors like computers, steel, and pharmaceuticals. The major result is a tendency to understate the degree of concentration, both spatially and sectorally, and to overstate the stability of sectors over time. A related problem is the inability to distinguish adequately among sectors at certain junctures. An example is the classification of knit outerwear in the textile sector when it produces not only the fabric but also, simultaneously, the item of apparel. Another is the interpenetration of computer and semiconductor manufacture, at least on a firm-by-firm basis, with the prospect of the computer on a chip becoming the state-of-the-art technology.

The expectation that firm growth would peak before job growth, which in turn would peak before output expansion, was overwhelmingly confirmed by the studies. The three-peak series held for all but aluminum and wineries. In aluminum the historic monopoly of Alcoa resulted in new firm entry very late in the sector's history; in wineries sequential cycles of firm entry can be explained by the long- and short-term effects of prohibition. In recent years a reversal in the tendency for firm populations to decline can be detected in a number of industries such as apparel; however, this may be a function of a secular trend in the economy at large and not related to passage through the profit cycle.

The case studies offer preliminary evidence that employment performance is also related to the degree of oligopoly, especially in consumer goods industries. Several consumer goods sectors—notably autos and brewing—posted a second round of employment gains once successful oligopolization had been completed. Both pharmaceuticals and tobacco, which spend large sums on advertising, may be creating demand at the expense of other commodities as well. Highly concentrated sectors in both consumer and producer goods appear to exhibit smoother output and employment growth curves than their more competitive counterparts, suggesting that both classic restriction of output and risk-averting behavior lead to less extravagant competition in earlier stages and longer, more drawn out expansionary stages. Aluminum is an outstanding example, as are autos, soybean mills, and steel. Yet, and perhaps as a consequence, several of these sectors—particularly autos and steel—are suffering unusually severe retrenchment now that their oligopolistic hegemony is being eroded by commodity substitutes and import competition. Nor did the top firms in many of these oligopolistic sectors maintain their hegemony over the long run; in aluminum, tobacco, and steel, for instance, medium-sized firms consistently increased their shares of the market at the expense of the top one, two, or three.

The case studies uncovered numerous instances of sectors gaining special protection or privileges from the state. Generally these tended to be correlated with either oligopolistic power or with extensive congressional support. Ineffective antitrust prosecution engendered oligopoly in autos, steel, aluminum, and other sectors like oil not studied here. Agriculturally related sectors like wineries and soybean mills benefited from agricultural policies of import protection, export promotion, and government research and development activities. Patent laws guaranteed Alcoa and many pharmaceutical companies an absolute monopoly over markets for an extended period. Finally the auto industry enjoyed an extensive infrastructure development program—housing and highways—that made its product more essential in the consumer budget.

The longitudinal evidence on patterns of agglomeration and dispersion is quite convincing. From a household locus of production, many early commodities such as shoes, textiles, apparel, tobacco, brewing, and winemaking were concentrated in one or a few centers—Lynn, Massachusetts; Lowell and New Bedford, Massachusetts; Manhattan; Milwaukee; and New York's Finger Lakes region, respectively. Commodities innovated in the trust-building era—autos, steel, aluminum—agglomerated in centers like Detroit, Pittsburgh, and the Pacific Northwest and Tennessee River valleys. More recent entries such as computers, semiconductors, and pharmaceuticals are agglomerated around new centers such as Silicon Valley, Route 128 outside Boston, and the Philadelphia-Trenton-New York hinterland industrial triangle. A distinction must be made between resource- and labor-oriented sectors, however. Resource industries tended to agglomerate but with much greater impermanence. Once a resource became mined out, fished out, or clearcut, its exploiters would move on to find new sources, where they would often reagglomerate. Similarly the studies confirm that once a sector has passed through its major period of innovation, it tends to disperse. Almost every sector, except semiconductors, pharmaceuticals, and computers, which are still in developmental stages, showed a tendency to disperse both employment and plants away from its historic centers. This took the form of both interregional movements and shifts from metropolitan areas to rural and outlying regions. Not only would the lead region lose its share of production, but the top four and eight states generally lost shares over time. In most cases, however, these industries remained relatively unevenly distributed across space, indicating that subcenters of production, rather than total diffusion, were the product of this dispersion. The emergence of labor unions, growth of a social wage, and other indicators of a bad business climate, such as a will to limit environmental degradation and to tax businesses for social services, figure as significant centripetal forces in this process.

As in expansionary eras, the spatial migration of mature or troubled resource-oriented sectors does not closely approximate the dispersion model. Nor are the reasons for interregional shifts as clear as those that dominate in labor-oriented sectors. In fact such movement may have as much to do with the vagaries of resource depletion, technological change, and public policy as with the search for cheaper labor and a better business climate. In some cases—iron ore for instance—decentralization may not occur at all, and in others—such as lumber—reversals may occur that carry the sector back to previous locations. Yet regional differentials in taxes, wages, and environmental regulations, often stiffer in those regions where resource sectors had matured, did provoke relocation in the lumber and fishing sectors. But it must be concluded that for the resource-oriented sectors, the hypothesized spatial patterns of agglomeration, decentralization, and reconcentration are not supported strongly, even though they are frequently and abruptly reoriented spatially in a way that causes severe displacement.

It is difficult to prove that the early presence of oligopoly retards decentralization, but secondary sources for a number of sectors do support this finding for steel, autos, pharmaceuticals, soybean mills, and even, to some extent, aluminum. Furthermore the present high density of computer and electronics firms in a few locations suggests that oligopolistic competition may be playing a role in these sectors as well. When oligopolistic sectors do decentralize, they tend to produce clusters of competitive plants rather than truly dispersed capacity. In brewing and auto assembly, for instance, major corporations have tended to site their market-oriented new capacity in the same metropolitan areas, while in contrast, the decentralization of shoemaking and apparel has a much more anarchic locational pattern.

Two problems complicate the interpretation of these long-term spatial trends. First, different functions within each sector are dispersing at different rates. The disparity between auto parts and assembly locations shows this clearly. The same is true of the management, design, prototype construction, and assembly portions of semiconductor manufacture. An electronics job in Phoenix is not the same as an electronics job in Santa Clara, but this difference is not broken out in the data. Headquarters functions for a number of the sectors studied remain in the original centers even though little actual production may be going on there. For instance, steel headquarters still occupy downtown Pittsburgh even though only one open hearth furnace is currently being fired in the entire Monongahela Valley. Sometimes, in fact, the continued presence of corporate headquarters protects the home region's jobs while nearby older centers are hard hit. An example was the reinvestment in Milwaukee brewing facilities by its caucus of brewing leaders while smaller branch breweries in medium-sized midwestern towns like Duluth closed down.

Second, the interpretation of dispersal rates is complicated by extraordinary postwar growth in international market penetration. Large corporations can now disperse production to overseas sites with rapidity and ease. Because the data set is limited to U.S. job and plant locations, this phenomenon tends to understate the actual shifts. It also may imply an incorrect assessment of the sector's profitability. Corporations in that sector may be thriving from highly profitable overseas production at the same time that the domestic segment of the industry is in trouble. The data do not permit us to distinguish between jobs being displaced by foreign production by domestic corporations and those displaced by foreign-owned competitors.

12.2 Cross-Sectional Comparisons

A second means of summarizing the empirical work on profit cycles consists of comparing the behavior of all industries during a particular stage. Absence of a consistent pre-1947 data series prevents a comparison of the behavior of, say, a steel or an auto industry in its infancy with the contemporary innovative sectors. But we can examine cases of stage II, III, IVa, and IVb behavior in the postwar period to see whether there is consistent behavior across the set. The number of identifiable cases amounts to six for each of the four intermediate stages (II, III, IVa, IVb) of the profit cycle. Their SIC codes, stage dates, average annual employment growth rates, and concentration ratios are shown in table 12.1. These cases constitute a quite small sample (six apiece) in each of the four stages covered, but they do offer an opportunity to compare magnitudes and rates of change across each set.

Before investigating the findings in this way, several points about the difficulties of doing so are in order. First, precision is hampered by the fact that some stages are only partially represented by the data, especially in cases where a sector has only recently entered the stage or where the stage dates from the prewar era. Second, census bracketing dates are not always coterminous with true stage length. Third, magnitudes measured by bracketing dates may be subject to cyclical swings, which depress or inflate their values. Finally, not all events hypothesized to accompany the profit cycle stage sequence operate perfectly in tandem. Decentralization may be clearly

Table 12.1
Sector stages from case studies, 1947-1977

Stage	Sector	SIC	Years	Job growth per year	Four-firm concentration ratio[a]
II	Semiconductors	3674	1963-1977	+ 5.2	42
	Computers	3573	1967-1977	+ 6.9	44
	Pharmaceuticals	2834	1947-1977	+ 2.2	24
	Aluminum	3334	1947-1972	+ 4.3	79
	Wineries	2084	1963-1972	+ 4.9	53
	Fish, frozen	2092	1954-1977	+ 4.6	14
III	Brewing	2082	1947-1958	− 1.3	28
	Textiles, knitted	2253	1958-1977	+ 1.0	17
	Apparel, dresses	2335	1947-1972	+ 0.6	9
	Apparel, suits and coats	2337	1947-1977	+ 0.4	15
	Wineries	2084	1947-1963	− 1.4	44
	Wineries	2084	1972-1977	− 0.4	49
IVA	Soybean oil	2075	1947-1977	+ 1.2	54
	Steel	3111	1900-1958	+ 1.4	53
	Autos	3711/4	1947-1972	+ 0.6	83
	Brewing	2082	1958-1977	− 2.5	64
	Aluminum	3334	1972-1977	+ 2.5	76
	Cigarettes	2111	1947-1977	+ 1.1	84
IVB	Steel	3111	1958-1977	− 0.8	45
	Textiles, cotton	2211	1947-1977	− 3.4	39
	Apparel, dresses	2335	1972-1977	− 4.5	8
	Shoes	3144	1947-1977	− 2.4	29
	Fish, canned	2091	1947-1977	− 0.8	52
	Sawmills	2421	1947-1977	− 2.6	17

Source: *Census of Manufactures.*
a. As of end of stage period.

detected in case study times-series data as a temporal phenomenon, and yet it may occur so rapidly that its incidence bunches up in stage III, with no change detected in stage IV. Despite these problems the data demonstrate interesting parallels and discontinuities across sectors that permit us to gauge the relative strength of the model's hypothesized features.

The tendency for firm growth rates to peak before either employment or value added is shown in table 12.2. In semiconductors, computers, and frozen fish, firm and plant growth exceeded job growth. In those sectors where the fusion of oligopoly power with innovation has been identified—aluminum and pharmaceuticals—this was not the case, but only because firm growth had peaked prior to the initiation of the period. Value added tended to outpace employment growth in almost all cases across all stages; only aluminum, soybeans, and apparel showed minor and probably short-lived tendencies for job growth to outpace value added. The hypothesis that firm growth would outpace plant additions in early stages is confirmed by the last two columns, while the presumption that the average number of plants per firm would decline in later stages, as larger firms rationalized capacity faster, is not.

The hypotheses on industry structure are generally confirmed by the cross-sectional analysis; the results are shown in table 12.3. Sectors in initial stages showed clear tendencies toward increasing competition and new firm entry. While five of the six postwar innovative sectors showed a decline in four-firm ratios, five of six stage III sectors showed gains. This pattern continued through the later stages, except that the top four firms were more likely to lose their share in the most highly oligopolized stage IVa sectors (for example, steel, aluminum, and cigarettes), while the top twenty firms still tended to increase their share of market power. Contrary to expectations, concentration increased more often than not in less-than-normal profit stages, suggesting that the hypothesized small firm survival effect is not very strong, at least with respect to total output. The relatively high initial ratios found in contemporary stage II sectors like electronics, computers, and pharmaceuticals suggest that oligopoly may indeed emerge more quickly now than in the past.

Ownership patterns attest to the general tendency for multiplant firm growth to accompany movement through the profit cycle. In initial stages, despite the heightened competition that the concentration ratios indicate, multiplant corporations (MPCs) nevertheless increased their shares of both establishments and employment in half

Table 12.2
Profit cycle stage results for employment, output, and plant growth

Stage	Sector	SIC	Years	Job growth	Average annual job growth	Real value added growth	Average annual value added growth	Firm growth	Plant growth
II	Semiconductors	3674	1963–1977	102.5%	5.2%	274.0%	9.9%	484%	+409%
	Computers	3573	1967-1977	94.7	6.9	123.6	8.4	+498	+423
	Pharmaceuticals	2834	1947-1977	93.3	2.2	375.0	5.3	− 42	− 13
	Aluminum	3334	1947-1972	187.6	4.3	515.9	7.5	+300	+181
	Wineries	2084	1963-1972	54.1	4.9	113.9	8.8	n.a.	− 4
	Fish, frozen	2092	1954-1977	181.0	4.6	509.2	8.2	+235	+235
III	Brewing	2082	1947-1958	− 10.8	− 1.3	6.9	− 48	− 40	− 21
	Textiles, knitted	2253	1958-1977	20.5	1.0	60.9	2.5	− 25	+ 25
	Apparel, dresses	2335	1947-1972	16.5	0.6	21.8	0.8	+ 16	− 48
	Apparel, suits and coats	2337	1947-1977	14.3	0.4	15.1	0.5	n.a.	− 14
	Wineries	2084	1947-1963	− 20.8	− 1.4	− 0.7	− 0.04	n.a.	+ 26
	Wineries	2084	1972-1977	− 2.1	− 0.4	− 10.8	− 2.3	n.a.	

Table 12.2 (continued)

Stage	Sector	SIC	Years	Job growth	Average annual job growth	Real value added growth	Average annual value added growth	Firm growth	Plant growth
IVA	Soybeans	2075	1947-1977	44.6	1.2	26.6	0.8	-38	-9
	Steel	3111	1899-1958	-28.1	1.4	521.4	3.1	n.a.	-56
	Autos	3711/4	1947-1972	16.4	0.6	186.7	4.3	+153	+210
	Brewing	2082	1958-1977	-38.6	-2.5	11.2	0.6	-62	-50
	Aluminum	3334	1972-1977	11.7	2.2	73.4	11.6	+8	+3
	Cigarettes	2111	1947-1977	40.8	1.1	281.0	4.6	-58	-50
IVB	Steel	3111	1958-1977	-13.6	-0.8	20.7	1.0	+167	+73
	Textiles, cotton	2211	1947-1977	-64.5	-3.4	-52.8	-2.5	-49	-45
	Apparel, dresses	2335	1972-1977	-0.5	-0.5	-18.5	-4.0	+28	+11
	Shoes	3144	1947-1977	-51.5	-2.4	-20.1	-0.7	-77	-75
	Fish, canned	2091	1947-1977	-20.8	-0.8	60.6	1.6	-29	-22
	Sawmills	2421	1947-1977	-54.3	-2.6	10.3	0.3	-63	-60

Source: *Census of Manufactures.*

Table 12.3
Profit cycle stage results for concentration and ownership

Stage	Sector	Concentration ratios				Ownership share			
		Four-firm[a]	Percentage change four firm	Twenty firm[a]	Percentage change twenty firm	Percentage of plants in multi-plant firms[a]	Percentage change in share of plants in multi-plant firms	Percentage in plants in multi-plant firms[a]	Percentage change in share of jobs in multi-plant firms
II	Semiconductors	42	− 9	79	− 12	29	− 46	91	− 2
	Computers	44	− 33	71	− 23	33	− 44	89	− 6
	Pharmaceuticals	24	− 14	73	+ 14	35	+278	93	+ 21
	Aluminum	79	− 21	100	0	97	− 3	97	− 3
	Wineries	53	+ 21	68	+ 11	29	+ 71	70	+ 30
	Fish, frozen	14	− 42	42	− 25	20	+150	50	+117
III	Brewing	28	+ 33	68	+ 55	56	+ 2	78	+ 16
	Textiles, knitted	17	+143	46	+130	15	+150	51	+ 89
	Apparel, dresses	9	+ 50	18	+ 29	8	+100	26	+ 71
	Apparel, suits and coats	15	+400	31	+182	15	+650	33	+267
	Wineries	44	+ 69	76	+ 38	17	+ 42	54	+ 69
	Wineries	49	− 8	62	0	29	0	76	+ 9

Table 12.3 (continued)

Stage	Sector	Concentration ratios				Ownership share			
		Four-firm[a]	Percentage change four firm	Twenty firm[a]	Percentage change twenty firm	Percentage of plants in multi-plant firms[a]	Percentage change in share of plants in multi-plant firms	Percentage in plants in multi-plant firms[a]	Percentage change in share of of jobs in multi-plant firms
IVA	Soybeans	54	+ 23	94	+ 16	64	+ 9	79	– 6
	Steel	53	– 28	84	+ 19	31	n.a.	99	n.a.
	Autos	83	+ 48	93	+ 19	32	+ 10	96	+ 3
	Brewing	64	+129	98	+ 44	42	– 24	96	+ 23
	Aluminum	76	– 4	100	0	94	– 3	94	– 3
	Cigars	84	– 9	100	+ 1	86	+ 8	100	+ 1
IVB	Steel	45	– 15	84	0	46	– 43	99	0
	Textiles, cotton	39	+117	79	+ 61	57	+ 16	94	+ 19
	Apparel, dresses	8	– 11	19	+ 6	6	– 25	24	– 8
	Shoes	29	+ 4	56	+ 24	51	+ 96	82	+ 61
	Fish, canned	52	+ 37	75	+ 41	38	+137	83	+124
	Sawmills	17	+ 55	36	+ 70	14	+367	56	+124

Source: *Census of Manufactures*.

a. Ratios and shares computed at end point of stage period

the cases. Multiplant corporations' shares rose universally in stage III cases. In normal-plus profit stages, single-plant corporations occasionally outgrew MPCs, particularly in brewing, where small, single-plant specialty breweries popped up although without increasing their employment shares. Generally, however, ownership domination by multiplant corporations became stronger as stages progressed.

The tendency for production workers to rise as a proportion of the work force relative to all manufacturing was pronounced in almost every sector studied (table 12.4). Even cross-sectionally this variable showed strong, consistent patterns. In the innovative stage the ratio was more than 20 percent below the national average for all but aluminum and frozen fish. In stage III examples, it was above 90 percent of the national average at the most recent period's end for all but wineries. In every stage IVa case recorded, the ratio was above the national average and increasing. Similarly in every stage IVb case, the ratio was above 120 percent of the national average and increasing. Thus the discipline of competition in later profit cycle stages raised the ratio even when a significant degree of oligopoly was present.

The case studies of labor-oriented sectors showed clear support for hypothesized spatial movement in profit cycle stages, although the timing of decentralization could clearly be stalled or speeded up by the particular nature of the oligopolistic competition. The cross-sectional results are less clear, due in large part to the imperfections in the data, particularly the ill fit of bracketing years, and to the uneven timing of centripetal tendencies within different sectors (table 12.5). Some, like aluminum, tend to disperse earlier in their cycles than others, like electronics and computers. Thus for stage II, four of the six sectors had already begun to decentralize while still growing rapidly, three of the four being resource-oriented sectors. Consumer goods too decentralized faster than producer sectors in initial stages, which may reflect the fact that consumer markets are more decentralized than industrial clients; however, this difference did not hold for later stages in the cycle.[1]

Sectors immersed in competition have tended to quicken their dispersion rates, except in the resource-oriented sectors. Brewing is the only instance of an industry in which the agglomerative core, Wisconsin, managed to modernize fast enough to maintain its preeminence. Sectors in the latter stages of the profit cycle generally exhibited continued decentralization, with mature industries such as cigarettes, shoes, apparel, textiles, and sawmills demonstrating

Table 12.4
Profit cycle stage results for production to total workforce

Stage	Sector	Ratio of production workers to total[a]	Percentage change in ratio of production workers to total	Normalized ratio of production workers to total[a]	Percentage change in normalized ratio of production workers to total
II	Semiconductors	55	− 17	.79	− 23
	Computers	40	− 14	.56	− 13
	Pharmaceuticals	49	− 25	.70	− 10
	Aluminum	78	− 5	1.10	+11
	Wineries	59	− 13	.83	− 12
	Fish, frozen	86	− 7	1.23	+ 3
III	Brewing	67	− 13	.92	− 1
	Textiles, knitted	85	− 2	1.21	+ 2
	Apparel, dresses	88	− 1	1.24	+16
	Apparel, suits and coats	86	− 2	1.23	+22
	Wineries	68	− 9	.94	+ 4
	Wineries	59	0	.77	− 7
IVA	Soybeans	70	− 11	1.00	+ 5
	Steel	82	− 7[b]	1.12	+ 3[b]
	Autos	83	− 5	1.17	+13
	Brewing	70	+ 5	1.00	+ 9
	Aluminum	79	+ 1	1.13	+ 3
	Cigarettes	83	− 10	1.19	+ 7
IVB	Steel	79	− 3	1.13	+ 1
	Textiles, cotton	91	− 5	1.30	+12
	Apparel, dresses	87	− 1	1.24	0
	Shoes	87	− 5	1.21	+11
	Fish, canned	86	− 9	1.23	+ 9
	Sawmills	88	− 8	1.20	+ 9

Source: *Census of Manufactures.*
a. Ratios taken at end point of stage period. Normalization refers to the expression of the ratio as found in column three as a proportion of the national manufacturing average. Sectors with normalized ratios below 1.00 have lower shares of production workers than does manufacturing nationally; above 1.00, greater shares.
b. Computed from 1939-1958.

reconcentration in newer locations. The net results on the locational question, then, indicate that almost all nonresource-based industries pass through the hypothesized sequence but that the strength and timing of interregional shifts are not precisely predictable at any given juncture.

12.3 Distinctions among Sectoral Types

The case studies were less conclusive about the differences between resource- and labor-oriented sectors and between producer and consumer goods sectors, in large part because the sample size is so small. Nevertheless some tentative conclusions for and against hypothesized differentials for sectoral types can be drawn. Resource-based sectors were more likely in later stages to experience output growth with severe employment declines, suggesting that greater prevalence of process innovations does hold for such sectors. Production to total worker ratios were higher for resource sectors in initial stages but not in later stages, suggesting a high but diminishing degree of labor intensity. Perhaps the addition of agricultural, mining, and fishing workers to these figures would heighten this effect. The hypothesis that resource-based sectors would show less oligopoly in later stages was also contradicted by the results, which suggest that such sectors are quite likely to show concentration even when their resource base is dominated by small-scale ownership or production units (soybeans, cigarettes).

Few distinctions hypothesized between producer and consumer sectors could be confirmed or disproved by the data.[2] Contrary to expectations, the producer goods sectors in the study set demonstrated higher concentration ratios than did consumer goods in initial stages. In the later stages, however, consumer goods sectors exhibited the higher ratios on average. This is consistent with a view that suggests that consumer goods sectors have a greater tendency to develop oligopolistic structure because of their ability to manipulate consumer tastes through advertising. Further research is needed to clarify whether distinctions by sectoral type are reflected in profit cycle experience.

12.4 Reflections on Corporate Behavior and
the Profit Cycle Model

These research results permit further speculation on several broader aspects of corporate decision making, industrial change, and spatial structure. The case studies reflect a greater economy-wide tendency for oligopoly to appear at an earlier stage than was true for sectors originating in the eighteenth or nineteenth centuries. Thus some support for the view that we have entered a monopoly capitalist era in the twentieth century can be drawn from this exercise.

On the other hand, the studies also show that significant competition continues to stalk even those sectors with large corporate leaders, especially in the form of new product substitutes and international competition. Indeed, within sectors, the corporate leaders of one era are often successfully challenged by those of the next, such as GM overtaking Ford, the three newer tobacco companies overtaking American Tobacco, the constantly eroding lead of U.S. Steel, the challenge to Alcoa in aluminum. In addition the rankings of national corporate leaders also change with sectoral succession. In 1906 U.S. Steel was the nation's largest corporation. By mid-century GM had displaced the steel maker, and by the mid-1970s Exxon had outpaced GM, reflecting the successive triumphs of steel, autos, and oil.

Concentrated U.S. industries compete in a very distinctive manner, the result of political intervention into a monopoly-bent business environment at the turn of the century. The antitrust movement, a by-product of agriculturally based populism, resulted in a compromise that engendered oligopoly as the dominant U.S. capitalist organizational form. Corporations have been encouraged to exercise extraordinary political power, to restrict output, to realize normal-plus profits, and to manipulate consumer tastes. At the same time competition among the few has often sharpened the drive to increase productivity, fashion new products, install new processes, and penetrate international markets.

Finally, the case studies underscore the historical specificity of the profit cycle model.[3] Since capitalism is constantly being transformed by both technical and social events, it is not surprising that the particular way in which profits are realized should be modified over time. Four secular trends distinguish sectors with their roots in the nineteenth century from those begun more recently.

First, the prevalence of oligopoly may foreshorten and perhaps eliminate stage III, the competitive experience on which most microeconomic models of business behavior are based. Oligopoly will tend to moderate the pace of innovation in the initial stages but

Table 12.5
Profit cycle stage results for spatial change

Stage	Sector	Share of top state[a]	Percentage change in share of top state	Share of top four states[a]	Percentage change in top four states[a]	Share of top eight states[a]	Percentage change in top eight states	Share of original top four states	Percentage change in original top four states
II	Semiconductors	36	+ 44	64	− 1	84	− 4	64	− 2
	Computers	35	+ 46	58	+ 6	75	− 2	57	+ 4
	Pharmaceuticals	18	− 6	53	+ 6	75	− 2	47	−17
	Aluminum	22	− 37	48	−33	74	−26	42	−42
	Wineries	57	− 3	74	− 6	100	n.a.	74	− 6
	Fish, frozen	13	− 21	43	−24	69	−12	34	−41
III	Brewing	15	+ 7	43	− 6	64	− 4	43	− 6
	Textiles, knitted	24	− 37	63	−14	79	− 1	51	−31
	Apparel, dresses	30	− 35	62	−13	77	− 8	54	−24
	Apparel, suits and coats	25	− 52	− 57	−21	− 73	−11	− 52	−28
	Wineries	59	+ 14	79	+ 8	100	n.a.	79	+ 8
	Wineries	61	+ 7	74	0	100	n.a.	74	0

IVA	Soybean oil	16	− 33	41	− 34	59	− 21	39	− 37
	Steel	32	− 53	54	− 26	92	− 7	64	− 26
	Autos	20	− 37	51	− 21	68	− 13	50	− 22
	Brewing	11	− 27	36	− 16	56	− 13	32	− 26
	Aluminum	22	− 3	44	− 10	69	− 7	41	− 3
	Cigarettes	43	+138	86	+72	100	n.a.	96	+72
IVB	Steel	27	− 14	66	− 2	81	− 2	66	− 2
	Textiles, cotton	30	+ 6	90	+25	98	+16	90	+25
	Apparel, dresses	31	+ 1	64	+ 3	80	+ 3	53	− 3
	Shoes	16	− 22	55	+ 2	87	+11	32	− 41
	Fish, canned	16	− 11	48	− 14	71	− 8	45	− 20
	Sawmills	14	+ 31	40	+ 20	57	+ 1	33	− 1

Source: *Census of Manufactures*.

a. Share is taken at the end point of the specified period. Shares correspond to employment, except in those cases where disclosure rules permitted only plant tracking.

may lead to severe adjustment problems later. The cases of autos and steel, for instance, suggest a revised employment growth curve comparable to that drawn in figure 3.2.

Second, and associated with the first, increasing power of large corporations undoubtedly will lead to yet greater state involvement in nurturing and protecting certain sectors. New high technology firms, for instance, are trying to get state protection of their young markets from international competitors. In older, troubled sectors, a debate on renewed protection of domestic production is heating up; however, the major advocates in this case are not the indigenous corporations, as in the past, but workers and communities affected by displacement.

Third, fundamental changes in the occupational structure of the economy are taking place as mechanization and a focus on marketing augment professional, technical, managerial, and clerical and sales jobs at the expense of blue-collar jobs. These may reshape locational patterns if white-collar-oriented plants seek and attract workers with different types of community roots and preferences. Since the decomposition of functions in the basic production process now permits sales, management, R&D, and assembly to be located in sites remote from one another, this could imply a heightening of interregionally segregated labor.

13   Sectoral Change and Regional Development

The ideas and evidence presented in the previous chapters suggest new interpretations of development prospects for contemporary regions. In particular two common themes in the regional development literature are called into question: the prescription of development strategies for generic types of regions, classified on the basis of the maturity and competitiveness of their aggregate industrial composition, and the presumption of the stability of urban hierarchies and core-periphery distinctions. The normalcy of the boom-bust evolutionary path, the role of oligopoly power in the fates of individual regions, and the unique labor, business, and political cultures associated with individual sectors at different stages argue for a new interpretation of regional development problems and prospects.

Most participants in the growth debate have assumed relatively greater regional homogeneity across and within regions than is the case. They speak or write as if Detroit and Providence have the same generic problems. Yet from the local or regional perspective, the issue is not a preponderance of industrial versus service or postindustrial sectors but a problem of adversity in steel, rubber, iron ore, or apparel industries. Recovery from the specific dilemmas left in the wake of restructuring is often a unique project, which requires an understanding of the exiting sectors.

Across U.S. regions sectoral structure is highly differentiated. In the broadly tagged manufacturing belt, for instance, there are great variations in industrial composition. Consider the list of leading states (at least until recently) in the following sectors: Michigan in autos, Pennsylvania in steel, New York in knitwear and apparel, Massachusetts in computers, New Jersey in drugs, Maine in shoes, and Wisconsin in brewing. On a national scale Iowa dominates soybeans, Oregon lumbering, North Carolina tobacco and cotton textiles, California electronics, wine, and aircraft bodies, Alaska canned fish, and Washington aluminum. To this we could add concentrations in aircraft engines (Connecticut), rubber (Ohio), farm machinery (Illinois), iron ore (Minnesota), oil (Texas), and so on from sectors not studied here, until a highly differentiated map emerged.

It is not only that sectors have discernably different centers of gravity. Across all regions, plants are unevenly distributed so that whether they are the original sites of agglomeration or not, few subregions have much in common with their neighbors or rivals. For instance, regions of relatively recent entry have highly differentiated local configurations. Among the maturer sectors in search of cheap labor, there are great differences in the attractiveness of specific sunbelt locations. Textiles are almost entirely confined to the eastern piedmont of the Appalachians, and apparel has reconcentrated in the southern portions of California and Florida; fishing and lumbering have concentrated in regions of the interior and coastal zones, respectively. Consider, too, the regions of recent innovation. Minnesota's high technology prominence is almost entirely dependent on mainframe computers, while Silicon Valley's future probably lies in the microchip and computer software. Singularity is perhaps most characteristic of towns dominated by the resource sectors. Two mountain mining towns within fifty miles of each other that are based on copper and uranium, respectively, have very different pasts and futures. And a salmon fishery in Alaska is highly distinct from a shrimping town on the Gulf.

Since each of these sectors is at a different stage in its evolution, the experience of individual states and subregions within a larger region, say the manufacturing belt, may be correspondingly quite disparate. This is not to say that there are not similarities binding the larger regions together, only that regional displacement is a very complicated and uneven phenomenon, more closely tied to individual sectoral and spatial dynamics than to broad designations such as manufacturing versus service economies, frostbelt versus sunbelt, industrial versus postindustrial, sunrise versus sunset, high tech versus low tech. Regional development policy cannot continue to be so simplistic that it focuses on attracting high tech sectors to an Akron or a Buffalo without close attention to the fit between the type of economy left in place by the demise of previously dominant sectors and the varieties of innovative sectors on the horizon.

The geographical work on systems of cities and innovation diffusion must be amended to cope better with the complexity of contemporary experience. Across the case study set, innovation was as likely to take place in a nonurban, or at least noncentral city, location as in a historic metropolitan center. The leading-edge new technologies—electronics and computers—have taken deeper root in new locations like Santa Clara Valley and Minneapolis rather than in the older centers of New York and Boston. Although some metropolitan centers, since they provide existing pools of skilled labor, both professional and technical and production, continue to spawn high technology growth, their lead is by no means secure. Areas like Santa Clara Valley, Los Alamos, and Oak Ridge have been able to import their entire skilled labor force and are generating their own financial and administrative centers.

The evidence also suggests more generally that core and periphery models contain a rigidity not supported by historical experience. Older, prominent regions have not been able to hold their lead unchallenged. Some corporate headquarters have remained in metropolitan centers like New York, Pittsburgh, and San Francisco, but the corresponding recomposition of the local labor force has not absorbed most workers displaced from older, industrial sectors. The forces propelling newer regions toward industrial leadership, at least in terms of capitalist growth experience, are complex and not limited to a single factor such as climate, cheap labor, ample resources, or a better business climate. Studying them by the particular sectors that are either entering or leaving the region seems to be the most fruitful way of distinguishing among causal forces of past and future regional differentiation.

13.1 Capitalist Movement and Regional Obsolescence

The rise and fall of employment over time is a quite normal experience, at least for the sectors studied here. Indeed all three of the major economic paradigms—institutional, Marxist, and neoclassical—would predict this. Geographically the manifestations of this boom-bust cycle are even more striking since the combination of dispersion and automation generally results in job losses in older centers long before total employment in a sector begins to decline. Thus it is not overstating the case to contend that most regions should expect their major industries to become job losers ultimately. Hope for long-term community growth or stability thus depends on the continual recruitment of newer sectors at younger stages in their profit cycles. Yet the evidence on the locations of innovative industries does not lend great credibility to the prospects for such a strategy.

What has the evolutionary cycle of individual industries meant for the communities involved? It is not difficult to find numerous examples of regions and communities where one or several related industries have had a dominating role in local development patterns. Agricultural regions are among the most outstanding examples. The poverty of the Tennessee Valley region in the 1930s was due in large part to the land-eroding agricultural practices of previous decades and the movement of agricultural capital farther to the west. The TVA project, one of the two most important regional development programs in U.S. history, attempted to make this depressed agricultural region attractive to new sectors, particularly manufacturing.

The valley was not the only region whose history was dominated by the prominence and restructuring of agriculture. The extraordinary rate of out-migration from rural counties from the 1930s to the 1960s portrayed dramatically how one sector's fortunes can profoundly shape demographic patterns. Agriculture is a somewhat unusual sector in that government aid in the form of both research and price supports has impeded corporate consolidation while simultaneously facilitating an extraordinary automation that has displaced many small farmers and farmworkers.[1] The inability of rural areas and small towns that had served as agricultural supply centers to recover from this restructuring is cogent proof of the ways in which one sector may tailor land uses, settlement patterns, labor force skills, and even cultural life to its needs and in ways that leave the area unattractive to job growth sectors in subsequent periods. This has been the legacy of an agricultural sector that remains vigorously competitive internationally, again proving that output expansion and the viability of larger operations is not synonymous with community stability and job maintenance.

In consumer goods a number of regions have formed their economies around a sector and then suffered from its exit. New England towns like Lynn, Massachusetts, specialized in early standardized commodities like shoes, displacing many small-town custom shoemakers in the process. Lynn drew around its town center more than a hundred shoe machine makers as well as dozens of shoe companies and for a short period at the end of the nineteenth century was the center of innovative ferment and competition. Subsequently a long period of dispersion of capacity to new centers like Chicago and St. Louis and then to more rural areas like Kentucky left increasing numbers of shoe workers idle as the older Lynn plants closed down.[2]

The history of midtown Manhattan illustrates the normalcy of a boom-bust trajectory in apparel. Once a bustling center of design, garment making, and wholesaling, "New York" once connoted the fashion center of the Western Hemisphere and the only respectable rival of Paris. By the 1950s midtown Manhattan hosted very little cutting or sewing. Old lofts where immigrant women had stitched clothing and organized the Ladies International Garment Workers Union were left empty and eventually converted into housing for artists. From 1950 to 1981 New York City lost 200,000 workers in apparel and textiles.[3]

Nor is it simply nondurable goods, often more labor intensive than consumer durables, that exhibit a normal tendency to desert regions of origin. Detroit and other automaking centers in the Midwest have suffered serious job losses. Southern cities that became the recipients of plants fleeing from more northerly locations in the 1950s and 1960s sometimes have found the tenure of the new entrants to be short-lived. In Memphis, for instance, an RCA color television plant that arrived there in 1966 from Indiana was closed by 1971 as production was again relocated to Taiwan.[4]

The producer goods sectors similarly have carried certain regions and towns along with them on their profit cycle trajectories. The New England region, for instance, has suffered textile-related job loss and community viability problems. In textiles a series of regional displacements can be charted within that larger region. In the early days small towns cropped up around the water-driven mills. When mill owners began to build elsewhere to avoid the militancy of women workers and to take advantage of steam power, these small towns saw their dormitories empty out and their local service sectors depressed. The relocated industry, in places like New Bedford, dominated local employment for the next eighty years (1850-1930). In the late 1920s cotton manufacturing still accounted for more than 80 percent of all capital invested in New Bedford factories and for 75 percent of the value of manufacturing output. Once the pull of cheap southern labor began to close down New Bedford's mills, there was little to take their place as a major employer. Indeed during the depression, New Bedford's unemployment rate was double that of the United States; one of every three workers was unemployed.[5] As late as the 1970s unemployment from the decline of textiles and related sectors was so high that in some New England towns, some policymakers were counseling inducements to out-migration as the preferred local economic development strategy.

Farm machinery is another example of a sector with an extraordinary impact on individual communities. In 1982 two cities—one in Ohio and one in Indiana—struggled to convince International Harvester to close down its other plant during the most recent profit squeeze. Each came up with more than $30 million in subsidies, tax abatements, workers' concessions, and so on because the shutdown consequences were so highly feared. In the end the corporation closed the older of the two plants but by pitting the two towns against each other had garnered significant community and worker concessions.

Resource sectors provide the textbook case of the normalcy of interregional migration and associated community displacement. The second major U.S. regional program, the Appalachian Regional Commission, was directed at a region whose adversities were the legacy of its specialization in coal and the mechanization and decline of that sector.[6] In the West the ubiquitous ghost town is the tombstone of this history. Mining often prompts the planting of communities where no other form of commodity production is profitable; total depopulation is the ultimate consequence of mineral development. The hard-rock mining communities of the West are perhaps the best examples, and by no means an event of the past. The hard-pressed copper industry, for instance, recently closed down mines that were the mainstay of both small and large communities. On Christmas day 1977 Anaconda Copper Company closed down its Weed Heights Mine in Yerington, Nevada, eliminating 450 jobs that formed one-third of the local economy. The same company recently closed the remainder of its historic copper mining operations in Butte, Montana, which had also been its corporate headquarters.[7] Uranium, lead, silver, gold, molybdenum, and other precious metals have left other communities in similar straits.

Iron mining in northern Minnesota is a similar case. In the early decades of the century Mesabi Range mines were so productive, and miners so well organized, that the Hibbing town hall was built of marble and the schools were among the best in the state. By the late 1950s deposits of high-grade ore had begun to be depleted. The University of Minnesota, through extensive R&D efforts, and the state legislature, through two rounds of extraordinary tax breaks, managed to promote a new round of innovation based on taconite, a low-grade ore that is crushed and reformed into pellets.[8] For another twenty years production was revived, although with far fewer jobs than in earlier decades and with locational shifts that required the construction of several new towns despite the excess housing capacity in older ones. The depression in steel, however, in part a product of the rise of plastics and aluminum, ricocheted back into iron mining so severely that some towns had unemployment rates of 85 percent in the summer of 1982.

Communities in forested regions are often the historical creatures of the timber industry. Certainly at least two major regions—the Great Lakes cutover and the Pacific Northwest—stand out as hosts of a vigorous lumbering trade followed by long-term economic decline. The cutover is a vast area of northern Michigan, Wisconsin, and Minnesota where rapid clear-cutting of white pine in the period from 1880 to 1920 abandoned the marshy, agriculturally unproductive soil to alder and willow swamps.[9] The coastal range redwood and douglas fir lumbering counties of California and farther north are the contemporary counterparts.[10]

It would be easy to extend this list to hundreds of other communities. The point is that the rise and decline of a region's economic base are predictable developmental events. This is not to say that all communities are equally vulnerable to the passage of industries through profit cycles. Clearly some regions are more dependent on individual sectors than others, an observation amply documented in the diversification literature. The long-term development potential of any community or region does appear to depend on its ability to attract newer sectors to supplant job losses in the older ones. Two final observations may be made about the contemporary prospects for succeeding at this task.

First, if the inferences of the previous chapter about the apparent acceleration of sectoral progression through the profit cycle are correct, then the problems of community adjustment will become even more severe. Initial developmental pressures for alterations in land uses, prompt provision of required infrastructure, and special subsidies for infant industries will intensify. At the same time the useful lifetime of a particular site to a firm or sector may shorten so that the community's ability to finance long-term capital expenditures associated with growth will become increasingly problematic. When managers do decide to close down a facility, they will do so with a rapidity that may catch workers, small businesses, and local governments with major liabilities on their hands. Increasingly entire communities, with their housing stocks, streets, public buildings, culture, and lives, will be scrapped in tandem with private relocation decisions. This has happened in agricultural towns over the past century; now we may witness the same fate for industrial towns, cities, and entire regions. The acceleration in spatial movement may make the transition from one set of basic activities to another even more difficult for communities facing the prospect.

Second, the movement of capital from one region to another is in large part a response to the maturation of the relationship between capital and labor. Sectors late in their profit cycle do try to flee the historically evolved social contract between the two, often manifested in the institutions of regularized bargaining over wages and work conditions, a publicly guaranteed level of unemployment compensation and welfare funding, and regulations preserving a decent living environment by restricting the degradation of air, land, and water quality. One can even argue that the appearance of new sectors in locations far from the original centers of industrial development is due to the fact that entrepreneurs are now preoccupied with issues of labor discipline and are adamant about the creation of working conditions that will obviate unions. As long as firms can find cheaper, more tractable labor at new sites, they will try to move production in that direction, despite the fact that plants may be profitable and workers highly productive in the older areas. The ability of older industrial regions to attract new business under these conditions is in doubt.

13.2 Role of Oligopoly in Regional Development

These developmental problems may be compounded by the presence of oligopoly in one or more sectors. The region that hosts the core of an oligopolistic industry may appear to enjoy a prolonged period of prosperity but may evolve a relatively nondiversified local economy with great vulnerability to the inevitable restructuring in that sector. Regions that host branch plants of the same oligopoly may find their own capacity underdeveloped, particularly with respect to supplier sectors. Overall strong spatially concentrated oligopolies may lend an excessive degree of regional differentiation to a national economy, which may become particularly dangerous during severe recessions.

Certain regions have become the home ports of individual oligopolies over the past century. The most obvious examples are Detroit (autos) and Pittsburgh (steel); others are Akron (tires), Minneapolis (flour milling), Milwaukee (brewing), Battle Creek (cereals), and

Silicon Valley (semiconductors). The spatial clustering of the lead corporations in these centers means that they come to occupy the center stage of these local economies and discourage entrepreneurs in unrelated sectors, for several reasons.[11]

First, members of the area labor force, whether entrepreneurial or production workers, may come to regard a job in this industry as preferable to other jobs. The local business culture will tend to be dominated by the management of these industries, so that for entrepreneurs, status in the community is defined by place in the hierarchy of firms. For production workers the oligopolistic industry will most likely offer better paying and more stable jobs than other sectors. This lure will be even greater if workers have successfully organized a union, as is generally the case in these regions. Indeed the greater-than-normal profits of these sectors tend to breed successful unions since the firms' ability to pay presumably is higher than it would be in a more competitive sector.

The orientation of the labor force toward the dominant industry will tend to restrict its availability to other employers. Especially at peaks of the business cycle, workers can be expected to respond first to job openings in the oligopolistic sector and may desert other employers to get a foot in the door. Other employers considering the region as one of several alternative sites will be loathe to shoulder this special difficulty in procuring workers. In addition, if the preeminence of a single sector is accompanied by rotational shift work, then the average incidence of moonlighting and working spouses will be lower, further restricting the labor pool. Chinitz (1960) argued that the labor force participation rates of women in both Detroit and Pittsburgh were far below those in metropolitan areas of comparable size, and he attributed this fact to the necessity of wives to cope with rotating shifts.

The preoccupation of entrepreneurs with events in the dominant industry will tend to starve the rest of the economy of innovative leadership. As Abernathy (1978) has argued, the maturation of the auto industry bred a shift from innovative activities toward those that enhanced productivity. Engineers become preoccupied with design changes, especially because of the importance of nonprice competition, and with perfecting the production process. Innovative ideas for unrelated products will be unlikely to surface in this kind of environment. In addition, capital for financing small, innovative sectors may be even scarcer in the oligopolistic center since corporate leaders are more likely to retain their earnings and transfer them directly to branch operations in other regions rather than deposit them in local banks and other financial institutions. In these circumstances entrepreneurs with a better idea may gravitate to a more wide-open regional economy for moral and financial support.

Finally, the social and economic prominence of the oligopoly's corporate leadership will tend to distort local political culture. Since the health of the regional economy is dependent on the profitability of the leading sector, a political environment favorable to the latter will prevail, even if corporate heads do not take an active role in local politics. In most cases, however, they do participate, ensuring that the problems of that industry are kept at the top of the agenda before city hall, the county board of supervisors, and the state capitol. Political scientists have confirmed that community decision making is more pluralistic when its economy is more diversified.[12] Fears of lack of access to political power may further deter entrepreneurs from other sectors from setting up shop. There are even documented instances of leadership in one sector denying access to others. In Greensboro, North Carolina, for instance, local textile mill owners successfully defeated a zoning change before the city council that would have permitted a northern employer in an unrelated sector to build a plant. They feared that the firm, which was highly unionized at other locations, would permit a union to form, raising area-wide wages and encouraging mill workers to organize.

Under these circumstances the weight of the oligopolistic sector may stunt the diversification of the regional economy. A relative shortage of labor, entrepreneurship, and capital may discourage unrelated sectors from setting up shop in the region. At first glance this might seem to be countervailed by the fact that supplier and client sectors may also gravitate toward this center. For instance, auto parts production, much of which is carried out by small firms, is highly concentrated in the Detroit area, even more so than is contemporary auto assembly. But although this is true, it does not lessen the area's dependency on the automobile since the fortunes of these related sectors will be closely linked to that of the oligopolized sector. Symptomatic of the identity of entire metropolitan areas with a single dominant and oligopolistic industry is the frequency with which major league teams bear the names of that industry — Milwaukee Brewers, Minneapolis Millers, Detroit Pistons, Pittsburgh Steelers, Houston Oilers.

A corollary of oligolistic overconcentration and host region underdiversification is the conspicuous absence of the oligopolized sector in neighboring regions. Regions that under competitive conditions might have hosted a branch plant or a new entrant will be neglected, which implies that these regions will be relatively less diversified than they might otherwise have been. The steel industry provides a distressing example of this tendency. The absence of a cost-efficient integrated steel works is a permanent testament to the underdevelopment of a West Coast steel industry. Others have made a similar argument with respect to the stunting of the Alabama steel sector. The detection of this phenomenon in other sectors lay beyond the boundaries of this research effort, but it is not unreasonable to assume that a similar pattern has prevailed in other sectors.

When a profit squeeze does strike an oligopolistic sector, the size and financial power of its leading corporations will afford them the means to restructure rapidly. They will be able to move resources out of the region through both intersectoral transfers of capital and through interregional relocation of production. Examples of the former strategy are the purported milking of Youngstown Sheet and Tube by its new conglomerate owners to finance new ventures in transportation and chemicals and U.S. Steel's use of recent retained earnings to purchase Marathon Oil Company. An example of the latter is Ford's decision to produce all engines for its North American market in Mexico. The consequences for the Detroit and Pittsburgh-Youngstown areas are severe. The restructuring has closed scores of auto assembly and parts plants in the former and over 50 percent of the steel-making capacity in the latter, all within the span of a few years. The primacy of these sectors in the respective local economies, combined with their role in discouraging regional diversification over the decades, has meant that unemployment and economic dislocation have been even more severe here than the adjustment problems of the garment district in New York or a textile town in New England.

This dramatic restructuring does not benefit the peripheral regions whose economies have been relatively neglected by these sectors. The time is long past when the attractive alternative to home base production of auto parts was Los Angeles or Kansas City. Many auto parts can now be more cheaply produced, including shipping charges, overseas than domestically. Restructuring decisions thus frequently involve leapfrogging the newer regions for entirely foreign production sites. The West Coast steel market is now almost entirely served by Asian mills.

Ironically the underdevelopment of regions peripheral to the original centers of oligopolistic gravity has been mitigated somewhat recently by new entrants in each sector, the same ones whose arrival has unsettled the prevailing configurations of market power. Michelin, for instance, the successful French challenger to the U.S. tire industry, set up its first plant in the South. A German company set up one of the original steel minimills in Georgetown, South Carolina. Volkswagen located its first assembly plant in western Pennsylvania. And there are glimmerings that the decisions by foreign firms to start up domestic production in the United States may also countervail the pace of plant closings in the older centers. Datsun has expressed interest in a Detroit plant. In a yet more startling harbinger of things to come, Toyota and GM in 1983 announced plans to reopen GM's Fremont, California, assembly plant as a joint venture.

The differences in contemporary adjustment experience between the Northeast and the Midwest may stem from the differential degree of oligopolistic industrial structure in each region's economic base. The Northeast, whose industrial structure was formed in the competitive era of the mid-nineteenth century, experienced the worst of its restructuring about five years ahead of the Midwest, peaking approximately in the mid-1970s. The timing of its crisis suggests that its relatively nonoligopolistic sectors (textiles, apparel, shoes) had little protection from the onslaught of new forms of competition. Its cities have been relatively more diversified and less dependent on any one sector so that the recycling of its resources, especially labor power, into new production activities was not as abrupt a process as in the Midwest. In the Midwest the worst of the restructuring crisis is perhaps yet to come. Beginning in about 1980 plant closings and unemployment accelerated in several basic sectors like autos and steel, reaching proportions much higher than they had farther east a few years before. Recovery promised to be even more difficult because the legacy of single industry dominance acted as a repellant discouraging new forms of economic activity.

13.3 Profit Cycles and Regional Structure

The evolutionary status of one or more sectors will play an important role in the structure of the region's political culture. Three important features stand out: the way in which a sector's age affects the labor force composition of the region, the size and diversity of the local business community, and the immediate planning issues and dilemmas that confront the region.[13]

The composition of the regional work force will be closely related to the maturation of dominant sectors. Regions with a predominance of youthful innovative sectors will have much higher proportions of professional and technical workers than other regions. Large numbers of these workers may be recent migrants, recruited by the industry from other regions or from the area's better universities. Relatively absent in this type of region will be a large production work force, and those who do work there will tend not to be organized. Silicon Valley, for instance, has a much lower than average proportion of production workers, most of whom are are Latina and Asian women, many of whom cannot even converse with each other.

Regions with a more mature sectoral structure will tend to have relatively low proportions of professional and technical workers. Those who do work in local industries will be involved with management, sales, worker discipline, and efforts to streamline the production process rather than with innovation and institution building. The regional work force will contain large concentrations of production workers, who will tend to be organized across ethnic, race, and gender lines and be fairly visible in regional politics. A much greater consciousness of management versus worker class lines will characterize these regions (the company person versus the union person), and intraregional residential segregation will reinforce these distinctions. Regions where older sectors are recent in-migrants will tend to have similar labor force structures, though less cohesive and more divided among race and ethnic lines. Examples are the divisive force of racism in the Old South and of language, culture, and bigotry in Florida and the Southwest.

Similarly the composition of the business community will vary substantially across these types of region. In the innovative regions the relatively widespread entrepreneurship in newer sectors will tend to breed a new type of local businessperson who may have a very different outlook from that of the traditional business community. In Silicon Valley, for example, the leaders of the new electronics and other high tech companies have formed the Santa Clara County Manufacturers Group, which is careful to distinguish itself from the older chamber of commerce. These indigenous entrepreneurs are more likely to favor a strong leadership role at the local level in ensuring the appropriate conditions for continued innovative preeminence, conditions that may not be synonymous with the traditional boosterism of the chamber. For instance, the former may favor industrial development while the latter may be more concerned with residential growth.

In regions where older sectors are based, corporate executives are likely to play a powerful role in the region's politics. This has been particularly true in oligopolistic centers such as Detroit and Pittsburgh, where auto and steel industry executives have taken a leading role in the home region's financial and industrial restructuring. Those regions that host branch plants will experience the relative absence of involvement by business elites and managers in local politics. Studies have shown that these branch plant representatives tend to dissociate themselves from political participation if their companies are outside owned or integrated into national markets.[14] Hewlett-Packard, a prominent Silicon Valley electronics firm, has adopted a policy of siting new plants in medium-sized communities in which its work force forms an insignificant portion of the local electorate. Mining communities in the West and textile towns in the South often have complained of outside absentee ownership, both because profits flow out of the area and because corporate decisions appear to be made with extraordinary indifference to the fate of the local community.

Planning agendas differ predictably across these regional types as well. In regions dominated by newly innovating sectors, internal conflicts over land space, open space, and provision of new infrastructure tend to dominate. Prior sectors and land users often find themselves opposed to the environmental needs of the new sectors. In Silicon Valley, for instance, farmers and long-time residents increasingly complain of the congestion, pollution, and escalating land and housing prices bred by the mushrooming of industrial users. In many small towns in the energy-rich West, ranchers, the tourist industry, and other long-time residents attempt to prevent an air- or land-altering mine or power plant from beginning operations.[15]

In the regions with a majority of mature sectors, the planning agenda is more likely to be dominated by economic development concerns. In the 1970s, for instance, the Northeast-Midwest Congressional Coalition was formed with the intention of redirecting as much federal spending as possible into the old manufacturing areas. Internally these regions have toyed with packages of tax incentives, industrial development bonds, product development corporations (Connecticut), and publicly funded development corporations (Massachusetts) to try to lower the cost of doing business.

Enterprise zones are an extreme form of this approach. Some of these regions have tried to deter as well as lure; plant-closing legislation has passed in Maine and Wisconsin in an attempt to raise the cost of destroying a business. As one might predict, considerable internal struggle takes place within these regions over the terms on which economic development planning will proceed.

Regions into which mature sectors have branched fall somewhere between these two extremes. On the one hand, they are concerned that recent growth not bring with it the mistakes of the North. In the early 1970s the newly formed Southern Growth Policies Board focused on issues of environmental regulation and regional planning as ways of managing the new prosperity. But by the middle of the decade issues of economic development came to the fore as the fragility of an economy built on émigrés from the North became apparent. Supplanting a concern for growth control, the necessity for preserving a good business climate became paramount, in many cases completely overriding the pressures for pollution control and land use planning since these might be taken as signs of an area-wide willingness to control the privileges of private developers.

13.4 The Development Potential of Individual Regions

The dynamics of sectoral evolution and their accompanying spatial tendencies suggest that the developmental potential of individual regions may be closely tied to that of their characteristic sectors. Regions like the old manufacturing belt or Appalachia, where significant portions have been dominated by a single or several closely related sectors, will continue to have relatively poor developmental prospects. The commitment of the population and regional politicians to the maintenance of the social wage, workers' rights to organize, and the protection of a healthful environment will make the region unattractive to profit-squeezed sectors seeking lower costs of production. Even the original sectors increasingly will choose to locate new capacity elsewhere and close down local facilities as they become relatively less competitive. Also the presence in the region of corporate headquarters for the mature sectors will tend to throttle attempts to pursue innovative strategies for regional development. Alternatives that stress maintenance of community jobs and income can succeed with new institutional forms that do not require rates of return as high as those in the private sector. Examples are worker and community buy-outs, community development corporates, and cooperatives. At present, for instance, union locals in the Pittsburgh area are trying to convince local boroughs (counties) to use eminent domain to permit workers to take over and run some idle steel mills. The downtown corporate leaders—U.S. Steel and other industry executives among them—are staunchly opposed. In Youngstown the steel corporations and other business leaders successfully opposed the Ecumenical Coalition's attempt to take over Youngstown Sheet and Tube mills, preferring instead the promotion of private sector small businesses.[16]

The prominence of corporate leaders in local politics will tend to keep public sector dollars focused on the plight of these older sectors. In Detroit the largest industrial redevelopment project in the city was the effort to clear and prepare the old Cadillac site for a new assembly plant. That project was indefinitely stalled by the deepening crisis in auto production, despite the expenditure by the city of millions of dollars. A second strategy preferred by oligopolistic corporate leaders is the construction of downtown enclaves for finance and management functions, sometimes at the expense of the older downtown blocks. An example is Detroit's Renaissance Center, conceived of by a business-dominated committee, Detroit Renaissance, which included Henry Ford among its members. Downtown Pittsburgh is being transformed into a corporate ghetto with a three-stop subway serving the compact business area. Critics such as Luria and Russell (1981) point out that a superior strategy for Detroit would be the investment of public dollars in relatively newer sectors, such as energy production equipment, that can use the metal-bending skills of the area's labor force.

Regions suffering from the rationalization of older sectors have few options. Resource regions have the greatest long-term adjustment problems, particularly if they are relatively remote and inaccessible. The Appalachian Regional Commission's program, while careful not to acknowledge the importance of the coal industry to the region's decline, pursued a program of conscious depopulation of the mountain hollows and small coal towns, hoping to concentrate residents in larger cities where they might become production workers. And to some extent, with the help of the TVA's cheap power, states like Kentucky and Tennessee did attract some plants in more mature sectors to this newly formed labor force. Most mining, fishing, and lumber regions, however, face a future of sustained unemployment once their resource base is depleted or substitute commodities capture the market.

The attraction of high technology industries, a euphemism for what many believe to be the fastest-growing sectors in the economy, has recently become a preferred development strategy for many older regions. This is an unlikely prospect for several reasons.[17] First, high technology industries have chosen for the most part to locate in newly developing regions free of labor unions and high tax rates, such as Silicon Valley, Dallas, and suburban Los Angeles. When they do open branch plants, these tend to be in even lower-cost locations such as Phoenix, Mexico, Taiwan, or the Philippines. Second, the extraordinary job growth rates of high technology industries today are in large part a function of their innovative age and the tremendous competition to perfect products like the microcomputer. Once these products become standardized, the employment growth curve will flatten out and may even decline. Third, these industries, as the studies on computers and semiconductors stress, are already becoming oligopolistic in nature, with negative implications for the rate of expansion, innovative performance, and the regional location of jobs.

The developmental implication of the profit cycle model is that regions with largely mature sectors will be able to sustain their local economies only by continually renewing the economic base with the addition of new sectors. There are many historical instances of such success: New Bedford switching from whaling to textiles, Minneapolis from a timber economy to flour milling, to computers, New York from apparel and cigar making to a center of financial exports. But they are increasingly less common. Because world capital markets have become so integrated, the profits from a region's local economy are no longer necessarily reinvested within the region, as was the case in the nineteenth century. The opening up of alternative sites in the Third World makes it easier for profit takers to escape the older economies that are dominated by corporate leadership and working-class cultures antagonistic to new sectors. And the evolution of the large oligopolistic corporation and of institutionalized capital-labor conflict tends to make older regions increasingly unattractive to the badly needed newer sectors.

The previously underdeveloped regions, such as rural areas and the Old South, which have more recently welcomed new plants in older industry, do not necessarily have better developmental prospects either. They are constrained by the same threat of capital flight to yet cheaper regions. Their attractiveness depends on their continued ability to woo plants away from other regions, since they have relatively few indigenous institutions (such as good universities or corporate headquarters cities) that encourage newly innovative sectors. The pressure to maintain a good business climate has its own developmental contradictions. It may thwart local efforts to attract plants in industries that have a history of unionization, as in the Greensboro case. And it easily leads to a starvation of the local public sector, due to tax abatements and low expenditure levels, which paradoxically makes the site less attractive to prospective entrants. These regions are likely to become temporary low-cost production platforms for sectors whose longer-run prospects are clearly grim yet whose short-term maintenance dictates planning approaches that discourage newer sectors from entering.

Perhaps the regions with expanding innovative sectors are to be most envied. Certainly this is what the popular literature and the haste to erect state high technology programs suggest. Yet there are developmental dangers in this type of region as well. There is no guarantee that these economies will not become similarly deformed by the dominance of the newer sectors, especially because the emergence of market power is increasingly prevalent at a youthful stage. Second, as large corporations increasingly dominate the innovative process, they are more able to redeploy plants overseas or in cheaper locations rapidly. Atari, for instance, recently announced that it is laying off 1,700 Silicon Valley workers with an impending move to Korea. Third, the hyperconcentration of innovative activities in a few centers raises the housing, transportation, and environmental costs to residents of the region.[18] As a result regions like Silicon Valley, the envy of most other U.S. communities, are in the anomalous position of trying to slow down growth and to limit the construction of new industrial facilities.

13.5 Concluding Remarks

The prospects for balanced regional development in a country like the United States are not encouraging. Troubled regions of capital out-migration do not seem well equipped to cope with transition to a new economic base. Unless they remake themselves in the image of more depressed and underdeveloped regions, they may confront permanent dislocation. Spatial separation of management, finance, and control from production seems increasingly to be leading toward a new form of regional differentiation where entirely class-specific enclaves exist—downtown New York, San Francisco, and suburban

Palo Alto for the professional-managerial class and entirely new complexes like Sparks, Nevada, for blue-collar workers.[19]

These new spatial tendencies have been created by the evolving forms of competition and corporate structure in the twentieth century and by the unique dynamic of capitalist expansion with its preoccupation with innovation and profitability. Regional obsolescence appears to be an increasing companion of this process. The costs of community dislocation—costs for workers as income earners and home owners and for state and local government in unused capacity and higher welfare burdens—seem to be escalating, and some believe they have reached unacceptable levels. It is time to face the fact that contemporary competition does not conform to the textbook economics model and that it does not lead to equilibrating regional growth. The preservation of our communities and the fates of our regions lie in the development of new mechanisms for industrial planning that will acknowledge the costs of community change as an integral part of the choice to set up and close down production facilities.

Notes

Chapter 2

1. Siebert (1969:1).

2. Nourse (1968:1). Dubey (1964) presents an extended version of this view.

3. Chinitz (1960) still provides the best overview of supply side issues, which have been relatively neglected in regional growth theory. Richardson (1973) is the best general treatment of regional growth theory.

4. An elegant critique of the substitution of characteristics of the victims for the causes of the victimizing process, told as an allegory, is found in Marcuse (1973).

5. For a parallel argument concerning the distribution of job slots in the case of occupational segregation, see Hartmann (1976).

6. Manners, Keeble, and Warren (1980:1).

7. See Glickman (1977) for an overview of both methods. By using input-output models and linear programming techniques for modeling firm decision making, demand models can be improved substantially; see, for instance, Harris (1973). But empirical implementation of linear programming models is quite difficult.

8. Massey and Meegan (1978:273).

9. Baumol (1968), Sayer (1976), and Krumme and Hayter (1975) make similar criticisms of the black box approach of economic models. An exception is the German-Austrian school, which shunned the strict neoclassical formulation and admitted corporate behavior into its analysis.

10. Long-run growth theories, pioneered by economists such as Harrod (1939) and Robinson (1963), have treated capital investment as the engine of employment expansion. Such capital-flow theories of investment (and the investment-subsidy policies associated with them) are not sufficient to plug the gap between demand and supply theories of regional growth; augmentation of the capital stock through increased investment is not necessarily linked to the expansion of employment prospects for regional workers

because of the substitution of capital for labor and speculative investment in unproductive assets. Varaiya and Wiseman (1980) found that while manufacturing investment climbed in New England from 1960 through 1976, production employment fell by 30 percent. See Massey and Meegan (1979b) for a similar point.

11. Implicit in this statement is the contention that workers' migration decisions are secondary in importance—that is, that workers follow job opportunities rather than vice-versa. The extensive literature on this question seems to favor the view that migration (and refusal to migrate) is very important but less so than capital movement. For overviews of migration theory and patterns in the United States, see Morrison (1975, 1977a, 1977b). I have been unable to explore the phenomenon of migration in this round of research, although I have found its results significant in the formation of regional consciousness.

12. In some usages industries are meant to connote merely manufacturing sectors. In this study I use the broader meaning of all economic activities in their specific forms. Furthermore to relieve the tedium of countless repetition of the word *sector,* I use both words to refer to sector, although not vice-versa.

13. Schumpeter (1939, 1961, 1962); Chandler (1962, 1977); Vernon (1966). Some argue that Schumpeter built his model of capitalist dynamics on Marx's but to a very different end, of course; see, for instance, Elliott (1980). Schumpeter's model was fashioned to air his admiration of capitalism rather than as a diatribe against it, as was Marx's. For an interesting evaluation of the Schumpeterian vision of creative destruction, see Strassman (1959). See Hall (1983) for an assessment of Schumpeter's status in the history of economic thought.

14. Equilibrium-oriented models may include disequilibrium paths yet belong to the same family of theory. Exceptions to this characterization exist, of course. See, for instance, Lynne Browne's (1979) work on capital formation.

15. In the 1970s macroeconomists were less interested in business cycles than in the shorter-term fine-tuning of econometric models for forecasting purposes. For a regional example, see Glickman (1977).

16. Myrdal (1957); Holland (1976).

17. In the value theory model, this amounts to saying that the governing class seeks to maximize relative surplus value rather than absolute surplus value. Brenner (1977) elaborates on this point at length, with salient examples from the Latin American transition from plantation agriculture to contemporary industrial production. The original insight belongs to Marx and Engels (1968), who wrote in the *Communist Manifesto,* "Constant revolutionizing of production, uninterrupted disturbance of all social conditions, everlasting uncertainty and agitation distinguish the bourgeois epoch from all earlier ones."

18. Schumpeter (1939, 1962); Kuznets (1953); Mensch (1979); Mandel (1980); Hall (1982); and Van Duijn (1983). For a skeptical view of the bunching argument, see Rosenberg and Frischtak (1983).

19. Mandel (1975). Most theorists of innovation accept some form of the same notion—Mansfield (1968); Chandler (1962). Most neoclassical treatments of innovation, however, concern themselves with changes in the aggregate level of output or capacity in the economy, or in one product line, rather than with displacement of one sector by another; see Solow (1957); Schmookler (1966); and Hollander (1965). For an excellent account of the role of invention and innovation in U.S. economic history, see Rosenberg (1972).

20. For a number of reasons, recorded profit rates of a particular firm may not reflect these superprofits. It may be plowing them back into research or marketing activities or using them to subsidize predatory competition or a failing product line in another sector. The superprofit notion refers to the potential realization of greater-than-normal profits and is specific to a sector, not to a corporation, which may have disparate activities in several sectors reflected in its profit rate. These problems with the interpretation of profit rates require the use of other indicators as proxies for profit experience.

21. Kuznetz (1930).

22. Burns (1934).

23. Hayes and Wheelwright (1979a, 1979b); Abernathy and Townsend (1975); Abernathy and Utterback (1975, 1978).

24. In Mensch's restatement (1979:52), for instance, he summarizes the theory as follows: "Over time, the market demand for any given type of industrial product usually does not grow uniformly. Over and over again it has been observed to follow a certain dynamic, which is called the product's life cycle. If an innovation brings a new product type or quality onto the market, the market accepts the product only hesitatingly at first. After a certain introduction period, the market rushes to acquire the novelty, first with growing and then later diminishing appetite. Finally, with time the demand for this entity dwindles in to a minimum. The cycle is complete." Mensch also refers to sales figures as the primary empirical indicator for stages of the product life cycle. Burns, in his original work, used physical output.

25. For the Marxist view, see Baran and Sweezy (1966) and De Vroey (1975). Two modifications have been developed in the business literature. First, some argue that firms maximize sales (Baumol, 1959) or growth (Penrose, 1959). Yet either of these maximands can be seen as instrumental to long-run profit and/or dependent on it. Furthermore there is no good empirical technique for distinguishing between the results of these two competing approaches. Second, others (Williamson, 1964) argue that some firms satisfice—that is, after achieving some minimal rate of return, corporate managers maximize personal utility in the form of perquisites or choose the first adequate alternative in the face of uncertainty, search costs,

and organizational instability.

26. See, for example, the collection in Wells (1972).

27. Wells (1972:19) mentions price-discriminating oligopoly in certain national markets, and both Wells (1972:12) and Stobaugh (1972:87) acknowledge market power in innovative stages. Vernon (1977) argues that new sectors will tend to become more competitive with time, moving from monopoly to oligopoly to workable competition.

28. See the empirical work of Bela Gold (1964). Gold finds that for many of the same sectors studied by Burns, diverse patterns of output growth have resulted from the peculiarities of each sector. Yet many of Burns's and successors' insights into corporate behavior can withstand the demise of the specific forecast of a bell-shaped output or sales path. Cox (1967) found that more narrowly defined products, as opposed to sectors, did exhibit life cycles of 22 to 26 months when measured by sales figures.

29. Chamberlin (1962).

30. Robinson (1969).

31. For a rich account of variations in target pricing and product differentiation strategies, see Ong (1981).

32. Regional economists who have advocated analysis of corporate behavior at the disaggregated sectoral level include Thompson (1965), Pred (1977), Perloff et al. (1960), Duncan and Lieberson (1970), Massey and Meegan (1982), Bluestone and Harrison (1982), and Norton (1979).

Chapter 3

1. See Sylos-Labini (1969:107) on this distinction.

2. Both Pred (1966) and OECD (1971) cite the literature on the inducements to innovation. For views that stress how innovations are often inspired by the desire to counter challenges from labor, see Stone (1974) and Marglin (1974).

3. When a new industry is spawned by an existing one, which happens only in a minority of cases, the distinction between the two is difficult to pinpoint precisely. The Census Bureau has dealt with this problem pragmatically. Generally I use a strict definition, considering an industry new if the major corporate actors have changed (for example, the emergence of semiconductor firms different from the old electron tube manufacturers) or (unlike some census decisions) the new product revolutionizes the production process (for example, taconite versus natural iron ore, strip versus underground mined coal).

4. See Danilov (1969) and Goldstein (1967) for examples from recent U.S. innovative sectors.

5. See Jewkes, Sawer, and Stillerman (1958), Scherer (1965), and OECD (1971).

6. Mansfield (1968), Thomas (1981:19). Others argue that the pace of innovation is accelerating, shortening the innovative stage. See Lasuen (1973:170), for example.

7. Sylos-Labini (1979); Nelson (1959); Averitt (1968).

8. Sherman (1968) shows that oligopoly sectors exhibit greater profit stability and less volatile investment patterns than competitive sectors in the U.S. Blumberg (1975) presents the evidence on the correlation between profit rates and concentration, suggesting that profits may be higher by 50 percent or more in oligopolized sectors. Crum (1953) shows that across all industries, age and size of firm are strongly correlated with profitability. See de Kluyver (1977), on the promotional push elongating the growth period.

9. Mensch (1979:57) colorfully calls this the dinosaur effect, where firms with market power are preoccupied with productivity, long-term market control, and furthering concentration rather than innovation. Abernathy (1978) shows why this occurred in autos and argues that it is endemic to capitalist dynamics.

10. See Bluestone and Harrison (1982:149-51).

11. This divergence between jobs and output is a result of high levels of investment in the early stages, as the accelerator model of macroinvestment patterns suggests. After an initial burst, new investment falls dramatically to more modest levels. In later periods firms may actually permit the rate of depreciation to outrun replacement investment, so that the capital stock is actually shrinking.

12. For this reason, the literature on product cycle would be vastly improved if it modeled the cyclical nature of employment rather than output. See Sylos-Labini (1979:6) for a similar argument regarding the use of employment change in studying oligopoly. It is precisely the failure to take into account the power of oligopoly in output restriction, consumer taste manipulation, and extraordinary political leverage that results in poor empirical verification of a product cycle. For an intriguing discussion of bell-shaped functions in the development literature at large, see Alonso (1980). He points out the neglect of the right-hand portions of these relationships generally.

13. Empirically the professional-technical class corresponds to the equivalent census occupational designations; the managerial-sales class corresponds to the managerial, clerical, and sales occupations; and the production work force corresponds to the operative, crafts, service, and laborer categories.

Chapter 4

1. Remarkably few spatial applications of the product cycle exist. Most have emerged from international trade theory. Vernon (1966) and Hirsch (1967) argued that nations with different developmental histories could best specialize in sectors at certain points of their product cycle. Mature

capitalist countries, they argue, do best with rapidly growing industries, less developed countries with maturer sectors where low labor costs put them at an advantage, and small developed countries like Sweden and Switzerland in very new, innovative sectors. Wells (1972) argues that the product cycle theory explained what the factor proportions theory of Hecksher-Ohlin could not—that the United States specializes in exports that have high labor content despite high prevailing domestic wage rates. Studies of specific industries (Hirsch, 1967, on electronics, and Stobaugh, 1972, on petrochemicals) have verified these international locational tendencies. See also Magee (1977). The best theoretical work at the subnational level has been done by Thomas (1974, 1975, 1981), who explores the developmental consequences of regions heavily specialized in sectors in certain evolutionary stages. For empirical applications to the U.S. case, see Norton and Rees (1979) and Krumme and Hayter (1975).

2. Hoover (1948:174).

3. See Stevens and Brackett (1967:10), for instance, for a review concluding that the wage and labor factor studies have been inconclusive. Book-length treatments of location studies in the United States and Great Britain, respectively, are Moriarity (1980) and Keeble (1976). Storper (1981) offers a critical review of the location literature. For bibliographical reviews, see Stevens and Brackett (1967), and Miller and Miller (1978).

4. Spatial concentration is not to be confused with concentration of market power, since an industry with many small firms nevertheless may be highly geographically concentrated.

5. Taylor (1975) argues that most firms originate in the founder's home town.

6. Feller (1975:91-93) argues that there is no necessary relationship between inventive activity and subsequent location, which he illustrates with the case of light bulbs in the United States. General Electric bought out the original innovator, located in Lynn, Massachusetts, and moved production to New Jersey.

7. Innovation has received substantial attention in the literature as an agglomerative activity and one that propels certain core regions to prominence. See Thompson (1962, 1965, 1975), Pred (1966, 1975), Friedmann (1972), Borchert (1972), and Struyk and James (1975). This body of work has been intertwined with the debate on the stability of urban hierarchies, in which the emphasis has been on the function of innovative activity in maintaining the primacy of certain large metropolitan areas and on the regular diffusion path of innovations outward from such centers. For critical assessments of this pattern, see Cohen (1972), Pred (1976), and Norton and Rees (1979). Webber (1972) argues that uncertainty reinforces central and historical locations. Malecki (1980a, 1980b) focuses on recent high tech activities as reinforcing agglomerative tendencies in the urban system.

8. Discussions of these tendencies may be found in Rees (1974), McDermott and Keeble (1978), and Hamilton and Linge (1979).

9. Osborn (1953) argues that automation and unionization interact as stimulants to decentralization. Automating companies prefer to introduce new technologies at remote locations to avoid the organized opposition of workers in the original site.

10. Chinitz (1960) argues persuasively that both Pittsburgh and Detroit have experienced growth rates well below those of comparable industrial cities because the steel and auto industries, respectively, have dominated the supply of labor, entrepreneurship, and capital in their regional factor markets.

11. It is in this sense that Holland (1976a) sees uneven regional development resulting from what he calls mesoeconomic power.

12. Hotelling's original article (1929) recently has been elaborated on by Eaton and Lipsey (1975) who argue that his results are wholly dependent on the existence of oligopoly in the industry.

13. For examples of arguments about state sector impacts on regional growth patterns, see Luger (1981), Hunker (1980), Krumme and Hayter (1975), Rees (1978, 1979), Taylor (1975), and Walker (1975). Glickman (1980) includes a number of case studies and techniques for charting the urban impacts of federal policies.

14. Bluestone and Harrison (1982); Mollenkopf (1981).

15. Bluestone and Harrison (1982:25-34).

16. Bluestone and Harrison (1982:149-160).

17. The interrelationship of high tech sectors and a professional-technical labor force is acknowledged in the literature, but no consensus exists as to whether one follows the other spatially. See Oakey, Thwaites, and Nash (1980), Stephens and Holly (1980), and Ewers and Wettman (1980).

18. Several researchers have documented that branch plants, particularly in more mature sectors, are less likely to spawn other new businesses and more likely to close down than nonbranch plants. See Thompson (1969), Thwaites (1978), Johnson and Cathcart (1979), Erickson and Leinbach (1979), Hansen (1979), and Erickson (1980). Bluestone and Harrison (1982) reported that textile plants were closing in the South at a faster rate than in the North, although their residence in the former region is more recent.

Chapter 5

1. Fisher (1935) and Clark (1940). See Martinelli (1981:1) on the use of stages in national accounting systems and development theory, including the application of development stages to the contemporary Third World. Hoselitz (1961) presents a skeptical view of stage theories.

2. The tertiary sectors lie outside the analysis of this book. Their spatial patterns are interesting primarily on the interurban and intraurban levels.

Students of city spatial organization could adapt the profit cycle model to the tertiary sector, particularly for modeling the shift toward the urban periphery of certain service industries.

3. Oligopoly may prevail in the distribution end, however, as in the case of grain merchants in the United States.

4. Dhalla and Yuspeh (1976) argue that the ability to reverse profitability through innovation within a sector destroys the product cycle model. I believe, on the contrary, that the model can cope with reversals and that in any case they cannot override the long-term tendency toward a bell-shaped development path. See also van Duijn (1983).

5. A finer disaggregation of resource sectors would differentiate between renewal and nonrenewable resource dependency. In the latter, because of the potential for exhaustion, fluctuations in profitability may be wilder, proportions of professional workers involved in exploration and in efforts to dominate resource ownership may be higher, and oligopolistic tendencies may be stronger.

6. Both Marxist and traditional macroeconomists distinguish between producer and consumer orientation of firms on the selling end. In Marxist terminology these spheres of production are referred to as department I and department II; in traditional macroeconomics the output of each is termed *investment goods* and *consumption goods,* respectively.

7. See Mueller (1967) for evidence on both these points, especially pp. 57, 64, 68, 74, 79. He shows here and in Mueller (1970) that producer goods sectors have lower concentration rates than consumer goods sectors, despite greater economies of scale, suggesting that product differentiation appears to account for the differences.

8. Mensch (1979:57-60) uses this notion of technological stagnation. He reviews evidence that minor changes in durability or safety may occur in consumer goods at this juncture to maintain sales or increase market share. But few major changes in product functionality can be found at this stage. He concludes that little quality competition thus prevails.

9. See Mueller (1967:74, 81) on these points.

10. Vernon (1960); Pred (1975).

11. See Hymer (1972, 1979); Dicken (1971); Cohen (1977); and Noyelle (1983).

Chapter 6

1. Mensch (1979). Mensch's basic inventions are not synonymous with sectors, since some, such as the electric arc furnace, take place within the same sector, steel, and do not necessarily reverse the profit cycle. Luger (1981) finds that new corporate tax breaks also bunch up at the troughs of business cycles. Brown (1957) shows how one sector, machine tools, has innovated when demand has been slack.

2. Burns (1934:135) offers some historical cases where new sectors bid significant quantities of factors away from others. For labor, for instance, he cites the wooing of workers from autos and furniture toward the aircraft industry, from the legitimate stage toward motion pictures, and from whaling to gold mining.

3. Known as the regional aggregation problem, this monotonic variation of a phenomenon with scale is quite common in regional economics and geography. See, for instance, the review of shift-share techniques by Houston (1967) and Dawson (1982). Massey and Meegan (1982) pose several structural forms of retrenchment which exhibit the same problem.

4. Numerous authors have confirmed the growing integration of the world economy, the role of U.S. corporations within it, and the effect on employment at home. See Bryant and Krause (1980), Castells (1980), Friedmann and Wolff (1982), Frobel, Heinrichs, and Kreye (1979), Marchesini (1974), Hymer (1979), Modelski (1979), and Perlmutter (1968). Governmental studies on this subject include United Nations (1973), U.S. Department of Housing and Urban Development (1979), and U.S. Senate Committee on Foreign Relations (1975). See the review in Schoenberger (1981).

Chapter 7

1. The most comprehensive cross-sectional studies examining the composition of shifts in industrial structure across U.S. regions are Perloff et al. (1960), Fuchs (1962), and Dunn (1980).

2. Examples are the case studies in Miller (1977) and Alexandersson (1967), as well as many individual locational studies in geographic journals. These studies are largely devoid of systematic data, although sometimes they list known plant locations. They often place the sector in its international context.

3. Perloff et al. (1960) examined sectoral shifts at the two- and three-digit level for superstate regions and states between the bracketing years 1939 and 1954. In addition they reconstructed two-digit equivalent series back to the latter decades of the nineteenth century. Fuchs (1962), using a specially prepared data base, is the only study that has come close to a universal study of manufacturing location at the four-digit level. More recently Dunn (1980) has constructed a novel and useful set of highly disaggregated urban regions; he analyzes thirty one sectors composed of variations on one-, two-, and three-digit categories. Burrows, Metcalf and Kaler (1971) use a nonlinear econometric model with employment data on thirty two sectors to project county and supracounty employment. Conroy (1975) estimates 3-digit employment for a set of fifty two SMSAs, covering about half the U.S. urban population. None of these studies includes evidence on variables other than employment. Their advantage is their total coverage of all regions and sectors, although only the Fuchs study is disaggregated enough to be of substantial help to the present project.

4. Examples of collections that proved helpful include Adams (1971) and

Lindahl and Carter (1959), as well as numerous journal articles from the economics and business professions. These generally omit a focus on location but are excellent on the structural changes within the sector. Often they provide historical details not available elsewhere.

5. An alternative method for studying contemporary regional change as a product of sectoral change involves direct interviewing of sectoral actors, such as corporate managers and workers. This approach has been pioneered by Bluestone and Harrison (1982) and Saxenian (1980).

6. In the following discussion, the descriptions of these statistics are drawn from U.S. Federal Trade Commission (1981) and U.S. Internal Revenue Service (1982). A time series of aggregate corporate profits is also available from the National Income Accounts data published in the Annual Economic Report of the President but is available only on a 2-digit basis, treats depreciation quite differently, and does not present data for computing profit rates. For fuller discussion of problems with identifying the appropriate base for profit rate calculation, see Luger (1981).

7. The numerical values of both of these measures apply only to the postwar period. No attempt has been made to see if earlier stages for more mature commodities exhibit values in the same ranges.

8. In general profit cycle stage boundaries were chosen to approximate as closely as possible the change in sign of the second derivative of the employment growth curve, especially in the prewar periods. In the postwar period the nearest census year was selected. The criterion used here for classifying industries as oligopolistic is quite conservative; industries historically have been considered highly concentrated if eight firms control over 50 percent of output or twenty firms control more than 75 percent, and simply concentrated if eight control more than a third. See Kaysen and Turner (1959).

9. This problem is magnified by the discontinuous nature of the census data, collected only at four- to seven-year intervals since the war. Census years bear no consistent relationship to short-term cycles. From 1958 to 1963 there were two business cycle troughs and one peak; from 1963 to 1967, steady expansion; from 1967 to 1972, a distinct downturn, followed by a period of stagnation (see Varaiya and Wiseman, 1978). On average, then, 1967 figures will be high and 1972 low. No attempt has been made to correct for these economy-wide variations in the case study data.

10. In all cases output is measured by value added, corrected for inflation by using the GNP deflator. In some industries measures of quantity output, such as number of cars or dresses, or board feet of lumber, are also used, drawn from sources other than the census. Value added measures the value of output minus material and equipment input costs. It represents the sum of labor costs plus profits. Fluctuations in its magnitude can be caused by changes in wages or productivity, as well as by external factors such as changes in demand. In the long run, however, it is a good indicator of changes in output.

11. Concentration ratios as indicators of degree of market power are the subject of debate. They are understated because of the geographical separation of regional markets and overstated by failure to take product substitutes into account. Both Mueller (1967, 1970) and Scherer (1980) conclude that they probably underestimate market power more often than overestimating it. See also Nutter (1951), Blair (1972), and Miller (1955). The more disaggregated the sector, the greater the degree of concentration detected. Concentration in manufacturing as a whole increased from 1947 to 1977. The top fifty companies controlled 24 percent of value added in 1977, compared to 17 percent in 1947.

12. There are instances of multiplant firms that are nonincorporated, but tax advantages generally militate against maintenance of this form as companies grow. In the economy as a whole, there has been a secular trend downward in the percentage of plants and upward in jobs accounted for by multiplant corporations. Since 1946 the percentage of manufacturing establishments accounted for by multiplant firms has fallen from 34 percent to 23 percent, while the percentage of jobs they account for has risen from 56 percent to 76 percent. But the raw data on this variable were distinct enough between stages to use without normalizing for the economy-wide trend.

13. The Census of Manufactures changes sectoral definitions from census year to census year, creating substantial comparability problems for many subsectors. In the cases chosen for study, these problems were transcended by reconstructing data sets through reaggregation or disaggregation, possible in most cases, or by presenting the data graphically in discontinuous form.

14. The decennial Census of Population yields detailed occupational breakdowns by industry for the nation as a whole. But the bracketing years bear insufficient correspondence to the Census of Manufactures years to be of much help in documenting profit cycle occupational shifts. The Bureau of Labor Statistics also produces estimates of production compared to total work force, and since their definition diverges significantly from the census definition, both measures are employed throughout the case studies.

15. Where possible, extrapolation was used to derive an employment estimate from interval data. In years bracketed by observations with data, employment in the given year was estimated to be proportional to the difference between bracketing years, correcting for national growth rates and for differences in numbers of years between censuses. If the number so generated fell outside the census interval, the overreached interval boundary was used. In cases where the most recent periods lacked data or where the interval "FF" was specified, an open-ended category meaning greater than 2,500, it became impossible to use the employment data. In such cases the number of establishments was used and, where possible, those with more than twenty employees. In cases where the year 1947 was judged important to include, this was not possible since data are available for total numbers of establishments only.

16. An alternative to this spatial concentration ratio would be Fuchs's

(1962:121-122) coefficient of scatter, which expresses the number of states required to account for 75 percent of the employment. My measure, however, is more sensitive and precise. For instance, the distribution of states' shares of employment in two successive periods might appear as follows:

Number of states	4	5	6	8	Year
Cumulative share of employment	62	74	83	86	1972
	70	74	76	78	1977

Fuchs's coefficient would remain unchanged at 6 across the two periods. Mine would show a four-state concentration ratio rising from 62 to 70 percent, while the eight-state ratio fell from 86 to 78 percent. See Hall and Tideman (1967) for a general discussion of statistical measures of concentration and Isard (1960:chap. 7) for a discussion of spatial measures of concentration.

17. In retrospect aluminum, and perhaps steel, may have been misclassified, belonging instead to the resource-oriented category.

18. See Fuchs (1962:165-167) for a discussion of the identification of labor-oriented sectors. His definition is narrow, encompassing those sectors with greater-than-average labor intensity. My definition also encompasses sectors that are capital intensive but whose successful operation relies heavily on access to skilled labor, whether professional-technical or blue collar.

19. See Perloff et al. (1960) for a technique derived from input-output analysis for delineating producer from consumer sectors.

20. See Ware, DiPasquale, and Bluestone (1978), New England Economy Project (1981), and Massey and Meegan (1979a) for a description of similar selection procedures.

21. Both Fuchs (1962:153) and Mueller (1967:appendix table 9) list four-digit sectors considered to be locally oriented. Fuchs lists 29 (out of his total of 221) and Mueller lists 18, among which are two chosen for the present study: sawmills and beer. However, these two probably would not be classified similarly today. Viewed another way, Perloff et al. (1950) show metropolitan employment-to-population ratios for major two-digit sectors; those chosen in my study span the gamut from highly locationally specialized to highly market-oriented sectors.

Chapter 8

1. It may be too soon to conclude that output will permanently fall from this point on, though the scale of plant closings would seem to suggest so.

2. Hogan (1971:53). Figures are for the year 1860.

3. The discovery of the coking process, where bituminous coal could be used in steel making, plus the high tariffs on iron and steel imports, favored

Pittsburgh over eastern seaboard producers. Allegheny County hosted eleven new large mills from 1853 to 1911, and in 1894 this single county produced 43 percent of all the nation's steel (Houston, 1979).

4. Figures are from Alexandersson (1967:35, 45).

5. Isard (1948); Pounds (1959); Mancke (1972).

6. Alexandersson (1967:45, 46); Hogan (1971:73-74, 193).

7. Stocking (1954); Lindahl and Carter (1959:280); Rodgers (1952:61).

8. Stocking (1954:100, 104, 131-134, 77); Alexandersson (1967:47); Isard and Capron (1949:132). U.S. Steel's Duluth plant proved only marginally profitable in the long run because of its remoteness from fabricators and failure to draw customers around its port (White and Primmer, 1937). See Alanen (1977) for a discussion of environmental versus job issues surrounding the plant's closing in the mid 1970s.

9. Stocking (1954:62, 68-74).

10. Hogan (1971:643-814); Warren (1973:202).

11. Boylan (1975:204).

12. Lindahl and Carter (1959:274-280); Rowley (1971:93); Stocking (1954:77); Warren (1973:203).

13. Hogan (1971:1473); Warren (1973:237).

14. Stocking (1954:150-151). The same conclusion is reached by Fetter (1937), Kaysen (1949), Machlup (1949), Weiss (1967), and Warren (1973). Fetter (p. 601) quotes industry spokesmen as saying, "It is not too much to say that the abolition of the basing-point system would change the whole industrial map of America." He charges that the system's arbitrary spatial concentration violated the "rights and interests of whole regions and of many individual citizens." Other authors have ignored or viewed as locationally inconsequential the basing point system, although no study as thorough as Stocking's has been undertaken. See, for example, Noren (1960). For a dissident note on the debate, see Federal Reserve Bank of Cleveland (1969:9).

15. Warren (1973:210-211). While many of the market and resource factors mentioned in this account are focused on in traditional accounts of the location of the iron and steel industry, most such accounts ignore the role of oligopoly power. The debate between Isard (1948) and Hekman (1978) over the relative importance of input costs versus market pull disregards monopoly power completely.

16. Grether (1946:66, 98, 121); Alexandersson (1967:47); Warren (1973:234-237). Grether et al. argue that high western wage rates in the prewar era were not a significant factor in retarding growth of steel-making capacity. Warren characterizes eastern shipments to the West as a form of dumping, especially during recession.

17. Warren (1973:240-275).

18. *Ibid.,* 243. Nor did government construction and procurement counter concentration. Wartime purchases favored the largest steel corporations, and these same firms won the lion's share of plant sales. See Adams and Mueller (1982:80).

19. Duke et al. (1977:155).

20. Shapiro and Volk (1979:8); Brody (1960); Betheil (1978).

21. Hogan (1971:2034-2035); American Iron and Steel Institute (1977); Duke et al. (1977:6, 69); Rowley (1971:72).

22. Rowley (1971:69-71).

23. These shares represent the proportions of a total employment base that is substantially shrinking. The Steelworkers' union estimates that 32,000 jobs were lost between 1972 and 1980 due to plant closings (Bolle, 1980). Thus an increase in share does not necessarily mean an increase in absolute numbers of jobs.

24. Changes in resource and market factors are of minor importance in the recent era. Resource costs diminished as a locational factor due to both improved techniques avoiding waste and to lower transportation costs, which helped the Pittsburgh and Youngstown areas to remain competitive (Boylan, 1975:204-205). But gains in fuel efficiency loosened the ties of the industry to Appalachian coal fields and hurt the inland steel-making centers in particular. Demand continued to pull the industry toward Chicago and the Southwest, although much of this market growth was met by imports. The growth of special markets like oil and gas pipelines in the Southwest has also contributed to growth in new regional steel centers. Benhart (1972:8); Warren (1973:277-278, 283); White (1957); Federal Reserve Bank of Cleveland (1969:10-11); Adams and Mueller (1982:80).

25. Nelson (1971). The basic oxygen process was innovated in Austria in the early 1950s and was slow to be accepted by U.S. Steel corporate leadership (Adams and Dirlam, 1966). In 1955 it accounted for 0.3 percent of U.S. Steel production; by 1978 it accounted for 61 percent (U.S. Bureau of Labor Statistics, 1980:2; Gold, Rosegger and Boylan, 1980:136).

26. *Business Week* (1966:75).

27. Schmidt and LeHeron (1976:541).

28. Benhart (1972:5); Davenport (1968:129-135). Davenport cites a number of firms—Latrobe, Carpenter, Alleghany Ludlum, and Cyclops—located within a suburban or ex-urban radius of Pennsylvania steel towns.

29. Kirkland (1981b); Sease (1981).

30. *Business Week* (1980a:64).

31. Thackray (1981:54); Kirkland (1981a:31); *Business Week* (1981:82); Adams and Mueller (1982:79). The best performances in the top eight for the same period were posted by LTV (11.7) and Armco (12.3) and were also below the average for all manufacturing.

32. *Business Week* (1979:78-79); Sease (1980b).

33. U.S. Bureau of Labor Statistics (1980:2). These figures must be interpreted cautiously because they are generated from the Trade Adjustment Assistance Act program, which considers a job destroyed by imports if it disappears during a period when imports quantitatively are on the rise.

34. Select Committee on Small Business (1980).

35. Ignatius (1977:220-221); *Business Week* (1977); Sease (1979:2, 32).

36. *Wall Street Journal* (1980a:10, 1980c:3).

37. Petzinger (1979:2); Sease (1980a:1, 20); Kelly and Shutes (1977).

38. *Wall Street Journal* (1979:15, 1980b:10); Petzinger (1979:2); Sease (1979:2).

39. Kirkland (1981a:29-31); Duke et al. (1977:64-67); Office of Technology Assessment (1980:35-36); Shapiro and Volk (1979:15).

40. European steel experienced the profitability squeeze and employment decline several years before the United States. From 1974 to 1978, the EEC countries averaged a decline of 14 percent in employment, or a total of 33,100 workers (equivalent to the loss in the United States over a somewhat longer period). Percentage declines were: Belgium, −24 percent; Britain, −16 percent; France, −16 percent; Germany, 12 percent; Italy, 1 percent; Luxembourg, −29 percent; Netherlands, −20 percent (Citibank, 1979:12-14). Since 1978 the unemployment situation has worsened. France lost 35,000 steel jobs between 1977 and 1980 (Curry, 1978). British Steel Corporation lopped off one-third of its capacity in 1980. Japan too has had to scrap some plants. *Economist* (1980); Hargreaves (1981); *Business Week* (1981:80-82); Thackeray (1981:54).

Chapter 9

1. Hall (1982).

2. The industry is defined here as SIC 3573. Before 1967 computer industry employment was counted with other business machine categories under electrical machinery (SIC 35), mostly in calculating and accounting machines. The computer manufacturing industry, despite its close links with semiconductor activities, is distinct from that sector in both business organization and geographical location. To date it is also distinct from computer software, a distinct SIC code.

3. In 1946 two researchers at the University of Pennsylvania developed the first digital computing system, funded by army research. In 1948 Bell Labs produced the transistor, the key to the transition from bulky electron tubes to compact electronic systems. In 1959 Texas Instruments developed the printed circuit. In the 1950s Jay Forrester at MIT experimented with a core memory. All of these became incorporated into commercial applications of the computer. My discussion is indebted to New England Project

(1981:79-100) and Kuhn (1981).

4. The largest New England computer firm was formed in 1957. The most prominent U.S. firm, IBM, had made its start in business calculating machines and entered the computer field in the late 1950s.

5. This section draws on business press sources on various details, particularly the following *Business Week* articles: "Computers: Discovering a Vast Potential Market," December 1, 1980:91-97; "Apple's Morning After: Lots of Competition," December 29, 1980:47; "Memorex Tries a Turnaround — Again," January 19, 1981:89-93; "Computers: A Burst of Critical Feedback," February 25, 1981:68-71; "Computers: A Mainframe on Three Chips," March 2, 1981:116-118; "Computers: A Capital Crunch That Could Change an Industry," March 23, 1981:82-84; "No Boom for Bubble Memory," May 4, 1981:152-155.

6. The mainframe computer, a physically large, expensive, and sophisticated system sold largely to research institutions such as universities and government agencies, and to corporations for automation, planning, and accounting purposes, has been the most established segment to date. The fastest-growing segment of the market is the so-called minicomputer industry, somewhat arbitrarily cordoned off as those machines that cost the buyer less than $100,000. These too are mainly employed by industry for automation and control purposes but increasingly are marketed to smaller businesses for accounting and data processing purposes. Even more difficult to demarcate clearly is the personal computer segment, machines that cost less than $10,000 and are aimed at small businesses, professionals, and corporate managers, some for home use. In addition there are peripherals manufacturers, which make system components but not entire systems, and industry jobbers, firms that buy hardware from manufacturers, add software packages, and sell them to customers. Kuhn (1981:12-21).

7. Grossman (1980). Several events may change the composition of this sector: the microprocessor, the entry of AT&T into the data processing industry, and the Japanese effort to produce a supercomputer. Another anticompetitive trend in the mainframe business is the integration of computer makers backward into semiconductor manufacture through both buy-outs and in-house expansions.

8. See Draheim (1964) for a description of the advantages of the upper Midwest for these high technology industries.

9. Kuhn (1981:81); Estall (1963).

10. The industry is defined here as semiconductors, SIC 3674, a category created in 1963. While some of the original semiconductor firms are nondiversified and independent, the structure of the industry underwent significant transition in the 1970s as more computer, communication, and aerospace firms integrated backward into semiconductor manufacturing. This complicates the identification of individual firms as belonging to either the computer or semiconductor sectors; however, on a plant-by-plant basis, the level at which the census operates, production is quite distinct. The

details of this industry are covered in Saxenian (1980), Borrus and Millstein (1980), and Siegel (1981). The following *Business Week* articles are also drawn on in the discussion: "New Starters in Silicon Valley," January 26, 1981:67-70; "Schlumberger: The Star of the Oil Fields Tackles Semiconductors," February 16, 1981:60-70; "Computers: Japan's Bid to Out-Design the U.S.," April 13, 1981:123-124; "Israel: A Bargain for the U.S. in High-Tech Engineers," April 20, 1981:44-45.

11. Saxenian (1980:3, 117-118).

12. Two types of chips are manufactured: the commodities chip, which is produced for the mass market, and the custom chip, which is manufactured to the user's specifications. Although the commodities chips were the fastest-growing market segment through the mid-1970s, the custom chip segment has boomed recently, partly because the individual chip has become so complex and partly because oligopsonist users prefer not to buy interchangeable parts that are also available to their competitors. Custom chips, now 10 percent of the market, may account for 50 percent by 1990. Saxenian (1980:119); Borrus and Millstein, (1980:24); Association of Bay Area Governments (1981:49).

13. Eckhouse (1981:9); Siegel (1981:13), Saxenian (1980:35).

14. Saxenian (1980:22); Borrus and Millstein (1980:290).

15. Saxenian (1980:30-172); Borrus and Millstein (1980:15); Siegel (1981:4).

16. At the same time semiconductor firms have tried to integrate forward or to diversify, with limited success. They feel compelled to avoid a monopsonistic situation in which their more highly oligopolized computer customers force down the price of chips. On the other hand, entry into mini computers would enable them to cash in on the oligopoly profits that reside in downstream markets. In the future, analysts predict, the larger semiconductor companies will have only 10 to 20 percent of their sales in components. Borrus and Millstein (1980:273-275); Eckhouse (1981); Saxenian (1980:25, 33, 124).

17. Eckhouse (1981); Siegel (1981:4, 126); Saxenian (1980:121, 130-131).

18. Siegel (1981:6); Saxenian (1980:43-44); Hirsch (1972:49).

19. In Texas an oil drilling instrument company became Texas Instruments and initiated electronics growth in that region. Engineers and scientists trained at Boston-area universities are credited with developing New England's agglomeration of firms.

20. Borrus and Millstein (1980:280-281); Siegel (1981:7); International Labor Organization (1976:11).

21. Saxenian (1980:39, 142, 154); Borrus and Millstein (1980:288).

22. As VLSI circuits and custom work become the norm, the flexibility and increased testing required will also contribute to this repatriation but with

little impact on job gains. Siegel (1981:7-8); Saxenian (1980:122).

23. Large firms like Hewlett-Packard, Varian, and AMD are building new, enlarged corporate headquarters in Silicon Valley, as Santa Clara is called, and the headquarters of many other semiconductor firms are sited there as well. Numerous large user companies, such as Western Electric and Westinghouse, have established research facilities in the valley, too, drawn to the exceptional pool of skilled engineering and design talent located there.

24. The concentration of semiconductor activities in Santa Clara Valley has brought its own contradictions, largely manifested in high levels of pollution, congestion costs, and housing costs and in the movement for industrial growth control. Saxenian (1980).

25. Aluminum is defined here as SIC 3334, primary aluminum production. Primary aluminum accounted for 28,600 workers in 1977; in both reduction and fabrication, aluminum employs about one-eighth of all basic metal workers in the United States. Aluminum rolling and drawing is a separate industry, whose location is not very closely spatially tied to primary aluminum because freight rate differentials encourage fabrication nearer to industrial users. Alumina, the intermediate form of ore, is also not included because it is not sited with reduction plants but at mine mouth or transshipment points. Perloff et al. (1960:453); Krutilla (1955); Brubaker (1967:156-157).

26. Alcoa, as it was later dubbed, launched aluminum production in 1888 in Pittsburgh with the ideas of the inventor of electrolytic reduction, Charles Marten, and the money of Mellon and others. The company was immediately profitable, making 100 pounds of aluminum, which sold for $5 a pound, in its first week. Alcoa grew from a monopoly corporation of $20,000 at its birth to $20 million by 1907, protected by a nineteen-year patent, which expired in 1909. Lindahl and Carter (1959:202-206).

27. Earnings were also kept up by tariffs that Alcoa won from Congress, so that aluminum imports never rose above 15 percent, and by partial control over the scrap market. Until 1940, in fact, Germany was the world's largest producer of aluminum. Lindahl and Carter (1959:209-213).

28. Brubaker (1967:122-124, 229); Miller (1977:208).

29. The later success of new corporate entrants suggests that the government could have done much more to structure competition at this juncture. The first new entrant was Anaconda, previously a metal mining corporation, in 1955. In 1956 Olin Matheson built one of the first coal-fired plants. In the 1970s, the only new plant was built by Alumax, a joint venture of Amax, a U.S. mining and metals corporation, and Mitsui, a Japanese company. Peck (1962); Perloff et al. (1960:453).

30. Lindahl and Carter (1959:209, 218); Miller (1977:205).

31. See "For Aluminum, A Shift Overseas," *Business Week,* December 8, 1980:108-110.

32. Krutilla (1955) offers the seminal study of mid-century regional cost advantages. See also Lindahl and Carter (1959:203); Perloff et al. (1960:452); Miller (1977:209-210); and Moran (1958) for locational summaries.

33. Shutdowns have also occurred in aluminum rolling and drawing, which historically located near primary aluminum plants but were drawn later toward markets. In the immediate postwar period, Kentucky lost 2,000 workers and Tennessee 6,000 in that sector. See Fuchs (1962:216-217).

34. These are two of the industry's largest subsectors, and they represent opposite ends of the industry's contemporary experience. Discussion of earlier profit cycle stages relies on aggregate data for the entire textile sector.

35. The substitution of synthetics for cottons and other natural fibers (wool, silk, linen) accounts for the difference between the two subsectors studied here. In 1958 77 percent of all U.S. textiles manufactured were cottons, 20 percent were synthetics, and 3 percent were woolens. By 1968 cotton had fallen to 58 percent, and synthetics had risen to 41 percent. Rowan (1970:3, 17); Thornblade (1971:277, 280-281); Loving (1970:86).

36. The import problem is compounded by even stiffer competition in apparel; while imports of textiles doubled in the 1960s, garment imports tripled.

37. See Zeisel (1968:49, 1973:19); Strassman (1959:111); Stanback (1969).

38. Perloff et al. (1960:409); Stelzer (1961); Chang (1977:79); Feller (1974:276).

39. Rowan (1970:13 14); English (1969).

40. The U.S. industry is far less concentrated than its Asian competitors. Five Japanese firms control 80 percent of that country's output.

41. For instance, a private firm, Milliken, became the third largest company by adopting faster than others the new generation of machinery, which has been raising productivity industry-wide at a rate of 4.5 percent per year. Only 15 percent of the industry has converted to these innovations, which include open-end spinning, automatic doffing, shuttleless looms, and continuous flow processes. Most such inventions emanated from the textile machinery makers rather than from within the textile sector. "How Roger Milliken Runs Textiles' Premier Performer," Business Week, January 19, 1981:62-72; Rowan (1970:13); Feller (1974:594); Miller (1977:272); Loving (1970:87); Zeisel (1973:19).

42. Rowan (1970:25); Loving (1970:86); Thornblade (1971:284). Zeisel (1973:21) argues that new machinery has largely had the effect of deskilling workers, although more mechanics are now also hired to tend the equipment.

43. Perloff et al. (1960:115); Alexandersson (1967:95); Miller (1977:274-275). See Gordon (1978) for an elaboration of the role of worker and community struggles in this shift.

44. Feller (1974) shows that new technological breakthroughs continued to emanate from northeastern machinery makers but that they were adopted in the South, not the North.

45. Although the value of output was still lower because southern weaves were coarser and commanded a lower price on the market. Chang (1977:85); Alexandersson (1967:95-96); Miernyk (1952:163).

46. Fuchs (1962:251, 262, 419); Perloff et al. (1960:420); Rowan (1970:20). Textiles were more mobile than almost any other industry group studied by Fuchs.

47. See Wolfbein (1954); Fuchs (1962); Chang (1977:80, 84-86); Hammond (1942); Marshall (1967); Thornblade (1971:281); Rowan (1970), Zeisel (1973:18). All conclude that wages were the most significant factor.

48. Wolfbein (1954:11).

49. Rowan (1970:32). See Marshall (1967) for documentation of the weak union presence in the South.

50. Chang (1977:86); Wolfbein (1954:74, 81-82); Montgomery (1970); Zeisel (1968:49).

Chapter 10

1. The following discussion draws on a number of excellent studies of the industry: Reekie and Weber (1979); Fletcher (1970); Silverman and Lee (1974); Brooke (1975); Walker (1971); Wardell (1979); Library of Congress (1979); Barrie (1977); Grabowski and Vernon (1976); and United Nations, Centre on Transnational Corporations (1979).

2. The industry is defined here as SIC 2834, a subsector of chemicals. On a plant-by-plant basis, it is distinct from the chemical industry, although some large chemical firms own and operate plants in the drug industry. Excluded from the definition are biological substances and medicinals, two subsectors whose employment amounts to less than 10 percent of the three-digit pharmaceuticals category. The pharmaceuticals sector includes both ethical (prescription) drugs and proprietary (over-the-counter) preparations.

3. Depending on their potency and potential abuse, drugs are classified as either ethical or proprietary. Ethical drugs form by far the more profitable segment. They are divided further into two classes—brand name drugs and generics. Eighty-nine percent of all ethical drugs are marketed as brand name products, and of these 75 percent are still patented. Ethical drugs differ from proprietary products in three important ways. Productivity is much higher in proprietary drugs. They require much less space, labor, and equipment than do ethical drugs, which require much more careful testing, greater security precautions, small batch production, special handling, complex production processes, and drastic remedial action if a drug is tainted. Second, the proprietary producers engage mainly in market research rather than product research, as do generic producers. Third, ethical drugs of both

types are much shorter-lived than proprietary drugs, as new innovations tend to displace previous therapeutic favorites. Silverman and Lee (1974:17); Reekie and Weber (1979:2-3); Fletcher (1970:17-19).

4. There is a debate over the interpretation of such profits. Some analysts claim that they represent reasonable returns on research and development expenditures that should be counted in the capital base. Brownlee (1979); Schwartzman (1976).

5. Walker (1971:5-7).

6. Fletcher (1970:10, 13); United Nations, Centre on Transnational Corporations (1979).

7. Fletcher (1970:5, 9-10, 14); *Financial World* (1979).

8. Walker (1971:32).

9. Brooke (1975:1); Walker (1971:36-51); Barrie (1977:32).

10. Walker (1971:10-12); Brooke (1975:13-18); Schwartzman (1976:4-9); and Grabowski and Vernon (1976). A great deal of controversy surrounds whether innovational competition justifies market power or indeed obviates market power. For complete reviews, see Chien (1979) and Comanor (1979).

11. Brooke (1975); Walker (1971:5, 14). Because of both excessive profits and drug abuse, congressional committees as early as the late 1950s began to investigate the industry. As a result quality oversight was introduced through the Food and Drug Administration. In some cases— amphetamines, for instance—regulation has clearly cut down on abusive use of drugs. It has probably increased the quality of drugs, though at the cost of slowing down the rate at which a new drug reaches the market. Some studies warn that regulation will discourage innovation, and at least one argues that regulation has aided the large multinationals at the expense of the smaller drug makers. See Chien (1979) for a preponderance of authors who believe that regulation will hinder innovation.

12. Fletcher (1970:24-26).

13. Oil, Chemical and Atomic Workers (1980:18-19).

14. The industry data used here include both the three-digit industry, 233, women's and misses' outerwear, and two four-digit subsectors, 2335, women's dresses, and 2337, women's coats and suits. The choice of women's outerwear was guided by its nodal position within the clothing industry. Outerwear includes the manufacture of blouses, waists, dresses, suits, coats, pants, and other miscellaneous clothing. Women's outerwear is less standardized than most men's items or women's underwear and yet more so than categories like furs and accessories. It is also the single largest subsector within SIC 23, apparel. The two subsectors were chosen both because they are significant in size and because they display different recent experiences with consumer demand. In 1977 these two subsectors accounted for 40 percent and 19 percent of total SIC 233 employment, or

almost 60 percent together.

15. A historical summary can be found in Alexandersson (1967:100-102).

16. The increase in consumption of clothing may also be related to the acceleration of women's incorporation into wage labor, which requires a separate set of work clothes, as well as diminishing the time available for home production of clothing.

17. No standardized measure exists for physical output in women's clothing. Dresses are perhaps the only item at all temporally comparable. Yet a dress may have so many diverse attributes—durability, color, comfort, functionality, maintenance costs—that numbers of dresses produced over time can be used only tentatively as a standard. The figures show steady output increases from the 1920s until 1950, notwithstanding the war or the depression. This underscores the fact that a rapid-growth sector will not succumb to economy-wide patterns if its place in the profit cycle is one of rapid market penetration.

18. North American Congress on Latin America (NACLA) (1977:6-7).

19. Prunty and Ojala (1974).

20. NACLA (1977:6); Prunty and Ojala (1974:117).

21. Hayes and Schul (1968:117); Prunty and Ojala (1974:106); Fuchs (1962:22-25, 188-189); Perloff et al. (1960:420-423). Between 1929 and 1954, Fuchs shows, New York lost 81,560 jobs in women's and children's clothing, offset by a gain in New Jersey and Pennsylvania of about 70 percent of that number, while the South gained 22,121 jobs in the same period.

22. NACLA (1977).

23. Prunty and Ojala (1974:109, 113). In their study raw materials comprised 45 percent of all costs and labor accounted for 39 percent.

24. Market orientation cannot account for the shift away from the Northeast, especially in the suits-coats category, since average consumption of high-value woolens would clearly tie the industry to the frostbelt. Obviously it did have an effect on the initial location of the industry, which evolved out of the northeastern furrier trade.

25. Prunty and Ojala (1974:109-113).

26. Garment making is relatively sensitive to the short-term business cycle, as figure 10.6 indicates. Thus care should be taken in comparing two years at different points in recessionary cycles.

27. The industry as studied here consists of two segments, auto parts and auto assembly. Until 1967 figures for these two were collected together in SIC 3717, and only after that date do census figures separate parts (3714) from assembly (3711). In 1980 the two together accounted for 91 percent of all motor vehicle production (SIC 317), each with just over 45 percent of all motor vehicle jobs. The subject here is the auto industry rather than motor vehicles because demand for cars is quite distinct from that for

trucks, tanks, and buses, all of which are producer goods. The data for figure 10.11, however, use the three-digit umbrella group of motor vehicles, because of the 1967 change in definition.

28. Hainer and Koslofsky (1979:4).

29. Historical data and descriptions are drawn from Alexandersson (1967); Lindahl and Carter (1959); Miller (1977); Hainer and Koslofsky (1979); and Hurley (1959).

30. *Time* (1980); Hainer and Koslofsky (1979:28-32).

31. GM, founded in 1908 as a holding company, bought up twenty parts and assembly companies in its first year. By 1920 it had incorporated all the larger companies except for Ford and Olds's Rea, and by the late 1920s, this combination exceeded Ford in sales. Chrysler was formed when a disgruntled GM executive left GM to form his own firm, which became one of the three largest by 1930.

32. The degree of concentration was highest in auto assembly, where the largest four producers control more than 92 percent of value of output. In contrast the largest four parts producers control about 62 percent of parts output. See White (1971) for a full postwar history of auto industry concentration.

33. Since the late 1960s there has been a rapid increase in new firms and plants in the U.S. auto industry. Most of these are quite small; the number of plants with more than twenty employees has grown much more modestly. Only in auto assembly does the reverse pattern hold; here the number of plants with more than twenty employees continued to decline in the most recent period. Thus parts production may be getting somewhat more competitive, while auto assembly faces its competition from abroad and among the oligopolists, not from newcomers to the field.

34. Lansing was the initial site of successful commoditization. In 1899 R. E. Olds mass produced and marketed a luxury car at Lansing, Michigan, selling 1,000 the next year and 4,000 per year by 1903. Olds subsequently was lured to Detroit in a fight over public sector taxes and incentives precursing the present era. And, as critics today caution, Olds was later to relocate his factory back to Lansing.

35. Hurley (1959:5-7).

36. Miller (1977:221); Lindahl and Carter (1959:317); Hurley (1959:4, 5, 9); Birch (1966:15).

37. As Hurley (1959:10) put it, "The moderate-sized community plant, with an autonomous divisional unit, can be placed in a semi-rural area, enabling an employee to ride from his bungalow-type home to a spacious parking lot near the plant, free from all the inconveniences of commuting."

38. Examination of the geographical data for the auto industry is hampered by the fact that the disaggregation of data into parts and assembly subsections in the latest census periods has resulted in the deletion of almost all of

the spatial data on location of auto assembly. In order to compensate for these missing data, two devices are employed. First, the data on establishments as well as employment are examined. The growth of establishments far exceeds the growth in employment, as the figures demonstrate. However, a change in the spatial array of establishments provides a proxy for regional job change. Second, the data for parts alone (SIC 3714) are used for the most recent period, assuming that parts location is not moving in directions radically different from auto production. This assumption bears further examination, particularly because the introduction of automated lines in production and parts manufacture and the standardization of parts across model lines may result in greater separation of stages in auto manufacture, which may have spatial manifestations. However, using parts estimates will tend to err on the conservative side since assembly has decentralized much more quickly than parts. Still, overall there remains a discontinuity in the spatial data between 1963 and 1967 on employment. Before 1963 the data represent both parts and assembly location; afterward, parts alone.

39. Hurley (1959:8, 11-13). See Boas (1961) for a complete history of auto assembly location.

40. Corporate form and strategy has had a modest effect on this process. GM, because of its five-divisional internal structure, is somewhat less decentralized because each division has at least one assembly plant in the Detroit area. Ford has the highest percentage of dispersed assembly plants; only three of thirteen are in Michigan. The smaller producers are too weak to leave the Detroit area.

41. Data disclosure rules make it difficult to detect where the employment gains have taken place. Of the sunbelt states, only California and Texas figures are published, though not for every year. California doubled its share of employment from 1947 to 1963; thereafter it nearly doubled again its share of parts-related employment (see table 10.5). While parts employment is minor in Texas, the state's share is increasing. States like Tennessee also have increased parts employment in the mid-1970s. The failure of employment gains to register on a state-by-state basis in the census figures must be ascribed to the evenness of dispersion of this industry across many states, as well as to relatively large new establishment size, which increases the possibility of the disclosure prohibitions coming into effect. A better idea of where new plants are going can be gotten from the data on establishments.

42. All data refer to establishments with more than twenty workers. The choice of this indicator rather than all establishments eliminates the distorting effect from the emergence of tiny, marginal operations or parts.

43. Greer (1971:207).

44. New, larger, more automated plants producing 8 million to 10 million barrels a year supplanted the older 4.5 million barrel plant of the 1960s. Advertising-induced changes in the market added to small brewer problems.

As throwaway bottles replaced returnables, small brewers had to subcontract out for the expensive containers. In addition the shift from draft beer to bottled, as drinkers exchanged the bar stool for the family room sofa, handicapped the small breweries. The key advantage to the large brewing corporation lay in its ability to secure and enlarge its market share through advertising. Since labor, raw material, and freight costs rose less rapidly than price, the major new costs of production were those associated with advertising and marketing, especially packaging. Horowitz and Horowitz (1965); Greer (1971:218); Fogarty (1981; 1984). The lowering of the drinking age to 18 and the decline in the number of dry counties, especially in the South, has also boosted sales (Fogarty, 1984).

45. One might argue, as two British researchers have done for a comparable trend in England, that national integration has increased competition in local and regional markets. Yet concentration ratios in U.S. regional markets also grew during the postwar period, from an average four-firm ratio of 58 percent to 80 percent. Hawkins and Radcliffe (1971); Greer (1971:205).

46. In 1978 Miller's (Phillip-Morris) spent $18.80 per barrel of beer on advertising its new domestic Lowenbrau. Fogarty (1983).

47. Colorado had three breweries in 1947 with 596 workers, and in 1977, its controversial and sole brewer, Coors, employed well over 2,500 workers in one plant. Employment figures are not available for most states because of disclosure requirements.

48. Fogarty (1984).

49. Fogarty (1983) and (1984).

50. Fogarty (1983).

51. The industry definition used here is SIC 3144 from 1947 through 1967 and its equivalent thereafter: SICs 3143, 3144, and 3149. The figures used here were summed over these three categories. This change in the census treatment was unfortunate because the splitting into categories brought the disclosure rule into play much more frequently for geographical data in the 1970s. However, for the larger states, it was possible to find the figures and extrapolate. Historical data on location are available from Hoover's (1937) classic study, and data for the interim period are available in limited form from other sources. A close relative of shoemaking, leather production, is not included because its output is consumed by other sectors such as luggage and because its locational pattern historically has differed substantially from shoemaking, its client.

52. The historical material in this section draws on Hoover (1937).

53. Davis (1940:22-24); Hoover (1937:274).

54. Hoover (1937:271, 201-202). This is an example of how firm strategy can have a severe effect on location that could not be anticipated. This strategy on the part of United Shoe was not a profit-maximizing one, at least in the short run. In the longer run it may have prevented competitors from

developing, and it certainly prevented a monopolization of shoemaking that might have threatened its dominant position as a seller in the market. I have not been able to find conclusive evidence on whether United Shoe enjoyed monopoly profits under these strategies; Carl Kaysen suggests that profits were not outrageous, but high dividends and ample internal surpluses did occur consistently. Lindahl and Carter (1959:240-241).

55. Seifried (1972:311, 319). He finds similar rationalizing behavior exhibited by Quebec firms in the postwar era.

56. Hoover (1937:207).

57. Harrison (1981:27).

58. Hoover (1937:179-180). Ironically, although Hoover presents detailed shares of output for each period, nowhere in his book-length treatment does he present figures on total U.S. output growth.

59. Harrison (1981:11); Hoover (1937:234, 274).

60. Perloff et al. (1960:274, 445); Fuchs (1962:255); Hoover (1937:180).

61. Fuchs (1962:271); Harrison (1981:125); Perloff et al. (1960:443-444). See Heitmann (1963) for an effort to distinguish econometrically among the causal factors.

62. Estall (1966).

Chapter 11

1. These are largely renewable resources. Only one, lumber, has been nonrenewable for most of its history, although that has changed as techniques for farming trees have been successfully innovated. Another, fisheries, is occasionally nonrenewable as either depletion or biological cycles diminish supplies. Several nonrenewable sectors were investigated in the preliminary stages of the research as well (iron ore, gold, and coal), but although their employment and production histories demonstrate clear profit cycle stages, their spatial patterns defy characterization by the profit cycle model. The model must be judged insufficient for the nonrenewable resource-oriented sectors. They are too tied to specific resource bases to enable the profit cycle locational component to be used.

2. The wine industry is proxied by SIC 2084, which encompasses the production of wine, brandy, vermouth, and champagne. The figures used in this chapter represent employment in the manufacturing end only, not the agricultural portions. Spatially, however, the vineyards are located close by the wineries and in many cases owned by the winery itself.

3. The historical data in the following paragraphs are drawn from Amerine (1981:1-20); Vine (1981:9-25); Wagner (1981:196-200); Amerine and Joslyn (1951:5-33).

4. Wagner (1981:200); Amerine (1981:20-25).

5. Amerine and Joslyn (1951:5); Vine (1981:20); Amerine (1981:5, 21).

6. Long (1981:37); Amerine (1981:10, 22-25). The University of California had begun its viticulture research in 1876, the state its subsidies for research and development in 1880. See Amerine (1981:10). Other states lent their educational and financial support to a local wine industry as well; see, for instance, Klein (1981) and Washington (1975) on the state of Washington.

7. Vine (1981:13, 18-20); Amerine (1981:3-20); Amerine and Joslyn (1951:23).

8. Secondary sources drawn on for the historical and contemporary description of this industry include Hieronymus (1969); Smith and Circle (1978); Houck, Ryan, and Subotnik (1972).

9. Initially industrial chemical producers formed the largest portion of the oil market, for soaps, paints, and varnish. Taste and stability problems had to be overcome before oil from soybeans could be used in food products, a project that agricultural research and development tackled in the 1920s. In the 1930s synthetic resins supplanted the soybean oil industrial uses. Up through World War II, oil needs so dominated the demand for soybeans that plants were bred to yield a high oil content. Today less than 10 percent of oil goes to nonfood uses; oil destined for food uses is sold to 100 manufacturers of margarine, shortening, and salad dressing.

10. John Deere Company (1929).

11. Kromer (1970). Since Bureau of Census figures allocate multiproduct plants to either one or another subsector (for example, cottonseed oil versus soybean oil), the decline in soybean oil mills may be understated.

12. Smith and Circle (1978:4); Tennessee Valley Authority (TVA) (1974:184); McMillen (1962).

13. Houck, Ryan, and Subotnik (1972:26, 58).

14. Smith and Circle (1978:4); Houck, Ryan, and Subotnik (1972:46); TVA (1974:132).

15. Venus and Walters (1965); TVA (1974:15); Houck, Ryan, and Subotnik (1972:32).

16. Houck, Ryan, and Subotnik (1972:11).

17. Canned and cured seafood is SIC # 2091; in 1967 and previously it was SIC 2031, and before 1958 cured seafood was listed separately as SIC 2032. Fresh and frozen packaged fish is SIC 2092; in 1967 and previously it was SIC 2036. I have corrected the figures to include Alaska and Hawaii before they became states, back to 1954. Prior to 1954 no data were available, so that series shown here do not include those territories in the 1939 and 1947 data. While fishing is treated here as a renewable resource, it has approached nonrenewable status in some areas when depletion has threatened. Catch limitations adopted in these situations have helped to keep the resource base renewable. In addition unexplained fluctuations in

specific fish populations, not related to the annual catch, affect the industry's performance.

18. The discussion here uses historical data on fishing activity, classified as part of the agricultural sector, to chart the earlier periods of growth and decline. For the postwar period it uses data on fish processing, disaggregated to show the differences between canned fish and frozen fish. Although the data series is discontinuous, it makes little difference to the interpretation of geographical trends since fish processing, because of the high perishability of fish, is done on site. Fishing employment and jobs in fish processing are thus very closely associated spatially. Altogether about 150,000 people currently are employed in fishing-related occupations. See Perloff et al. (1960:375).

19. White (1954:2, 5); Bell and Hazleton (1967:9).

20. White (1954:12, 14-15); Stansby (1976).

21. Bell and Hazleton (1967:3, 16).

22. White (1954:5); Bell and Hazleton (1967:7-8); O'Rourke (1967:81-22); Farrell and Lampe (1967:45-60); Whitaker (1974).

23. Perloff et al. (1960:150).

24. The New England fishing industry was revived somewhat by two developments in Maine. First, fishing limits had helped to restock the beds, and second, an extensive canning industry was set up there. A combination of depleted beds and high wages kept similar investment in processing from reviving the Middle Atlantic fishing industry. Perloff et al. (1960:366, 476) show how poultry raising and fish processing are related to low wages and part-time fishing employment in Maine.

25. White (1954:4, 6, 177); Bell and Hazleton (1967:16); Barsh (1979).

26. Loss of plant share, however, does not necessarily mean a loss of employment share. Unfortunately no complete series can be constructed because of disclosure problems. The calculations for California show that a 3 percent plant share loss from 1967 to 1972 corresponded to a 1.2 percent increase in employment share. Since this was a period in which total employment declined, California still lost 300 jobs during that five-year period. Generally establishment share understates Pacific states' employment shares and overstates, though not by a lot, the job shares of all other states.

27. The industry is defined here as cigarette manufacturing, SIC # 2111, which now accounts for 64 percent of employment and 83 percent of value-added in the larger two-digit category, 21, which also includes cigars, chewing and pipe tobacco, and tobacco stemming and redrying. This last, the second largest in the category, corresponds today quite closely to cigarette making locationally. Cigars, on the other hand, which account for about 13 percent of employment in tobacco today, are heavily concentrated in quite different locations. The historical data used in this section cover all of these

subsectors.

28. Once cigarettes were under control, the trust turned to plug tobacco, employing similar practices with its aptly named Battle Ax brand. By 1898 it had engineered the Continental Tobacco Company, the plug trust. It spawned the American Snuff Company in 1901 and the American Cigar Company a year later, though in this last arena it was never able to control more than 25 percent of the market. It set up a string of retail outlets, called the American Cigar Stores. In 1901 it joined with the British trust to form the British American Tobacco Company. Lindahl and Carter (1959:180-195).

29. Perloff et al. (1960:391, 572).

30. "Cigarette Sales Keep Rising," *Business Week,* December 15, 1980.

31. Tennant (1950:280-297); Lindahl and Carter (1959:196-197).

32. "Cigarette Makers Rush to Ultra-Low-Tar Brands," *Business Week,* May 25, 1981; Schnabel (1972) argues that cigarette advertising outlays are designed to increase total demand as well as market share. This could be reinterpreted to mean that cigarette corporations fear that in the absence of advertising, significant erosion of aggregate demand would occur.

33. Fuchs (1962:250, 283).

34. Ibid. (261); Perloff et al. (1960:670). To the extent that cigar making survived, it became concentrated in Pennsylvania and Florida where early mechanization had given it an edge.

35. The industry is defined here as sawmills and planing mills, SIC 2421, the single largest category, which includes more than 40 percent of the employment in the lumber and wood products industry, although much of the discussion applies to all segments. The rest of the industry includes many operations that are sequentially linked to lumber mills, specifically logging and wood product processing such as plywood, pressboard, and matchmaking, whose locations are spatially linked to the mills. Of lumber harvested, one-fourth is classified as hardwood and the rest as softwood. The industry definition does not include pulpwood used for making paper, nor does it include finished wood products such as furniture.

36. Perloff et al. (1960:215-216); Howard (1970:2).

37. Zaremba (1963); Row (1962).

38. Already by 1965, acquisitions in lumber and wood products showed one of the highest rates for any other U.S. sector. See Mueller (1967:appendix, table 6).

39. Bennett (1981); Perloff et al. (1960:216).

40. William Duerr, chair, Department of Forestry Economics, State University College of Forestry, Syracuse University, cited by Howard (1970:20).

41. Burton and Alpert (1981:n. 4). They argue that tax write-offs and capital gains treatment of land appreciation encouraged this concentration of

ownership. Christensen (1981).

42. Ojala and Prunty (1968); Bennett (1981); Howard (1970:12-13); Holley (1970:127).

43. Howard (1970:12); Rowlands (1952).

44. Burton and Alpert (1981:4); Howard (1970:9); Bennett (1981); Holley (1970:127).

45. Howard (1970:7, 13, 22); Stoddard (1961); Krutilla (1981).

46. Logging operations, however, increased in the South during the same period, almost entirely to supply the growing pulp and paper industry, and so offset somewhat the declines in mill employment. Howard (1970:13, 45).

47. Holley (1970:127); Howard (1970:14); Burton and Alpert (1981:1). Fuchs (1962:252, 283) found an increase in concentration in the lumber industry from 1929 to 1954, which he too ascribed to resource availability.

49. Georgia-Pacific had begun a southern plywood industry in 1963, and subsequently the region became a major plywood producer. Holley (1970:131); Howard (1970:22); Christensen (1980:23).

49. Burton and Alpert (1981); Christensen (1980).

50. Harris (1981); Christensen (1980). See Burton and Alpert (1981) for a lengthy discussion of policy issues in the redwood region.

Chapter 12

1. The problems with using the cross-sectional cut show up most clearly in this category. Ironically, the instances of stage III development identified in the postwar period show a greater tendency to agglomerate than the stage II sectors. The leading state in half of the cases actually increased its share, although equivalent agglomerative gains were registered for the top four and top eight states in only one of six cases; however, two of these instances involved the winemaking business, a resource-oriented industry. When it was excluded from the sample, the expected decentralizing behavior held for the rest of the sectors studied, with the remarkable exception of brewing in Wisconsin.

2. The small sample problem was further complicated by the fact that producer goods sectors tended to be more resource oriented than consumer goods.

3. See also the reflections of Vernon (1979), and Giddy (1978).

Chapter 13

1. See Averitt (1968:161-167) on the uniqueness of the agricultural sector. Lively (1932) has an excellent discussion of the growth and decline of farm trade centers in rural areas. See Hansen (1973) for an empirical account of the thousands of rural counties that have experienced decline in the postwar

period.

2. See Harrison (1983) for a brief history of community causes and effects of restructuring in shoes. Klein and Kantor (1976) trace the dependence on industrial cities on their major industry for the period 1850 through 1920.

3. Ross and Trachte (1982), Sassen-Koob (1982), and Council on Wage and Price Stability (1978) offer greater detail on apparel displacement in New York City.

4. See Ciscel and Collins (1977) for an extended discussion of plant closings in Memphis.

5. Wolfbein (1944:29-37). His book on New Bedford offers an excellent study of the adverse effects of cotton mill closings on a New England town.

6. See Simon (1980).

7. "Mine Closing Hits Town Hard at Christmastime," *Denver Post,* December 27, 1977; "All Coppered Out in Montana," *High Country News,* February 4, 1983.

8. American Iron and Steel Institute, "Minnesota's Iron Mining Industry: Striving to Meet the Challenge," *Steel '82* (1982).

9. See Nelson (1960) for a discussion of the cutover region and its problems.

10. See, for instance, Michael Harris, "High Prices, Hard Times for Loggers," *San Francisco Chronicle,* November 12, 1981, p. 23.

11. The notion that the presence of a dominant oligopolistic industry could stunt the growth of a metropolitan area was first put forward by Chinitz (1960), who made a number of points to which I am indebted.

12. See Prethus (1964) and Clark (1974).

13. See the companion volume, *The Politics of Regions.*

14. Schultze (1958); Clelland and Farm (1964).

15. See Markusen (1978) for an analysis of this conflict.

16. See my account of this battle in *The Politics of Regions,* chap. 8.

17. See Markusen (1983).

18. See Noyelle (1983) for an extended treatment of this theme.

19. See Saxenian (1981).

References

Abernathy, William J. 1978. *The Productivity Dilemma: Roadblock to Innovation in the Automobile Industry.* Baltimore: Johns Hopkins University Press.

Abernathy, William, and Philip Townsend. 1975. "Technology, Productivity and Process Changes." *Technological Forecasting and Social Change* 7, no. 4:379-397.

Abernathy, William, and James Utterback. 1975. "Dynamic Model of Process and Product Innovation." *Omega* 3, no. 6:639-656.

Abernathy, W. J., and J. M. Utterback. 1978. "Patterns of Industrial Innovation." *Technology Review* 80 (June-July): 40-47.

Adams, Walter. 1971. *The Structure of American Industry.* 4th ed. New York: Macmillan.

Adams, Walter, and Joel Dirlam. 1966. "Big Steel, Invention and Innovation." *Quarterly Journal of Economics* 80, no. 2:167-189.

Adams, Walter, and Hans Mueller. 1982. "The Steel Industry." In Walter Adams, ed., *The Structure of American Industry.* Sixth Edition. New York: Macmillan.

Alanen, Arnold. 1977. *Economics and Environmentalism in a Company Town.* Research Series 1977, 806. Madison: University of Wisconsin.

Alexandersson, Gunnar. 1967. *Geography of Manufacturing.* Englewood Cliffs, N.J.: Prentice-Hall.

Alonso, William. 1980. "Five Bell Shapes in Development." *Papers of the Regional Science Association* 45:5-16.

American Iron and Steel Institute. Annual. *Annual Statistical Report.* Washington, D.C.: AISI.

American Iron and Steel Institute. Annual. *Directory of Iron and Steel Works of the United States and Canada.* New York: AISI.

Amerine, Maynard. 1981. "Development of the American Wine Industry to 1960." In Maynard Amerine, ed., *Wine Production Technology in the United States.* Washington, D.C.: American Chemical Society.

Amerine, M. A. and M. A. Joslyn. 1951. *Table Wines: The Technology of Their Introduction in California.* Berkeley: University of California Press.

Association of Bay Area Governments. 1981. "Silicon Valley and Beyond: High Technology Growth for the San Francisco Bay Area." Working Papers on the Region's Economy, No. 2. Berkeley, December.

Averitt, Robert. 1968. *The Dual Economy: The Dynamics of American Industry Structure.* New York: W. W. Norton.

Baran, Paul and Paul Sweezy. 1966. *Monopoly Capital.* New York: Monthly Review Press.

Barrie, James. 1977. *Future of the Multinational Pharmaceutical Industry to 1990.* New York: Wiley.

Barsh, Russel Lawrence. 1979. *The Washington Fishing Rights Controversy: An Economic Critique.* Rev. ed. Seattle: Graduate School of Business Administration, University of Washington.

Baumol, William. 1959. *Business Behavior, Value and Growth.* New York: Macmillan.

Baumol, William. 1968. "Entrepreneurship in Economic Theory." *American Economic Association, Papers and Proceedings* 58 (May): 64-71.

Bell, Frederick, and Jared Hazleton, eds. 1967. *Recent Developments and Research in Fisheries Economics.* Dobbs Ferry, N.Y.: Oceana Publications.

Benhart, John E. 1972. "Location Factors and Location Theory Influencing the Iron and Steel Industry." *Pennsylvania Geographer* 10 (December): 3-11.

Bennett, Marjorie. 1981. "Industrial Change in the Softwood Industry." Paper presented at the University of California, Berkeley, May 6.

Betheil, Richard. 1978. "The ENA in Perspective: The Transformation of Collective Bargaining in the Basic Steel Industry." *Review of Radical Political Economics* 10, no. 2:1-24.

Birch, B. P. 1966. "Locational Trends in the American Car Industry." *Geography* 51:372-375.

Blair, John M. 1972. *Economic Concentration.* New York: Harcourt Brace Jovanovich.

Bluestone, Barry, and Bennett Harrison. 1982. *The Deindustrialization of America.* New York: Basic Books.

Blumberg, Phillip. 1975. *The Megacorporation in American Society.* Englewood Cliffs, N.J.: Prentice-Hall.

Boas, Charles. 1961. "Locational Patterns of American Automobile Assembly Plants 1895-1958." *Economic Geography* 37 (July): 218-230.

Bolle, Mary Jane. 1980. "Plant Closings and Relocations." Issue Brief no. IB80068. Washington, D.C.: Congressional Research Service, July 22.

Bond, Ronald, and David Lean. 1977. *Economic Report on Sales, Promotion, and Product Differentiation in Two Prescription Drug Markets.* Washington, D.C.: Government Printing Office.

Borchert, J. R. 1972. "America's Changing Metropolitan Regions." *Annals of the Association of American Geographers* 62:352-373.

Borrus, Michael, and James Millstein. 1980. "Trade and Development in the Integrated Circuit Industry." In Laura Tyson and John Zysman, *American Industry in International Competition.* Berkeley: Institute for Governmental Studies, University of California.

Boylan, Myles G., Jr. 1975. *Economic Effects of Scale Increases in the Steel Industry: The Case of U.S. Blast Furnaces.* New York: Praeger.

Braverman, Jordan. 1978. *Crisis in Health Care.* Washington, D.C.: Acropolis Books.

Brenner, Robert. 1977. "The Origins of Capitalist Development: A Critique of Neo-Smithian Marxism." *New Left Review* 104 (July-August): 25-92.

Brody, David. 1960. *Steelworkers in America: The Non-union Era.* Cambridge: Harvard University Press.

Brooke, Paul. 1975. *Resistant Prices: A Study of Competitive Strains in the Antibiotics Markets.* New York: Council on Economic Priorities.

Brown, William H. 1957. "Innovation in the Machine Tool Industry." *Quarterly Journal of Economics* 71:406-425.

Browne, Lynn. 1979. "Regional Capital Formation." Federal Reserve Bank of Boston, *New England Economic Indicators* (June): A3-A8.

Brownlee, Oswald. 1979. "Rates of Return to Investment in the Pharmaceutical Industry: A Survey and Critical Appraisal." In Robert Chien, *Issues in Pharmaceutical Economics.* Lexington, Mass.: Lexington Books, D. C. Heath.

Brubaker, Sterling. 1967. *Trends in the World Aluminum Industry.* Baltimore: Johns Hopkins Press.

Bryant, Ralph, and Lawrence Krause. 1980. "World Economic Interdependence." In Joseph A. Pechman, ed., *Setting National Priorities: Agenda for the 1980's.* Washington, D.C.: Brookings Institution.

Burns, A. F. 1934. *Production Trends in the United States.* New York: Bureau of Economic Research.

Burrows, James, Charles Metcalf, and John Kaler. 1971. *Industrial Location in the United States.* Lexington, Mass.: D. C. Heath.

Burton, Dudley, and Irvine Alpert. 1981. "The Decline of California's North Coast Redwood Region." *Policy Studies Journal* 10: no. 2:272-284.

Business Week. 1966. "Billions Build Chicago into a Steel Titan." November 19:68-75.

Business Week. 1977. "Lay Offs Are Spreading across Steel Country." October 3:39.

Business Week. 1979. "Big Steel's Liquidation." September 17:78-96.

Business Week. 1980. "The Reindustrialization of America." New York: McGraw-Hill.

Business Week. 1980a. "Kaiser Steel: The Strategic Question Is Whether to Liquidate." September 8:64-68.

Business Week. 1981. "Steel: Hopes That Could Be Easily Derailed." January 12:80-85.

Castells, Manuel. 1980. "Multinational Capital, National States, and Local Communities." Working Paper No. 334. Berkeley: Institute of Urban and Regional Development, University of California.

Chamberlin, Edward. 1962. *The Theory of Monopolistic Competition: A Reorientation of the Theory of Value.* 8th ed. Cambridge: Harvard University Press.

Chandler, Alfred. 1962. *Strategy and Structure: Chapters in the History of Industrial Enterprise.* Cambridge: MIT Press.

Chandler, Alfred D. 1977. *The Visible Hand.* Cambridge: Harvard University Press.

Chang, Hui. 1979. "A Study of Industry Location from Pooled Time-Series and Cross-Section Data: The Case of Cotton Textile Mills." *Quarterly Review of Economics and Business* 19, no. 3:75-88.

Chien, Robert. 1979. *Issues in Pharmaceutical Economies.* Lexington, Mass.: Lexington Books, D. C. Heath.

Chinitz, Benjamin. 1960. "Contrasts in Agglomeration: New York and Pittsburgh." *American Economics Association, Papers and Proceedings* 50:279-289.

Christensen, Kathryn. 1981. "Northwest Timbermen Hit by Housing Slump and Shortage of Trees." *Wall Street Journal,* April 10:1.

Citibank Economics Department. 1979. "World Steel Shatters Its Mold." *Citibank* (March): 12-14.

Clark, Terry. 1974. "Can You Cut a Budget Pie?" *Policy and Politics* 3 (December): 3-32.

Clelland, Donald, and William Farm. 1964. "Economic Determinants and Community Power: A Comparative Analysis." *American Journal of Sociology* 69 (March): 511-521.

Cohen, Robert. 1977. "Multinational Corporations, International Finance, and the Sunbelt." In David Perry and Alfred Watkins, eds., *The Rise of the Sunbelt Cities.* Beverly Hills: Sage Publications.

Cohen, Yehoshua. 1972. *Diffusion of an Innovation in an Urban System.* Research Paper No. 140. Chicago: Department of Geography, University of Chicago.

Comanor, William. 1979. "Competition in the Pharmaceutical Industry." In Robert Chien, *Issues in Pharmaceutical Economics.* Lexington, Mass.: Lexington Books, D. C. Heath.

Conroy, Michael. 1975. *Regional Economic Diversification.* New York: Praeger.

Cox, William E., Jr. 1967. "Product Life Cycles as Marketing Models" *The Journal of Business* 40, no. 4:375-384.

Council on Wage and Price Stability. 1978. "A Study of Textile and Apparel Industries." Washington, D.C.: Government Printing Office, July.

Crum, William Leonard. 1953. *The Age Structure of the Corporate System.* Berkeley: University of California Press.

Curry, David. 1978. "France's Lame-Duck Steel Industry Appeals for Second Rescue." *Financial Times,* June 14.

Danilov, V. 1969. "The Spin Off Phenomenon." *Industrial Research* (May).

Davenport, John. 1968. "The Special Case of Specialty Steel" *Fortune,* November: 129-135.

Davis, Horace B. 1940. *Shoes: The Workers and the Industry.* New York: International Publishers.

Dawson, John. 1982. *Shift-Share Analysis: A Bibliographic Review of Technique and Applications.* Monticello, Ill.: Vance Bibliographies.

De Vroey, Michel. 1975. "The Separation of Ownership and Control in Large Corporations." *Review of Radical Political Economics* 7, no. 2:1-10.

Dhalla, N. K. and S. N. Yuspeh. 1976. "Forget the Product Life Cycle Concept." *Harvard Business Review* 54 (January-February): 102-112.

Dicken, P. 1971. "Some Aspects of the Decision-Making Behavior of Business Organizations." *Economic Geography* 47:426-437.

Draheim, Kirk. 1964. *Technological Industry in the Upper Midwest.* Upper Midwest Economic Study, Technical Paper No. 11. Minneapolis: University of Minnesota.

Dubey, Vinod. 1964. "The Definition of Regional Economics." *Journal of Regional Science* 5, no. 2:25-30.

Duncan, Beverly, and Stanley Lieberson. 1970. *Metropolis and Region in Transition.* Beverly Hills: Sage Publications.

Duke, Richard, Richard Johsonson, Hans Mueller, and P. David Qualls. 1977. *The United States Steel Industry and Its International Rivals: Trends and Factors Determining International Competitiveness.* Staff Report to the U.S.

Federal Trade Commission. Washington, D.C.: Government Printing Office, November.

Dunn, Edgar, Jr. 1980. *The Development of the U.S. Urban System.* Baltimore: Johns Hopkins Press for Resources for the Future.

Eaton, B. C., and Richard Lipsey. 1975. "The Principle of Minimum Differentiation Reconsidered: Some New Developments in the Theory of Spatial Competition." *Review of Economic Studies* 42 (January): 27-49.

Eckhouse, John. 1981. "Silicon Valley: Forced to Change." *San Francisco Examiner,* December 27.

Economist. 1980. "Maybe There Is No World Steel Crisis." April 12:72-73.

Elliott, John. 1980. "Marx and Schumpeter on Capitalism's Creative Destruction: A Comparative Restatement." *Quarterly Journal of Economics* 95, no. 1:45-68.

English, W. 1969. *The Textile Industry.* Harlow: Longmans.

Erickson, Rodney. 1980. "Corporate Organization and Manufacturing Branch Plant Closures in Non-Metropolitan Areas." *Regional Studies* 14, no. 6:491-501.

Erickson, Rodney, and Thomas Leinbach. 1979. "Characteristics of Branch Plants Attracted to Nonmetropolitan Areas." In Richard Lonsdale and H. L. Seyler, eds., *Nonmetropolitan Industrialization.* New York: Halsted Press.

Estall, R. C. 1963. "The Electronic Products Industry of New England." *Economic Geography* 39, (July):189-216.

Estall, R. C. 1966. *New England: A Study in Industrial Adjustment.* London: G. Bell and Sons.

Ewers, H. J., and R. W. Wettmann. 1980. "Innovation-Oriented Regional Policy." *Regional Studies* 14:161-179.

Farrell, James, and Harlan Lampe. 1967. "The Revenue Implications of Changes in Selected Variables Examined in the Context of a Model of the Haddock Market." In Frederick Bell and Jared Hazleton, eds., *Recent Developments and Research in Fisheries Economics.* Dobbs Ferry, N.Y.: Oceana.

Federal Reserve Bank of Cleveland. 1969. "Regional Trends in Steel Production." *Economic Review.* (October): 3-18.

Feller, Irwin. 1974. "The Diffusion and Location of Technological Change in the American Cotton-Textile Industry, 1890-1970." *Technology and Culture* 15 (October): 569-593.

Feller, Irwin. 1975. "Invention, Diffusion and Industrial Location." In Lyndhurst Collins and David Walker, eds., *Locational Dynamics of Manufacturing Activity.* London: Wiley.

Fetter, Frank A. 1937. "The New Plea for Basing Point Monopoly." *Journal of Political Economy* 45:577-605.

Fletcher, F. Marion. 1970. "The Negro in the Drug Manufacturing Industry." The Racial Policies of American Industry, Report No. 21. Philadelphia: University of Pennsylvania Press.

Fogarty, David. 1983. "Some Locational Aspects of the Brewing Industry in California." Working Paper. Berkeley: Department of City and Regional Planning, University of California.

Fogarty, David. 1984. "From Saloon to Supermarket: Packaged Beer and the Shaping of the Modern U.S. Brewing Industry." Working Paper, Berkeley: Department of City and Regional Planning, University of California.

Friedmann, John. 1972. "A General Theory of Polarized Development." In Niles Hansen, ed., *Growth Centers in Regional Economic Development.* New York: Free Press.

Friedmann, John, and Goetz Wolff. 1982. "World City Formation: An Agenda for Research and Action." World Cities Project 3. Los Angeles: School of Architecture and Urban Planning, University of California.

Frobel, Folker, Jurgen Heinrichs, and Otto Kreye. 1979. *The New International Division of Labour.* Translated by Pete Burgess. Cambridge. Cambridge University Press.

Fuchs, Victor. 1962. *Changes in the Location of Manufacturing in the United States Since 1929.* New Haven: Yale University Press.

Giddy, Ian H. 1978. "The Demise of the Product Cycle Model in International Business Theory." *Columbia Journal of World Business,* 13, no. 1:91-97.

Glickman, Norman. 1977. *Econometric Analysis of Regional Systems: Explorations in Model Building and Policy Analysis.* New York: Academic Press.

Glickman, Norman, ed. 1980. *The Urban Impact of Federal Policies.* Baltimore: Johns Hopkins University Press.

Gold, Bela. 1964. "Industry Growth Patterns: Theory and Empirical Results." *Journal of Industrial Economics* 13:53-73.

Gold, Bela, Gerhard Rosegger, and Myles Boylan, Jr. 1980. *Evaluating Technological Innovations.* Lexington, Mass.: D. C. Heath.

Goldstein, J. 1967. "The Spin-Off of New Enterprises from a Large Government Funded Industrial Laboratory." Master's thesis, MIT.

Goodman, Charles. 1948. *The Location of Fashion Industries, with Special Reference to the California Apparel Market.* School of Business Administration, Bureau of Business Research. Ann Arbor: University of Michigan Press.

Gordon, David. 1978. "Capitalist Development and the History of American Cities." In William K. Tabb and Larry Sawyers, eds., *Marxism and the Metropolis.* New York: Oxford University Press.

Gordon, David. 1981. "Capital Labor-Conflict and the Productivity Slowdown." *American Economic Review* 71, no. 2 (May): 30-35.

Grabowski, H. G., and J. M. Vernon. 1976. "Structural Effects of Regulation of Innovation in the Ethical Drug Industry." In Robert T. Masson and P. David Qualls, eds., *Essays in Industrial Organization in Honor of Joe S. Bain.* Cambridge, Mass.: Ballinger.

Greer, Douglas F. 1971. "Product Differentiation and Concentration in the Brewing Industry." *Journal of Industrial Economics* 19 (July): 201-219.

Grether, E. T. 1946. *The Steel and Steel-Using Industries of California.* Sacramento: California Reconstruction and Reemployment Commission.

Grossman, Robin. 1980. "IBM Drops the Other Shoe—and the Industry Relaxes." *Business Week,* December 1: 88.

Hainer, Mary, and Joanne Koslovsky. 1979. "Car Wars." North American Congress on Latin America, *Report on the Americas* XIII, no. 4.

Hall, M., and N. Tideman. 1967. "Measures of Concentration." *American Statistical Association Journal* 62:162-168.

Hall, Peter. 1982. "Innovation: Key to Regional Growth." *Transaction/Society* 19, no. 5 (July-August).

Hall, Peter. 1983. "The Third Man of Economics." *New Society,* no. 1:351-354.

Hamilton, F. E. Dan, and G. J. R. Linge, eds. 1979. *Spatial Analysis, Industry and the Industrial Environment.* Vol. 1: Industrial Systems. New York: Wiley.

Hammond, Seth. 1942. "Location Theory and the Cotton Industry." *Journal of Economic History* supplement, vol. 2:101-117.

Hansen, Niles. 1973. *The Future of Non-Metropolitan America: Studies in the Reversal of Rural and Small Town Population Decline.* Lexington, Mass.: D. C. Heath.

Hansen, Niles. 1979. "The New International Division of Labor and Manufacturing Decentralization in the United States." *Review of Regional Studies* 9, no. 1:1-11.

Haren, Claude, and Ronald Holling. 1979. "Industrial Development in Nonmetropolitan America: A Locational Perspective." In Richard Lonsdale and H. L. Seyler, eds., *Nonmetropolitan Industrialization.* New York: Wiley.

Hargreaves, Ian. 1981. "Pleasant Surprise for Wall Street." *Financial Times,* February 5.

Harper, Ann K. 1977. *The Location of the United States Steel Industry 1879-1919.* New York: Arno.

Harris, Curtis. 1973. *The Urban Economics 1985: A Multiregional Multi-Industry Forecasting Model.* Lexington, Mass.: Lexington Books, D. C. Heath.

Harris, Michael. 1981. "High Prices, Hard Times for Loggers." *San Francisco Chronicle,* November 12.

Harrison, Bennett. 1983. "Regional Restructuring and 'Good Business Climates': The Economic Transformation of New England since World War II." In William K. Tabb and Larry Sawers, eds., *Frostbelt-Sunbelt: The Political Economy of Urban Development and Regional Restructuring.* New York: Oxford University Press.

Harrod, R. F. 1939. "An Essay in Dynamic Growth Theory." *Economic Journal* (March): 14-33.

Hartmann, Heidi. 1976. "Capitalism, Patriarchy and Job Segregation by Sex." *Signs* 1, no. 3, pt. 2:137-169.

Hawkins, Keirn, and Rosemary Radcliffe. 1971. "Competition in the Brewing Industry," *Journal of Industrial Economics* 28 (November):20-41.

Hayes, C. R., and N. W. Schul. 1968. "Why Do Manufacturers Locate in the Southern Piedmont?" *Land Economics* 44 (February).

Hayes, Robert, and Steven Wheelwright. 1979a. "The Dynamics of Process-Product Life Cycles." *Harvard Business Review* 57, no. 2:127-136.

Hayes, Robert, and Steven Wheelwright. 1979b. "Link Manufacturing Process and Product Life Cycles." *Harvard Business Review* 57, no. 1 (January-February): 133-140.

Hekman, John S. 1978. "An Analysis of the Changing Location of Iron and Steel Production in the Twentieth Century." *American Economic Review* 68, no.1:123-133.

Heitmann, George. 1963. "An Econometric Study of the Regional Growth of the Footwear Industry." Ph.D. dissertation, Princeton University.

Hieronymus, T. H. 1969. "Soybeans: End of an Era." *Journal of Illinois Agricultural Economics* 9 (July).

Hirsch, Seev. 1967. *Location of Industry and International Competitiveness.* London: Oxford University Press.

Hirsch, Seev. 1972. "The United States Electronics Industry in International Trade." In Louis Wells, Jr., ed., *The Product Life Cycle and International Trade.* Cambridge: Harvard University Press.

Hogan, William. 1971. *Economic History of the Iron and Steel Industry in the United States.* 5 vol. Lexington, Mass.: D. C. Heath.

Holland, Stuart. 1976. *Capital versus the Regions.* New York: Macmillan.

Hollander, Samuel. 1965. *The Sources of Increased Efficiency: A Study of Du Pont Rayon Plants.* Cambridge: MIT Press.

Holley, D. L. 1970. "Location of the Softwood, Plywood, and Lumbering Industries: A Regional Programming Analysis." *Land Economics* 46 (May): 127-137.

Hoover, Edgar M. 1937. *Location Theory and the Shoe and Leather Industries.* Cambridge: Harvard University Press.

Hoover, E. M. 1948. *The Location of Economic Activity.* New York: McGraw-Hill.

Horowitz, Ann, and Ira Horowitz. 1965. "Firms in a Declining Market: The Brewing Case." *Journal of Industrial Economics* 13 (March): 129-153.

Hoselitz, Bert F. 1961. "Theories of Stages of Economic Growth." In Bert Hoselitz, Joseph Spengler, J. M. Tetiche, Erskine McKinley, John Buttrick and Henry Burton, *Theories of Economic Growth.* Glencoe, Il.: The Free Press.

Hotelling, Harold. 1929. "Stability in Competition." *Economic Journal* 39 (March): 41-57.

Houck, James, Mary Ryan, and Abraham Subotnik. 1972. *Soybeans and Their Products: Markets, Models and Policy.* Minneapolis: University of Minnesota Press.

Houston, David. 1967. "The Shift Share Analysis of Regional Growth: A Critique." *Southern Economic Journal,* 33, no. 4:577-580.

Houston, David. 1979. "A History of the Process of Capital Accumulation in Pittsburgh: A Marxist Interpretation." *Review of Regional Studies* 9, no. 1 (Spring): 12-32.

Howard, John. 1970. "The Negro in the Lumber Industry." The Racial Policies of American Industry. Report No. 19. Philadelphia: University of Pennsylvania Press.

Howes, Candace, and Ann Markusen. 1981. "Poverty: A Regional Political Economy Perspective." In Amos Hawley and Sara Mazie, *Nonmetropolitan America in Transition.* Chapel Hill: University of North Carolina Press.

Hunker, Henry. 1980. "The Evolution of Industrial Development Planning in North America." In David Walker, ed., *Planning Industrial Development.* New York: Wiley.

Hurley, Neil P. 1959. "The Automobile Industry: A Study in Industrial Location." *Land Economics* 35:1-14.

Hymer, S. H. 1972. "The Multinational Corporation and the Law of Uneven Development." In J. W. Bhagwati, ed., *Economics and the World Order.* New York: Macmillan.

Hymer, Stephen. 1979. "The Multinational Corporation and the International Division of Labor." In S. H. Hymer et al., eds., *The Multinational Corporation: A Radical Critique.* Cambridge: Cambridge University Press.

International Labor Organization. 1976. *The Impact of Multinational Enterprises on Employment and Training.* Geneva, Switzerland: ILO.

Isard, Walter. 1948. "Some Locational Factors in the Iron and Steel Industry since the Early Nineteenth Century." *Journal of Political Economy* 56 (June).

Isard, Walter. 1949. "The Future Locational Pattern of Iron and Steel Production in the United States." *Journal of Political Economy* 57, no. 1:118-133.

Isard, Walter. 1960. *Methods of Regional Analysis.* Cambridge: MIT Press.

Isard, Walter, and William M. Capron. 1949. "The Future Locational Pattern of Iron and Steel Production in the United States." *Journal of Political Economy* 57, no. 1:118-133.

Ignatius, David. 1977. "Bethlehem Meets Crisis Drastic Pruning of Plants, Personnel." *Wall Street Journal,* October 10.

Jewkes, J., D. Sawer, and R. Stillerman. 1958. *The Sources of Invention.* London: St. Martin's Press.

John Deere Company. 1929. *Soybeans for Profit.* Chicago: Soil Culture Department, John Deere.

Johnson, P. S. and D. G. Cathcart. 1979. "New Manufacturing Firms and Regional Development: Some Evidence from the Northern Region." *Regional Studies* 13:269-280.

Karlson, Stephen. 1983. "Modeling Location and Production. An Application to U.S. Fully-Integrated Steel Plants." *Review of Economics and Statistics* 65, no. 1:41-50.

Kaysen, Carl. 1949. "Basing Point Pricing and Public Policy." *Quarterly Journal of Economies* 63 (August).

Kaysen, Carl, and Donald Turner. 1959. *Antitrust Policy: An Economic and Legal Analysis.* Cambridge: Harvard University Press.

Keeble, D. 1976. *Industrial Location and Planning in the U.K.* London: Methuen.

Kelly, Edward, and Mark Shutes. 1977. "Lyke's Responsibility for Closing the Youngstown Campbell Works." Cleveland: Ohio Public Interest Campaign, November.

Kirkland, Richard, Jr. 1981a. "Big Steel Recoasts Itself." *Fortune,* April 6:28-34.

Kirkland, Richard, Jr. 1981b. "Pilgrim's Profits at Nucor." *Fortune,* April 6:43-46.

Klein, Joel D. 1981. "Wine Production in Washington State." In Maynard Amerine, ed., *Wine Production Technology in the United States.* Washington, D.C.: American Chemical Society.

Klein, Maury, and Harvey Kantor. 1976. *Prisoners of Progress: American Industrial Cities. 1850-1920.* New York: Macmillan.

de Kluyver, Cornelis. 1977. "Innovation and Industrial Product Life Cycles." *California Management Review* 20, no. 1 (Fall): 21-33.

Kromer, G. W. 1970. "Structural Changes in the Soybean Industry." In U.S. Department of Agriculture, *Fats and Oils Situation* (July): 16-37.

Krumme, Gunter, and Roger Hayter. 1975. "Implications of Corporate Strategies and Product Cycle Adjustments for Regional Employment Changes." in Lyndhurst Collins and David Walker, eds., *Locational Dynamics of Manufacturing Activity.* London: Wiley.

Krutilla, John. 1955. "Locational Factors Influencing Recent Aluminum Expansion." *Southern Economic Journal* 21 (January): 275-276.

Krutilla, John. 1981. "Managing the National Forests." *Resources, Newsletter of Resources for the Future Spring,* p. 10.

Kuhn, Sarah. 1981. *Computer Manufacturing in New England: Structure, Location and Labor in a Growing Industry.* Cambridge: Harvard-MIT Joint Center for Urban Studies.

Kuznets, Simon. 1930. *Secular Movements in Production and Prices.* Boston: Houghton Mifflin.

Kuznets, Simon. 1953. *Economic Change.* New York: W. W. Norton & Co.

Lall, Sanjaya. 1978. *The Growth of the Pharmaceutical Industry in Developing Countries.* New York: United Nations Industrial Development Organization.

Lasuen, Jose R. 1973. "Urbanization and Development—The Temporal Interaction between Geographic and Sectoral Clusters." *Urban Studies* 10:163-188.

Library of Congress. Congressional Research Service. 1979. *Competitive Problems in the Drug Industry: Psychotropic Drugs.* Washington, D.C.: Government Printing Office.

Lindahl, Martin, and William Carter. 1959. *Corporate Concentration and Public Policy.* 3d ed. Englewood Cliffs, N.J.: Prentice-Hall.

Lively, C. E. 1932. *Growth and Decline of Farm Trade Centers in Minnesota 1905-30.* Bulletin 287. St. Paul: Minnesota Agricultural Experiment Station.

Long, Zelma. 1981. "White Table Wine Production in California's North Coast Region." In Maynard Amerine, ed., *Wine Production Technology in the United States.* Washington, D.C. : American Chemical Society.

Loving, Rush, Jr. 1970. "What the U.S. Textile Industry Really Needs." *Fortune* 82 (October): 84-87.

Luger, Michael. 1981a. "Federal Business Tax Incentives: A Critical View." Working Paper, Public Policy Studies. Durham, N.C.: Duke University.

Luger, Michael. 1981b. "The State against Itself: A Study of the Micro-Consequences of Macro Policy." Unpublished paper, University of California, Berkeley.

Luria, Dan, and Jack Russell. 1981. *Rational Reindustrialization: An Economic Development Agenda for Detroit.* Detroit: Widgetripper Press.

McDermott, P. J. and D. Keeble. 1978. "Manufacturing Organization and Regional Employment Change." *Regional Studies* 12, no. 2:247-266.

Machlup, Fritz. 1949. *The Basing-Point System.* Philadelphia: Blakiston Company.

McMillan, Dale, Jr. 1962. "Decision at the Crossroads." Speech at the National Soybeans Processors Association Convention, August 20.

Magee, S. P. 1977. "Multinational Corporations, the Industry Technology Cycle and Development." *Journal of World Trade Law* 11:297-321.

Malecki, E. J. 1980a. "Corporate Organization of R and D and the Location of Technological Activities." *Regional Studies* 14:219-234.

Malecki, Edward. 1980b. "Science and Technology in the American Metropolitan System." In Stanley Brunn and James Wheeler, eds., *The American Metropolitan System: Present and Future.* New York: Wiley.

Mancke, Richard. 1972. "Iron Ore and Steel: A Case Study of the Economic Causes and Consequences of Vertical Integration." *Journal of Industrial Economies* 20 (July 1972): 220-229.

Mandel, Ernest. 1975. *Late Capitalism.* London: New Left Books.

Mandel, Ernest 1980. *Long Waves of Capitalist Development: The Marxist Interpretation.* Cambridge: Cambridge University Press.

Manners, Gerald, David Keeble, Brian Rodgers, and Kenneth Warren. 1980. *Regional Development in Britain.* 2 ed. Chichester: Wiley.

Mansfield, Edward. 1968. *Industrial Research and Technological Innovation.* New York: Norton Press.

Marchesini, Roberto. 1974. "Impact of Multinational Corporations on Domestic Employment." Ph.D. dissertation, University of Texas.

Marcuse, Peter. 1966. "Scholarship and the Burning Issues." *New Republic,* August 13:23-24.

Marglin, Stephen. 1974. "What Do Bosses Do? The Origins and Functions of Hierarchy in Capitalist Production." *Review of Radical Political Economics* 6, no. 2:60-112.

Markusen, Ann. 1978. "Class, Rent, and Sectoral Conflict: Uneven Development in Western U.S. Boomtowns." *Review of Radical Political Economics* 10, no. 3:177-129.

Markusen, Ann. 1983. "High-Tech Jobs, Markets and Economic Development Prospects: Evidence from California." *Built Environment* 9, no.

1:18-28.

Markusen, Ann. 1984. *The Politics of Regions.* New Jersey: Rowman and Allenheld.

Marshall, Ray. 1967. *Labor in the South.* Cambridge: Harvard University Press.

Martinelli, Flavia. 1981. "Services, Employment and the Urban Economy." Unpublished paper. Department of City and Regional Planning, June 29.

Marx, Karl, and Friedrich Engels. 1968. *The Communist Manifesto.* New York: Monthly Review Press.

Massey, Doreen, and Richard Meegan. 1978. "Industrial Restructuring versus the Cities." *Urban Studies* 15, no. 3:273-288.

Massey, Doreen, and Richard Meegan. 1979a. "The Geography of Industrial Reorganization." *Progress in Planning* 10, pt. 3:155-237.

Massey, Doreen, and Richard Meegan. 1979b. "Labour Productivity and Regional Employment Change." *Area* 11, no. 2:137-145.

Massey, Doreen, and Richard Meegan. 1982. *The Anatomy of Job Loss.* London: Methuen.

Mensch, Gerhard. 1979. *Stalemate in Technology.* Cambridge, Mass.: Ballinger.

Miernyk, William. 1952. "Labor Costs and Labor Supply as Determinants of Industrial Location." Ph.D. Dissertation, Harvard University.

Miller, E. Willard. 1977. *Manufacturing: A Study of Industrial Location.* University Park, Pa.: Pennsylvania State University Press.

Miller, E. Willard, and Ruby Miller. 1978. *Industrial Location: A Bibliography.* Worcester, Mass.: Clark University Press.

Miller, J. P. 1955. "Measures of Monopoly Power and Concentration: Their Economic Significance." In George Stigler, ed., *Business Concentration and Price Policy.* Princeton: Princeton University Press.

Modelski, George. 1979. "International Content and Performance among the World's Largest Corporations." In George Modelski, *Transnational Corporations and the World Order.* San Francisco: W. H. Freeman and Company.

Mollenkopf, John. 1981. "Paths toward the Post Industrial City: The Northeast and the Southwest." In Robert Burchell and David Listokin, eds., *Cities under Stress.* Piscataway, N.J.: Center for Urban Policy Research, Rutgers University.

Montgomery, Austin H., Jr. 1970. "The Importance of Water Pollution Control Laws to Textile Plant Locations." *Atlantic Economic Review* 20 (February): 33-35.

Moran, Ramsay. 1958. "Locational Advantages in the Aluminum Industry." M.B.A. thesis, University of Pennsylvania.

Moriarty, Barry. 1980. *Industrial Location and Community Development.* Chapel Hill: University of North Carolina Press.

Morrison, Peter. 1975. "Population Movements and the Shape of Urban Growth: Implications for Public Policy." In John Friedmann and William Alonso, *Regional Development and Planning: A Reader.* Cambridge: MIT Press.

Morrison, Peter. 1977a. "The Functions and Dynamics of the Migration Process." In Alan Brown and Egon Neuberger, *Internal Migration: A Comparative Perspective.* New York: Academic Press.

Morrison, Peter. 1977b. "Urban Growth and Decline in the United States: A Study of Migration's Effects in Two Cities." In Alan Brown and Egon Neuberger, *Internal Migration: A Comparative Perspective.* New York: Academic Press.

Mueller, Willard. 1967. *Concentration Trends and Merger Activity in the U.S. Manufacturing Industries since World War II.* Washington, D.C.: Government Printing Office.

Mueller, Willard F. 1970. *Monopoly and Competition.* New York: Random House.

Myrdal, Gunnar. 1957. *Economic Theory and Underdeveloped Regions.* London: Duckworth.

Nelson, J. P. 1971. "An Interregional Recursive Programs Model of Production, Investment and Technological Change." *Journal of Regional Science* 11:33-47.

Nelson, Lowry. 1960. *The Minnesota Community: Country and Town in Transition.* Minneapolis: University of Minnesota Press.

Nelson, Ralph. 1959. *Merger Movements in American Industry, 1895-1956.* Princeton: Princeton University Press.

New England Economy Project. 1981. *Case Study Summaries, Policy Analysis and Research Methodology.* Cambridge: Joint Center for Urban Studies of MIT and Harvard University.

Noren, James Herbert. 1960. "The Effects of Basing Point Pricing on Pricing and Location in the Steel Industry." Ph.D. dissertation, Princeton University.

North American Congress on Latin America. 1977. "Capital's Flight: The Apparel Industry Moves South." *Latin America and Empire Report,* March 5.

Northrup, Herbert. 1970a. "The Negro in the Tobacco Industry." The Racial Policies of American Industry, Report No. 13. Philadelphia: University of Pennsylvania Press.

Norton, R. D. 1979. *City Life Cycles and American Urban Policy.* New York: Academic Press.

Norton, R. D. and John Rees. 1979. "The Product Cycle and the Spatial Decentralization of American Manufacturing." *Regional Studies* 13:141-151.

Nourse, Hugh O. 1968. *Regional Economics.* New York: McGraw-Hill.

Noyelle, Thierry. 1983. "The Implications of Industry Restructuring in the United States." In Frank Moulaert and Patricia Wilson Salinas, eds., *Regional Analysis and the New International Division of Labor.* Boston: Kluwer-Nijhoff.

Nutter, Warren. 1951. *The Extent of Enterprise Monopoly in the United States: 1899-1939.* Chicago: University of Chicago Press.

Oakey, R. P., A. T. Thwaites, and P. A. Nash. 1980. "The Regional Distribution of Innovative Manufacturing Establishments in Britain." *Regional Studies* 14: 235-253.

Office of Technology Assessment. U.S. Congress. 1980. *Technology and Steel Industry Competitiveness.* Washington, D.C.: Government Printing Office.

Oil, Chemical and Atomic Workers International Union. 1980. "OCAW Plant Shutdowns: The Oil and Chemical Industry." Mimeographed. Denver: OCAW Headquarters.

Ojala, Carl F., and Merle C. Prunty, Jr. 1968. "The Rise of the Pine Plywood Industry in the South." *Southeastern Geographer* 8:11-22.

Ong, Nai-Pew. 1981. "Target Pricing, Competition and Growth." *Journal of Post Keynesian Economics* 4, no. 1:101-116.

Organization for Economic Cooperation and Development. 1971. *The Conditions for Success in Technological Innovation.* Paris: OECD.

O'Rourke, Hugh. 1967. "Comment on the Market for Fresh Fish That Originate from Boston Fish Pier Landings." In Frederick Bell and Jared Hazleton, *Recent Developments and Research in Fisheries Economics.* Dobbs Ferry, N.Y.: Oceana Publications.

Osborn, David. 1953. *Geographical Features of the Automation of Industry.* Chicago: University of Chicago Press.

Peck, M. 1962. "Invention in the Post War Aluminum Industry." In National Bureau of Economic Research, *The Rate and Direction of Inventive Activity.* New York: NBER.

Pekkaner, John. 1973. *The American Connection: Profiteering and Politicking in the "Ethical" Drug Industry.* Chicago: Follett Publishing.

Penrose, Edith. 1959. *The Theory of the Growth of the Firm.* New York: Wiley.

Perlmutter, Howard. 1968. "Supergiant Firms of the Future." *Wharton Quarterly,* (Winter): 13-14.

Perloff, Harvey, Edgar Dunn, Jr., Eric Lampard, and Richard Muth. 1960. *Regions, Resources and Economic Growth.* Baltimore: Johns Hopkins Press.

Petzinger, Thomas, Jr. 1979. "Youngstown Is Numb As It Faces Closing of Two More Steel Mills." *Wall Street Journal,* November 28.

Pounds, Norman. 1959. *The Geography of Iron and Steel.* London: Hutchinson University Library.

Pred, Allan. 1966. *The Spatial Dynamics of U.S. Urban-Industrial Growth, 1800-1914: Interpretative and Theoretical Essays.* Cambridge: MIT Press.

Pred, Allan. 1975. "Diffusion, Organization Spatial Structure, and City-System Development." *Economic Geography* 51:252-268.

Pred, Allan. 1976. "The Interurban Transmission of Growth in Advanced Economies: Empirical Findings vs. Regional-Planning Assumptions." *Regional Studies* 10:151-171.

Pred, Allan. 1977. *City Systems in an Advanced Economy.* New York: Wiley.

Prethus, Robert. 1964. *Men at the Top: A Study in Community Power.* New York. Oxford University Press.

Prunty, Merle C., and Carl F. Ojala. 1974. "Locational Stability Factors in the Men's Apparel Industry in the Southeast." *Southeastern Geographer* 14 (November): 106-120.

Reekie, W. Duncan, and Michael H. Weber. 1979. *Profits, Politics and Drugs.* New York: Holmes and Meier.

Rees, John. 1974 "Decision-Making, the Growth of the Firm and the Business Environment." In F. E. Ian Hamilton, ed., *Spatial Perspectives on Industrial Organization and Decision-Making.* London: Wiley.

Rees, John. 1978. "Manufacturing Change, Internal Control and Government Spending in a Growth Region of the U.S." In F. E. Ian Hamilton, ed., *Industrial Change: Challenge to Public Policy.* London: Longman.

Rees, John. 1979. "Technological Change and Regional Shifts in American Manufacturing." *Professional Geographer* 31:45-54.

Richardson, Harry. 1973. *Regional Growth Theory.* London: Macmillan.

Robinson, Joan. 1963. *Essays in the Theory of Economic Growth.* London: Macmillan.

Robinson, Joan. 1969. *The Economics of Imperfect Competition.* 2d ed. London: Macmillan.

Rodgers, Allen. 1952. "Industrial Inertia, A Major Factor in the Location of the Steel Industry in the United States." *Geographical Review* 42, no. 1 (January): 56-66.

Rosenberg, N. C. 1972. *Technology and American Economic Growth.* New York: Harper & Row.

Rosenberg, Nathan C. and Claudio R. Frischtak. 1983. "Long Waves and Economic Growth: A Critical Appraisal." *American Economic Association, Papers and Proceedings* 73, no. 2:146-151.

Ross, Robert, and Kent Trachte. 1982. "Global Cities and Global Classes: The Peripheralization of Labor in New York City." Working Paper. Worcester, Mass.: Clark University, Departments of Sociology and Government.

Row, Clark. 1962. "Regional Competition in Softwood Lumber." *Society of American Foresters Proceedings* (October): 97-103.

Rowan, Richard. 1970. "The Negro in the Textile Industry." *The Racial Policies of American Industry,* Report No. 20. Philadelphia: University of Pennsylvania Press.

Rowlands, W. A. 1952. "The Great Lakes Cutover Region." In Merrill Jensen, ed., *Regionalism in America.* Madison: University of Wisconsin Press.

Rowley, Charles. 1971. *Steel and Public Policy.* London: McGraw-Hill.

Sassen-Koob, Saskia. 1982. "Recomposition and Peripheralization at the Core." *Contemporary Marxism,* no. 5 (Summer): 88-100.

Saxenian, Annalee. 1980. "Silicon Chips and Spatial Structure: The Semiconductor Industry and Urbanization in Santa Clara County, California." Master's thesis. University of California.

Saxenian, Annalee. 1981. *Silicon Chips and Spatial Structure: The Industrial Basis of Urbanization in Santa Clara County, California.* Berkeley: Institute for Urban and Regional Development, University of California.

Sayer, R. Andrew. 1976. "A Critique of Urban Modelling." *Progress in Planning* 6, pt. 3:187-254.

Scherer, Frederick. 1965. "Size of Firm, Oligopoly and Research: A Comment." *Canadian Journal of Economics and Political Science* 31, no.2:256-266.

Scherer, Frederick. 1980. *Industrial Market Structure and Economic Performance.* Chicago: Rand-McNally.

Schmidt, Charles, and Richard B. LeHeron. 1976. "Mini-plants in the United States: Some Technological and Locational Characteristics." *Land Economics* 52:530-544.

Schmookler, Jacob. 1966. *Invention and Economic Growth.* Cambridge: Harvard University Press.

Schnabel, Morton. 1972. "An Oligopoly Model of the Cigarette Industry." *Southern Economic Journal* 38 (January): 325-335.

Schoenberger, Erica. 1981. "International Direct Investment: A Review of the Literature." Unpublished paper. Berkeley: Department of City and Regional Planning, University of California.

Schultze, Robert. 1958. "The Role of Economic Dominants in Community Power Structure." *American Sociological Review* 23 (February): 3-9.

Schumpeter, Joseph. 1939. *Business Cycles: A Theoretical, Historical and Statistical Analysis of the Capitalist Process.* New York: McGraw-Hill.

Schumpeter, Joseph. 1961. *The Theory of Economic Development.* Cambridge, MA: Harvard University Press.

Schumpeter, Joseph. 1962. *Capitalism, Socialism and Democracy.* New York: Harper and Row.

Schwartzman, David. 1976. *Innovation in the Pharmaceutical Industry.* Baltimore: Johns Hopkins Press.

Sease, Douglas. 1979. "U.S. Steel Is Set to Close over 12 of Its Facilities." *Wall Street Journal,* November 28.

Sease, Douglas. 1980a. "Closing of a Steel Mill Hits Workers in U.S. with Little Warning." *Wall Street Journal,* September 23.

Sease, Douglas. 1980b. "Steel Companies Face Difficult Decisions in Dealing with Major Slump in Demand." *Wall Street Journal,* May 16.

Sease, Douglas. 1981. "Mini-Mill Steelmakers, No Longer Very Small, Out Perform Big Ones." *Wall Street Journal,* January 12: 1,19.

Seifried, Neil. 1972. "Locational Change in the Canadian Leather Footwear Industry." *Canadian Geographer* 16, no. 4:309-322.

Select Committee on Small Business. U.S. Senate. 1980. "Effects of Steel Closing on Small Businesses and Local Communities." Washington, D.C.: Government Printing Office, February 5.

Shapiro, Helen, and Steven Volk. 1979. "Steelyard Blues: New Structures in Steel." *NACLA: Report on the Americas* 12, no. 1 (January-February): 2-40.

Sherman, Howard J. 1968. *Profits in the United States.* Ithaca, N.Y.: Cornell University Press.

Siebert, Horst. 1969. *Regional Economic Growth: Theory and Policy.* Scranton, Pa.: International Textbook Co.

Siegel, Lenny. 1981. "Delicate Bonds: The Global Semiconductor Industry." *Pacific Research* 11, no. 1.

Silverman, Milton, and Philip Lee. 1974. *Pills, Profits and Politics.* Berkeley: University of California Press.

Simon, Richard. 1980. "The Labor Process and Uneven Development in the Appalachia." *International Journal of Urban and Regional Research* 4, no. 1:46-72.

Smith, Allan K., and Sidney Circle, eds. 1978. *Soybeans: Chemistry and Technology.* Vol. 1. Revised. Westport, Conn.: AVI Publishing.

Solow, Robert. 1957. "Technical Change and the Aggregate Production Function." *Review of Economics and Statistics* (August): 312-320.

Stanback, Thomas, Jr. 1969. *Tax Changes and Modernization in the Textile Industry.* New York: National Bureau of Economic Research.

Stansby, Maurice. 1976. *Industrial Fishery Technology: A Survey of Methods for Domestic Harvesting, Preservation and Processing of Fish Used for Food and for Industrial Products.* Huntington, N.Y.: R. E. Krieger.

Stelzer, I. H. 1961. "The Cotton Textile Industry." In Walter Adams, ed., *The Structure of American Industry.* New York: Macmillan. Third Edition.

Stephens, John, and Brian Holly. 1980. "The Changing Patterns of Industrial Corporate Control in the Metropolitan United States." In Stanley Brunn and James Wheeler, eds., *The American Metropolitan System: Present and Future.* New York: Wiley.

Stevens, Benjamin, and Carolyn Brackett. 1967. *Industrial Location: A Review and Annotated Bibliography of Theoretical, Empirical and Case Studies.* Philadelphia: Regional Science Research Institute.

Stobaugh, Robert. 1972. "The Neotechnology Account of International Trade: The Case of Petrochemicals." In Louis Wells, Jr., ed., *The Product Life Cycle and International Trade.* Cambridge: Harvard University.

Stocking, George. 1954. *Basing-Point Pricing and Regional Development.* Chapel Hill: University of North Carolina Press.

Stoddard, C. 1961. *The Small Private Forest in the United States.* Washington, D.C.: Resources for the Future.

Stone, Katherine. 1974. "The Origins of Job Structure in the Steel Industry." *Review of Radical Political Economics* 6, no.2:113-173.

Storper, Michael. 1981. "Technology, the Labor Process and the Location of Industries." Ph.D. dissertation, University of California.

Storper, Michael, and Walker, Richard. 1983. "The Theory of Labor and the Theory of Location." *International Journal of Urban and Regional Research:* 7,1:1-41.

Strassman, Paul. 1959a. *Risk and Technological Innovation.* Ithaca: Cornell University Press.

Strassman, W. Paul. 1959b. "Creative Destruction and Partial Obsolescence in American Economic Development." *Journal of Economic History* (September): 335-349.

Struyk, Raymond and Franklin James. 1975. *Intrametropolitan Industrial Location: The Pattern and Process of Change.* Lexington, Mass.: Lexington Books.

Sylos-Labini, Paolo. 1969. *Oligopoly and Technical Progress.* Cambridge: Harvard University Press.

Taylor, M. J. 1975. "Organizational Growth, Spatial Interaction and Locational Decision-Making." *Regional Studies* 9:313-323.

Tennant, Richard. 1950. *The American Cigarette Industry.* New Haven: Yale University Press.

Tennessee Valley Authority. 1974. *Soybean Production, Marketing and Use.* Muscle Shoals, Ala.: National Fertilizer Development Center, Tennessee Valley Authority.

Thackray, John. 1981. "The Steel Sickness." *Management Today.* (January): 54-57.

Thomas, Morgan. 1974. "Structural Change and Regional Industrial Development." In Frederick Helleiner and Walter Stohr, eds., *Spatial Aspects of the Development Process.* Proceedings of the Commission on Regional Aspects of Development of the International Geographical Union, vol. 2. London, Ontario.

Thomas, M. D. 1975. "Growth Pole Theory, Technological Change and Regional Economic Growth." *Regional Science Association, Papers and Proceedings* 34:3-25.

Thomas, Morgan. 1981. "Growth and Change in Innovative Manufacturing Industries and Firms." Working paper. Lauenburg, Austria: International Institute for Applied Systems Analysis, February.

Thompson, Wilbur. 1962. "Locational Differences in Inventive Activity and Their Determinants." In Richard Nelson, ed., *The Rate and Direction of Inventive Activity.* Princeton: Princeton University Press.

Thompson, Wilbur. 1965. *A Preface to Urban Economics.* Baltimore: Johns Hopkins.

Thompson, Wilbur. 1969. "The Economic Base of Urban Problems." In Neil Chamberlain, ed., *Contemporary Economic Issues.* Homewood, Ill.: Richard Irwin.

Thompson, Wilbur. 1975. "Internal and External Factors in Urban Economies." In John Friedmann and William Alonso, *Regional Development and Planning: A Reader.* Cambridge: MIT Press.

Thornblade, James B. 1971. "Textile Imports from the Less-Developed Countries: A Challenge to the American Market." *Economic Development and Cultural Change* 19 (January): 277-286.

Thwaites, A. T. 1978. "Technological Change, Mobile Plants and Regional Development." *Regional Studies* 12:445-461.

Time. 1980. "Detroit's Uphill Battle." September 8:46-47.

United Nations. 1973. *Multinational Corporations in World Development.* New York: United Nations.

United Nations. Centre on Transnational Corporations. 1979. *Transnational Corporations and the Pharmaceutical Industry.* New York: United Nations.

U.S. Bureau of Labor Statistics. 1980a. *Industry Wage Survey: Basic Iron and Steel.* Bulletin 2064. Washington, D.C.: Government Printing Office.

U.S. Bureau of Labor Statistics. 1980b. *Occupational Outlook Handbook.* 1980-1981 ed. Washington, D.C.: Government Printing Office.

U.S. Department of Housing and Urban Development. 1979. *The Impact of Foreign Direct Investment on U.S. Cities and Regions.* Washington, D.C.: Government Printing Office.

U.S. Federal Trade Commission. 1981. *Quarterly Financial Report for Manufacturing and Trade Corporations.* Washington, D.C.: Government Printing Office.

U.S. Internal Revenue Service. 1982. *Source Book, Statistics of Income. Active Corporation Income Tax Returns, 1980-1981.* Washington, D.C.: Government Printing Office.

U.S. Senate Committee on Foreign Relations. 1975. *Direct Investment Abroad and the Multinationals' Effects on the United States Economy.* Washington, D.C.: Government Printing Office.

van Duijn, Jacob J. 1983. *The Long Wave in Economic Life.* London: George Allen.

Varaiya, Pravin, and Michael Wiseman. 1978. "The Age of Cities and the Movement of Manufacturing Employment, 1947-72." *Papers of the Regional Science Association* 41:127-140.

Varaiya, Pravin, and Michael Wiseman. 1980. "Investment and Employment in Manufacturing in U.S. Cities, 1960-1976." Working Paper. Berkeley: Department of Economics, University of California.

Venus, Charles and Marsha Walters. 1965. *Market Potential for Producing Soybeans End-Products in Arkansas.* Little Rock: Industrial Research and Extension Center, College of Business Administration, University of Arkansas.

Vernon, Raymond. 1960. *Metropolis 1985: An Interpretation of the Findings of the New York Metropolitan Region Study.* Cambridge: Harvard University Press.

Vernon, Raymond. 1966. "International Investment and International Trade in the Product Cycle." *Quarterly Journal of Economics* 80, no. 2:190-207.

Vernon, Raymond. 1971. *Sovereignty at Bay: The Multinational Spread of United States Enterprises.* New York: Basic Books.

Vernon, Raymond. 1977. *Storm over the Multinationals: The Real Issues.* Cambridge: Harvard University Press.

Vernon, Raymond, and Louis Wells, Jr. 1976. *Manager in the Multinational Economy.* 3d ed. Englewood Cliffs, N.J.: Prentice-Hall.

Vernon, Raymond. 1979. "The Product Cycle Hypothesis in a New International Environment." *Oxford Bulletin of Economics and Statistics* 41, no. 4: 255-267.

Vine, Richard. 1981. *Commercial Winemaking: Processing and Controls.* Westport, Conn.: AVI Publishing.

Wagner, Philip. 1981. "Grapes and Wine Production in the East." In Maynard Amerine, ed., *Wine Production Technology in the United States.* Washington, D.C.: American Chemical Society.

Walker, Hugh D. 1971. *Market Power and Price Levels in the Ethical Drug Industry.* Bloomington: Indiana University Press.

Walker, David F. 1975. "Governmental Influence on Manufacturing Location: Canadian Experience with Special Reference to the Atlantic Provinces." *Regional Studies* 9.

Wall Street Journal. 1979. "U.S. Steel to Close Fabricating Plant Near Los Angeles." April 27.

Wall Street Journal. 1980a. "U.S. Steel Considering More Production Cuts in the Pittsburgh Area." May 23.

Wall Street Journal. 1980b. "U.S. Steel to Lay Off 3,000 More Workers at Alabama Plant." June 3.

Wall Street Journal. 1980c. "Johns and Laughlin Steel to Close Part of Pittsburgh Works." November 14.

Wardell, William. 1979. "The History of Drug Discovery, Development and Regulation." In Robert Chien, *Issues in Pharmaceutical Economics.* Lexington: Lexington Books, D.C. Heath.

Ware, Lynn B., Denise DiPasquale, and Barry Bluestone. 1978. *Selection of Industries for Case Study Analysis.* New England Economy Project, Working Paper No. 1. Cambridge: Joint Center for Urban Studies, MIT-Harvard.

Warren, Kenneth. 1973. *The American Steel Industry, 1850-1970: A Geographical Interpretation.* Oxford: Clarendon Press.

Washington, State of. 1975. *Technical and Economic Assistance in Fostering the Economic Development of the Wine-Grape Industry of Washington.* Pullman: Washington State University.

Webber, M. J. 1972. *Impact of Uncertainty on Location.* Cambridge: MIT Press.

Weiss, Leonard. 1967. *Case Studies in American Industry.* New York: Wiley.

Wells, L. T., Jr., ed. 1972. *The Product Life Cycle and International Trade.* Cambridge: Harvard University Press.

Whitaker, R. 1974. "Analysis and Characteristics of United States Demand for Fishery Products." In Rudolf Kreuzer, *Fishery Products.* London: Food and Agricultural Organization of the United Nations.

White, C. Langdon, and George Primmer. 1937. "The Iron and Steel Industry of Duluth: A Study on Locational Maladjustment." *Geographical Review* 27 (January): 82-91.

White, Donald. 1954. *The New England Fishing Industry: A Study in Price and Wage Setting.* Cambridge: Harvard University Press.

White, Langdon. 1957. "Water-Neglected Factor in the Geographical Literatures of Iron and Steel." *Geographical Review* 47, no. 4 (October): 464-489.

White, Lawrence J. 1971. *The Automobile Industry since 1945.* Cambridge: Harvard University Press.

Williamson, Oliver. 1964. *The Economies of Discretionary Behavior: Managerial Objectives in a Theory of the Firm.* Englewood Cliffs, N.J.: Prentice-Hall.

Wolfbein, Seymour. 1954. *The Decline of a Cotton Textile City: A Study of New Bedford.* New York: Columbia University Press.

Zaremba, Joseph. 1963. *Economics of the American Lumber Industry.* New York: Robert Speller and Sons.

Zeisel, Rose N. 1968. "Technology and Labor in the Textile Industry" *Monthly Labor Review* 91 (February): 49-55.

Zeisel, Rose N. 1973. "Modernization and Manpower in Textile Mills: Technological Changes Are Altering Skill Requirements, But Modernization Lags behind Other Industries." *Monthly Labor Review* 96 (June): 18-25.

Index